Human Rights in Twentieth-Century Australia

This groundbreaking study understands the "long history" of human rights in Australia from the moment of their supposed invention in the 1940s to official incorporation into the Australian government bureaucracy in the 1980s. To do so, a wide cast of individuals, institutions and publics from across the political spectrum are surveyed who translated global ideas into local settings and changed meanings of a foreign discourse to suit local concerns and predilections. These individuals created new organisations to spread the message of human rights or found older institutions amenable to their newfound concerns, adopting rights language with a mixture of enthusiasm and opportunism. Governments, on the other hand, engaged with or ignored human rights as its shifting meanings, international currency and domestic reception ebbed and flowed. Finally, individuals understood and (re-)translated human rights ideas throughout this period: writing letters, books or poems and sympathising in new, global ways.

Jon Piccini is a historian at Australian Catholic University. He wrote *Global Radicals: Transnational Protest, Australia and the 1960s* (2016), which looks at Australian protest movements in the transnational "Sixties", and edited a collection of essays entitled *The Far Left in Australia since 1945* (2018).

Human Rights in History

Edited by

Stefan-Ludwig Hoffmann, University of California, Berkeley

Samuel Moyn, Yale University, Connecticut

This series showcases new scholarship exploring the backgrounds of human rights today. With an open-ended chronology and international perspective, the series seeks works attentive to the surprises and contingencies in the historical origins and legacies of human rights ideals and interventions. Books in the series will focus not only on the intellectual antecedents and foundations of human rights but also on the incorporation of the concept by movements, nation-states, international governance and transnational law.

A full list of titles in the series can be found at:
www.cambridge.org/human-rights-history

Human Rights in Twentieth-Century Australia

Jon Piccini
Australian Catholic University

CAMBRIDGE
UNIVERSITY PRESS

University Printing House, Cambridge CB2 8BS, United Kingdom

One Liberty Plaza, 20th Floor, New York, NY 10006, USA

477 Williamstown Road, Port Melbourne, VIC 3207, Australia

314-321, 3rd Floor, Plot 3, Splendor Forum, Jasola District Centre, New Delhi - 110025, India

79 Anson Road, #06-04/06, Singapore 079906

Cambridge University Press is part of the University of Cambridge.

It furthers the University's mission by disseminating knowledge in the pursuit of education, learning and research at the highest international levels of excellence.

www.cambridge.org
Information on this title: www.cambridge.org/9781108460279
DOI: 10.1017/9781108659192

© Jon Piccini 2019

This publication is in copyright. Subject to statutory exception and to the provisions of relevant collective licensing agreements, no reproduction of any part may take place without the written permission of Cambridge University Press.

First published 2019
First paperback edition 2021

A catalogue record for this publication is available from the British Library

Library of Congress Cataloging in Publication data
Names: Piccini, Jon, author.
Title: Human rights in twentieth-century Australia / Jon Piccini.
Description: Cambridge, United Kingdom ;New York,NY:Cambridge University Press, 2020. | Series: Human rights in history | Includes bibliographical references and index.
Identifiers: LCCN 2019018397 | ISBN 9781108472777
Subjects:LCSH:Human rights – Australia – History – 20th century. | Civil rights – Australia – History – 20th century.
Classification: LCC JC599.A8 P53 2020 | DDC 323.0994/0904–dc23
LC record available at https://lccn.loc.gov/2019018397

ISBN 978-1-108-47277-7 Hardback
ISBN 978-1-108-46027-9 Paperback

Cambridge University Press has no responsibility for the persistence or accuracy of URLs for external or third-party internet websites referred to in this publication, and does not guarantee that any content on such websites is, or will remain, accurate or appropriate.

For Teena

Contents

Acknowledgements		*page* viii
	Introduction: Bereft of Words	1
1	Inventing Rights	21
2	Cold War Rights	53
3	Experimental Rights	86
4	Whose Rights?	119
5	Implementing Rights	153
	Epilogue: Cascade or Trickle?	188
	Index	203

Acknowledgements

While perhaps a worn cliché, that it takes a village to make a book has certainly been true in my experience. This book began life in the dying days of my doctoral studies at the University of Queensland (UQ) in 2013, as I considered what became of the transnational 1960s social movements my thesis had explored when their passions ebbed in the late 1970s. My chance discovery of Samuel Moyn's then recently published provocation *The Last Utopia* both provided a partial answer to this question and drove me in the direction of what was then becoming the burgeoning field of human rights historiography.

After several post–PhD years in the wilderness, it was back at UQ that I received a postdoctoral fellowship in 2016 and an Early Career Research Award in 2018, providing the necessary time and funding to turn this project from vague idea to (almost) finished product. All those employed at the Faculty of Humanities and Social Sciences' Research Office, and in particular Rachel Smith, were instrumental in ensuring my project was appropriately translated into the language of the Grant Writing Industrial Complex. Thanks must also go to Australian Catholic University, and in particular Michael Ondaatje and Maggie Nolan, for recognising this book and its author as worthy of support in the form of an ongoing lectureship in 2019, during which the rougher edges of the manuscript have been ironed out.

This book pulled together multiple seemingly disconnected archives, facilitated by the patience of numerous librarians and repository staff. Diligent archivists at the State Library of New South Wales, the State Library of Victoria, the National Library of Australia, the National Archives of Australia, the Fryer Library at the University of Queensland and the Bodleian Library at Oxford University deserve many thanks. Particularly helpful has been the digitisation work undertaken by the National Library of Australia via its Trove website, the National Archives and the State Library of Victoria, endeavours which are not only state of the art in archival practice but infinitely helpful in an era of smaller, more competitive research grants.

viii

Acknowledgements

In proposing this book to the esteemed publishers at Cambridge University Press, and in particular the Human Rights in History series, I knew that my chances were slim. It was as such a delight to hear such positive initial feedback from the series' editors, Samuel Moyn and Stefan Ludwig-Hoffman, followed by more detailed readings from three anonymous reviewers. Their kind, instructive words have done much to shape the final manuscript, while the work of Cambridge University Press staff, particularly Michael Watson and Lisa Carter, has ensured it stayed to deadline (my lateness notwithstanding). The editors and anonymous reviewers at *Journal of Australian Studies* and *Australian Historical Studies*, where sections of Chapters 3 and 4 have appeared in extended form, are also owed a great deal of thanks for allowing me to workshop and troubleshoot my emerging ideas.

It is my many wonderful colleagues, comrades and friends who are owed most of the intellectual debt for this project. Opportunities to present drafts of this work in diverse forums – including twice at the Australian Historical Association's annual meetings and at conferences of the Australian Society for the Study of Labour History and the Australia New Zealand Law and History Society – have been invaluable. Invitations from Amanda Nettelbeck to her "Civil and Human Rights in Australia" symposium in Dublin, Ireland, and from Madeleine Chaim to a workshop on Australian histories of international law at La Trobe University in Melbourne were particularly helpful, not only in terms of the comments and guidance received but also because they demonstrated that I was doing something right.

Unendingly giving of their time and intellects have been those esteemed scholars who have voluntarily read drafts of this manuscript throughout its germination. Jane Lydon, Kate Darian-Smith, Michelle Arrow, Jessica Whyte, Madeleine Chaim, Lisa Featherstone, Konstantina Tzouvala, Frank Bongiorno and Dirk Moses have each gone above and beyond the call of duty in carefully and thoughtfully reading chapters. My research mentors at the University of Queensland, Chris Dixon in 2016 and then Anna Johnston during the "crunch years" of 2017–18, have however put in the lion's share of labour, not just reading but seemingly endlessly discussing the ideas herein over numerous cups of coffee. The support and encouragement I have received from mentors and collaborators within the Australian historical profession has been truly awe-inspiring, and I can only hope to return in kind the generosity which I have experienced. Any errors herein, however, are entirely my responsibility.

Beyond readership, numerous friends have passed on helpful guidance and comments over the years, including Dave Eden, Evan Smith, Ana Stevenson, Gemmia Burden, Kate Ariotti, Elizabeth Humphreys and

Simon Copland. This is in no way a thorough list, which would no doubt require a further volume, a fact which speaks to the necessarily collective nature of all intellectual endeavour. Last, and certainly not least, I want to thank my family. Teena's love has gotten me through the peaks and troughs of tumultuous post–PhD life, while her intellectual rigour and targeted questioning has informed this book in so many ways. My son Francis, despite his preference for more vividly illustrated books than this one, always inspires me to work harder and do better. Without both of them, none of this would have been possible.

Introduction: Bereft of Words

On 3 May 1963, Shirley Andrews strode to the podium of Canberra's Rex Hotel to reveal a secret Australia's government wanted kept hidden. Delegates from over twenty Asian nations were gathered in the hotel's conference room to attend a United Nations seminar on "Human Rights and Policing", fourth in a series of gatherings on the topic of human rights and the legal system held in the Philippines, Japan and New Zealand since 1956. The head of the UN's Division on Human Rights, John Humphrey, praised Australia's hosting. The nation had "done quite a thing in taking the initiative in the seminar", which was to be "one of the most significant" human rights activities undertaken by the UN.[1] The gathering had set before it an agenda of global concerns – asking whether members of police forces should join political parties, as well as the veracity of compulsory fingerprinting and wiretapping. Australia's Minister for External Affairs, Paul Hasluck, hoped the seminar would allow for "views [to be] exchanged on concrete problems, and participants [to] learn at first hand of the difficulties faced in other countries".[2] The hosting doubled as a way for Australia, something of a pariah owing to support for South African apartheid alongside discriminatory immigration and indigenous policies, to present itself as a participant in global affairs.[3]

Andrews – communist, scientist, aboriginal rights campaigner and nationally renowned folk dancer – was an odd participant in the high-level goings-on. While open to the public, speakers at the meeting were to be "ministers and deputy ministers, attorneys general, solicitors-general, judges, lawyers, government officials, senior police officials and professors" – with members of the public relegated to

---

[1] *The Canberra Times*, 27 April 1963, 13.
[2] "United Nations Seminar on the Role of Police in the Protection of Human Rights: Statement by the Minister for External Affairs", 23 April 1963, available at http://parlinfo .aph.gov.au/parlInfo/search/display/display.w3p;query=Id%3A%22media%2Fpressrel% 2FHPR10012082%22.
[3] On Australia's pariah status, see Jennifer Clark, *Aborigines & Activism: Race, Aborigines and the Coming of the 1960s to Australia* (Crawley, WA: University of Western Australia Press, 2008), chapter 2.

2   Introduction: Bereft of Words

a spectator's role.[4] Andrews found herself amongst such luminaries due to her nomination as delegate, via expatriate Australian Jessie Street, for the London-based, UN-affiliated Anti-Slavery Society. Acknowledging her willingness to attend, Andrews wrote to Street that it was "not quite clear" if there was anywhere in the program, running from 29 April to 11 May, in which she could discuss Australia's treatment of Indigenous peoples.[5] Andrews' initial scepticism was vindicated at the gathering, where attempts to speak were confronted with "quite a bit of pressure", including a stern rebuke from Australia's Solicitor General Sir Garfield Barwick. "It would not be tactful to raise an issue that concerned only Australia when so many of the participants were Asians", Barwick suggested, as they "had so many much more serious problems ... terrorists, secret societies, etc that the Aboriginal problem would seem very unimportant to them".[6]

When Andrews was finally able to mount the podium, after effectively inserting herself into the program against the chair's wishes, she opened by criticising the seminar's overriding approach: noting the lack of "ordinary human beings" on the agenda, despite "the protection of their rights [being] the topic of this discussion", Andrews also railed against the dictatorial powers of Australian police over Aborigines, including the use of neck chains, forced removals and searches without warrant.[7] Despite receiving "quite a lecture" from the Victorian Commissioner of Police for having caused him "great personal mortification" by "mentioning these matters in front of Asian people", Andrews noted her intervention had "received very good publicity". A reporter for the *Canberra Times* remarked how the audience sat in "stunned silence" as Andrews explained how police were regarded as "instruments of tyranny" by Indigenous Australians. A Singaporean delegate remarked that Andrews' testimony had left him "bereft of words".[8]

Andrews' interruption of proceedings points towards several significant breaks in dominant understanding of human rights history, a field which has undergone a spectacular renaissance over the past twenty years.[9]

---

[4] "United Nations Seminar".

[5] Shirley Andrews to Jessie Street, 3 March 1963, Council for Aboriginal Rights Papers (henceforth CAR), Box 8, Folder 4, State Library of Victoria (henceforth SLV).

[6] Shirley Andrews to Thomas Fox-Pitt, 7 May 1963, CAR Records, Box 8, Folder 4, SLV.

[7] Shirley Andrews, "Speech made at UN Seminar on the Role of the Police in the Protection of Human Rights. Canberra, May 3rd, 1963", CAR Papers, Box 8, Folder 4, SLV.

[8] *The Canberra Times*, 4 May 1953, 3.

[9] A vast corpus of work now exists, with selected key works including Paul Gordon Lauren, *The Evolution of International Human Rights: Visions Seen* (Philadelphia: The University of Pennsylvania Press, 2003); Samuel Moyn, *The Last Utopia: Human Rights in History* (Cambridge, MA: Harvard University Press, 2010); Lynn Hunt, *Inventing Human Rights: A History* (New York: W. W. Norton & Company, 2007); Jean H. Quataert, *Advocating*

Introduction: Bereft of Words 3

Andrews' intervention at once placed matters of Australian activist concern in the middle of a global UN gathering – something many scholars have noted as a rarity in an organisation resigned to proceduralism – and translated the Universal Declaration of Human Rights (UDHR), and particularly the prohibition on denial of liberties in Article 3, into an environment it was never intended to impact. The use of this international forum to raise a fundamentally national issue illustrates how a binary understanding of global and local events is unhelpful, particularly when understanding a truly global ideal. For while Samuel Moyn is correct to argue that historians of the local may become "jealous of the specificities of their geographical domain", as such "losing the integrative view that the larger view tends to afford", it is equally impossible to ignore the lessons of transnational history, which demonstrate the deep interconnectedness of these two levels.[10] It is the task of historians, as Timothy S. Brown argues, to "situate[e] the local within the global while locating the global at work locally".[11] For it is sometimes at the most local of levels that historians can best come to understand the true meaning of global, abstract ideas. "The idea of the universal applicability of human rights norms needs to be distinguished clearly in our minds from how people actually apply the language of human rights", as Lora Wildenthal puts it in her work on West Germany.[12] Indeed, Mark Philip Bradley has recently argued that a focus on the local can in fact work to "provincialise" the nation, by "lifting up the critical role of processes initially set in motion well beyond U.S. shores."[13] Australia, too often viewed as isolated from global events, had its local political and cultural life shaped by events and ideas far beyond its borders.

Equally, arguments for the primacy of a particular decade in the emergence of human rights are left aside in this book. For while Dominique Clément talks of a "moment in history beginning in the 1970s when human rights replaced civil liberties as the primary language of rights"

Dignity: Human Rights Mobilizations in Global Politics (Philadelphia: University of Pennsylvania Press, 2009); Roland Burke, *Decolonization and the Evolution of International Human Rights* (Philadelphia: University of Pennsylvania Press, 2010).

[10] Samuel Moyn, "The 1970s as a Turning Point in Human Rights History", in Jan Eckel and Samuel Moyn (eds.), *The Breakthrough: Human Rights in the 1970s* (Philadelphia: University of Pennsylvania Press, 2013), 13.

[11] Timothy S. Brown, "'1968' East and West: Divided Germany as a Case Study in Transnational History", *The American Historical Review* 114, no. 1 (February 2009), 70.

[12] Lora Wildenthal, *The Language of Human Rights in West Germany* (Philadelphia: University of Pennsylvania Press, 2012), 2.

[13] Mark Philip Bradley, *The World Reimagined: Americans and Human Rights in the Twentieth Century* (Cambridge: Cambridge University Press, 2016), 9. Bradley here repurposes Dipesh Chakrabarty, *Provincialising Europe: Postcolonial Thought and Historical Difference* (Princeton, NJ: Princeton University Press, 2007).

4   Introduction: Bereft of Words

in his Canadian case study, this was no mere transition for Australians but a decided, decades-long contest over the meaningfulness of an array of modes of political identification.[14] The influence of human rights waxed and waned, while other possible utopias – communism, women's liberation and demands for Indigenous sovereignty, to name but a few – engaged with, questioned and proposed alternative futures to human rights. New scholarship is today unearthing the tangled relationship between rights and these other forms of claim making throughout the twentieth century, for as Stefan-Ludwig Hoffmann writes, "liberal-democratic, socialist and postcolonial human rights norms competed in the international arena … each claim[ing] for itself moral universalism".[15] Andrews – whose Marxism had initially led her to the Indigenous cause – is one of those activists, like Greek communist women or anti-democratic British conservatives, who set their existing ideologies to new coordinates, if with only sparing success. This uptake of human rights rhetoric by different forces, from communist internationalists to Catholic puritans, conservative politicos and liberal humanitarians, was a remarkable process and one best observed locally and outside of decadal confines.[16] A broader temporal reach is required, alongside a deeper archival analysis, to unearth the complexities of translation and reception. It is not sufficient to accept well-publicised utterances by presidents and prestigious NGOs in the late 1970s as a moment of rupture: instead one must consult the papers of groups who upheld the idea of rights well before this time frame, as well as those who questioned their validity.[17] The year 1963, the fifteenth anniversary of the UDHR, was not marked by any great ceremony in Australia. Bureaucrats refused to issue more than a "routine press release" at least "while we have discriminatory racial laws in the states and a racial immigration policy", and local organisations

---

[14] Dominique Clément, *Human Rights in Canada: A History* (Waterloo, Canada: Wilfrid Laurier University Press, 2016), 21.

[15] Stefan-Ludwig Hoffmann, "Genealogies of Human Rights", in Stefan-Ludwig Hoffmann (ed.), *Human Rights in the Twentieth Century* (New York: Cambridge University Press, 2011), 16–17.

[16] On Communist Internationalism, see Celia Donert, "From Communist Internationalism to Human Rights: Gender, Violence and International Law in the Women's International Democratic Federation Mission to North Korea, 1951", *Contemporary European History* 25, no. 2 (2016), 313–33. For Catholic and Conservative responses, see Marco Duranti, *The Conservative Human Rights Revolution: European Identity, Transnational Politics, and the Origins of the European Convention* (Oxford: Oxford University Press, 2017).

[17] Work "decentring" the 1940s and 1970s as key moments in human rights are growing; see in particular Steven L. B. Jensen, *The Making of International Human Rights: The 1960s, Decolonisation and the Reconstruction of Global Values* (Cambridge: Cambridge University Press, 2016).

More than a "Fair Go"? 5

failed to engender any wide enthusiasm.[18] Andrews' adherence to these beliefs – and her ability to exercise them to public value – demonstrates the continued persuasive power and utility of the idea of human rights even during a low – seemingly terminal – point in its global influence.

This book understands the "long history" of human rights in Australia from the moment of its invention in the 1940s to a long-delayed official incorporation into the Australian government bureaucracy in the 1980s. To do so, a wide cast of individuals, institutions and publics are surveyed. Andrews is but one of many proponents of human rights from across the political spectrum who translated global ideas into local settings, making meaning of a foreign discourse and melding it to suit local concerns and predilections. These individuals both created new organisations to spread the message of human rights – Amnesty International, the Ex-Services Human Rights Association of Australia, Right to Life – or found older institutions amenable to their newfound concerns, adopting rights language with a mixture of enthusiasm and opportunism. Governments, on the other hand, engaged with or ignored human rights as its shifting meanings, international currency and domestic reception ebbed and flowed, revealed through the dialogue between human rights groups and different levels of the bureaucracy. Finally, individuals understood and (re)translated human rights ideas throughout this period: writing letters, books or poems and sympathising in new ways. Each of these levels was essential, intersecting and contributing to the uptake of human rights into Australian political life and everyday vocabulary.

More than a "Fair Go"?

"Human rights" is a term with a complicated and politicised history, and nowhere is this more the case than in Australia. Having given the world the eight-hour working day and earned a reputation as the "workingman's paradise" in the late nineteenth century, Australia also birthed a harsh regime of domestic racism and immigration restriction that informed South African apartheid.[19] Australia was amongst the first

---

[18] J. Pomeroy, "Fifteenth Anniversary of the Universal Declaration of Human Rights", 24 September 1963, National Archives of Australia (henceforth NAA): A1838, 929/1/1/1. For more on commemorating human rights in the 1960s, see Roland Burke, "'How Time Flies': Celebrating the Universal Declaration of Human Rights in the 1960s", *The International History Review* 38, no. 3 (2016), 394–420.

[19] On the eight-hour day, see Ken Buckley and Ted Wheelwright, *No Paradise for Workers: Capitalism and the Common People in Australia 1788–1914* (Melbourne: Oxford University Press, 1988), 166; on Australia as example of racism, see Marilyn Lake and Henry Reynolds, *Drawing the Global Colour Line: White Men's Countries and the Question of Racial Equality* (Melbourne: Melbourne University Press, 2008), chapter 6.

6   Introduction: Bereft of Words

nations to grant white women full suffrage in 1902, a feat not to be achieved by Indigenous women for a further sixty years.[20] The notion of the "fair go" – a colloquial expression of Australia's supposedly egalitarian sentiment – was claimed by Australian Attorney General and 1940s human rights apostle Herbert Vere Evatt to "express the real spirit behind" the UDHR. Yet, this common sense cultural understanding has never been extended to include any constitutional or legislative guarantee of the rights of its peoples.[21] Untangling these and many other contradictions which plague Australia's long engagement with the idea of human rights is the object of the present study. Australia provides a particularly contradictory exemplar of human rights' disputed history. Unlike Canada, a nation born of a similar process of procedural, often begrudging decolonisation from Britain, Australia has never constitutionally embraced the idea of human rights, relying instead on common law principles. Despite Evatt's larger-than-life presence at the United Nations founding conference in 1945 and Australia's position as one of only eight nations to draft the UDHR in 1947–8, Australia did not become a signatory to the "twin covenants" that made its pronouncements enforceable until 1972, nor did it seek to ratify the documents until later in that decade. From 1981, Australia has had a Commonwealth Human Rights body, which, along with a series of state-based anti-discrimination bureaucracies, has provided provisional, ad hoc protections while coming under near-constant attack and criticism. Proposals for a Commonwealth Bill of Rights, now a common feature of nearly all Western liberal democracies, have never moved beyond the level of vocal public debate.

Yet, despite the term's lack of domestic traction, Australians from all walks of life have sought to make meaning of the idea of human rights in diverse contexts since the 1940s, finding a place for this global language in existing, politically divergent social movements, political parties and cultural contexts that already possessed their own specific vernaculars. Australia's religious community – and particularly Catholics – were amongst the first appropriators of the term, hoping it might protect such sacred notions as the family and private property from the

---

[20] On the global significance of Australia's extended franchise, see Clare Wright, "'A Splendid Object Lesson': A Transnational Perspective on the Birth of the Australian Nation", *Journal of Women's History* 26, no. 4 (Winter 2014), 12–36.

[21] On the history of Australian vernacular egalitarianism, see Nick Dyrenfurth, *Mateship: A Very Australian History* (Melbourne: Scribe, 2015). For Evatt's remark, see Herbert V. Evatt, "Untitled draft of a speech concerning the outcomes of the Third General Assembly of the United Nations", available at http://parlinfo.aph.gov.au/parlInfo/down load/media/pressrel/EFMA6/upload_binary/efma61.pdf;fileType=application%2Fpdf# search=%22human%20rights%201940s%20media%22.

More than a "Fair Go"?

totalitarian impulse of the social-democratic state.[22] This began a long tradition of religious rights claiming in Australia, from Social Justice statements in the 1940s to the wave of "conscientious objection" during the 1960s and their judicious employment by the anti-abortion activists from the 1970s onward. On the progressive side of politics, human rights also served as a tool to shine light on darkened corners of the national imagination – treatment of Indigenous Australians, conscription of young men for overseas service and discrimination against LGBTIQ persons, to name but a few. As Wildenthal puts it, to call something a human rights violation is "to intervene in politics as usual in order to place that example of violence or inequality in a new context".[23] Deportation controversies in the 1940s, the struggles for Indigenous rights – political and civil in the 1950s and economic and cultural in the 1970s – and women's and queer rights in later decades have seen the definition of the "human" extended to encapsulate more persons on the Australian continent than ever before. Yet, the ability of human rights language to provoke publicity and redraw lines of political debate has been jeopardised by the unenforceability of its universal pretensions at either local or global levels. What Roland Burke calls the "human rights proceduralism" of the UN and like bodies and the relative ineffectiveness of rights bodies locally has meant that little account was given to individual violations during the period surveyed.[24]

This book is divided into five chapters – each broadly covering a decade in Australian history. The first chapter explores the invention of human rights in the 1940s, paying close attention to how forces with widely divergent political goals articulated their ambitions in this new language. Catholics, the Labour Movement and Chinese seamen threatened with deportation all sought to capture the wartime rights zeitgeist, proposing human rights as central to their imaginings of Australia's postwar future. The Cold War occupies Chapter 2, particularly focusing on how this superpower conflict dramatically limited the usability of human rights

---

[22] For histories of Australian religion, see Roger C. Thompson, *Religion in Australia: A History* (Melbourne: Oxford University Press, 1994); Patrick O'Farrell, *The Catholic Church and Community: An Australian History* (Sydney: UNSW Press, 1985); and Meredith Lake, *The Bible in Australia: A Cultural History* (Sydney: NewSouth Press, 2018).

[23] Lora Wildenthal, *The Language of Human Rights in West Germany* (Philadelphia: University of Pennsylvania Press, 2012), 1.

[24] See Roland Burke, "Premature Memorials to the United Nations Human Rights Program: International Postage Stamps and the Commemoration of the 1948 Universal Declaration of Human Rights", *History and Memory* 28, no. 2 (Fall/Winter 2016), 156; and Roland Burke, "Human Rights Day after the 'Breakthrough': Celebrating the Universal Declaration of Human Rights at the United Nations in 1978 and 1988", *Journal of Global History* 10, no. 1 (2015), 147–70 and Roland Burke, "The Rites of Human Rights at the United Nations", *Humanity* 9, No. 1 (Spring 2018): 127–42.

8   Introduction: Bereft of Words

and how it impacted the slow transition from a vocabulary of British rights and civil liberties to more universal equivalents amongst campaigners. Communists who fell foul of sedition laws became human rights champions, while the narrow defeat of a 1951 referendum on the banning of the Communist Party saw frequent recourse by both opponents and supporters to infringements of the UDHR. Conflicts over rights are also found to have been central to the Labor Party's "great schism" of 1955, as many of the organisation's Catholic constituents sought a more independent, anti-communist body. Andrews' organisation – the Council for Aboriginal Rights – is explored as a case study of human rights activism in the 1950s. The group's early alignment with the principles enumerated in the UDHR encountered the difficult reality of translation and frustration at the limitations of their enforceability.

Chapter 3 engages with the decade of the 1960s – popularly remembered as years of revolt and revolution, but which were relatively quiet ones for rights advocates, who set about experimenting with their usability in diverse contexts. Three groups occupy the chapter's focus – the Communist Party of Australia, the Ex-Services Human Rights Association of Australia and Amnesty International. Each group adopted a different frame for its human rights activism: reform-minded communists saw it as a way of breaking the party's Stalinist stranglehold, war veterans used it to cast as outmoded the ideas of the conservative Returned Servicemen's League, and a new crop of humanitarian-moralists set about bringing to light the rights of forgotten prisoners at home and abroad. Revolution and backlash defined the 1970s in Australia, and Chapter 4 is concerned with how (re)emerging political forces – women's liberationists, Indigenous nationalists and anti-abortion evangelicals – engaged with a swiftly changing domestic context and international rights landscape. Indigenous Australians found that calls for economic restitution, cultural recognition and land rights chimed well with international advocates of third-world uplift and a New International Economic Order to redress the wrongs of colonialism, while those feminists who managed Australia's intervention into the UN's International Women's Year (1975) saw such a focus on the centrality of economic and cultural rights as conveniently ignoring the nature of women's oppression. All the while, conservatives sought to have human rights extended to the supposed victims of the decade's "permissive society": unborn children. The 1980s marked the period of human rights' final absorption within governmental bureaucracies. Chapter 5 focuses on how government and social movements responded to the human rights "breakthrough", seeking to turn it to their various agendas. Calls for a Bill of Rights to enshrine protections in Australia's minimalist constitution and the establishment of Australia's first Human Rights Commission are analysed alongside two of the decade's most prominent campaigns: those seeking a treaty between settler and Indigenous Australians; and those seeking the decriminalisation of homosexuality. The rancorous debates that rights engendered demonstrate not their ascendency but continued contestation. An epilogue brings the book into the twenty-first century, looking at moments of possibility in the 1990s – particularly around queer rights and settler–Indigenous relations – and the end of such dreams in a twenty-first century marked by closing borders and minds. Was Australia's rights revolution less of a cascade than a trickle?

Literature on post-war Australia pays little attention to human rights, whether because of the term's ahistorical pretences or lack of easily discernible domestic impact. Biographies of political leaders and public figures, even those with records of human rights advocacy like Evatt and Dame Roma Mitchell, shy away from close analysis of the ideas they upheld or how they came to hold them.[25] Studies of political parties abound, largely written by their respective devotees or detractors, while Mark McKenna and Judith Brett's work on republicanism and the idea of the middle class, respectively, offer analyses of the confluence of political ideas and pragmatic realities.[26] Yet, work specifically on political ideas in Australia is slim. The most recent contribution by James Walter makes no space for human rights or the United Nations in general.[27] Taken broadly, the various struggles Australians have waged for various causes – in particular those for just treatment of Indigenous peoples, equality of women and acceptance of homosexuality – have been given ample attention by historians in both liberal and more radical variants. In these studies, however, human rights appear as one amongst many demands articulated by protest movements seeking citizenship, liberation, or civil or land rights and is presented as just another way of articulating the same thing. John Chesterman frames the Indigenous struggle for dignity in the nineteenth and twentieth centuries as one "civil rights", while Bain Attwood speaks simply of "rights".[28] Marilyn Lake's history of

[25] John Murphy, *Evatt: A Life* (Sydney: NewSouth Publishing, 2016); Susan Magarey and Kerrie Round, *Roma the First: A Biography of Dame Roma Mitchell* (Kent Town, SA: Wakefield Press, 2007).

[26] Mark McKenna, *The Captive Republic: A History of Republicanism in Australia 1788–1996* (Melbourne: Cambridge University Press, Melbourne, 1996); Judith Brett, *Australian Liberals and the Moral Middle Class: From Alfred Deakin to John Howard* (Melbourne: Cambridge University Press, 2003).

[27] James Walter with Todd Moore, *What Were They Thinking: The Politics of Ideas in Australia* (Sydney: UNSW Press, 2010).

[28] John Chesterman, *Civil Rights: How Indigenous Australians Won Formal Equality* (Brisbane: University of Queensland Press, 2005); Bain Attwood, *Rights for Aborigines* (St Leonards, NSW: Allen & Unwin, 2003).

10 Introduction: Bereft of Words

Australian feminism and Robert Reynolds on gay politics each pay careful attention to the ways language and demands have changed over time, but neither pays significant attention to the idea of human rights as distinct from other forms of claim making, instead focusing on "citizenship" and "liberation".[29]

Annemarie Devereux, a human rights lawyer by training, has taken up the challenge of Australia's human rights history in an international context, from Evatt's 1940s enthusiasm for international law to attempts by his conservative successors at stalling and undermining progress towards the 1966 "twin covenants". Deep concerns around international perception of statutory discrimination against women, migrants and Indigenous people saw Australia abstain or vote against core principles like minority rights and equal opportunity in a policy that was "hypocri[tical] and mean-spirited".[30] While Devereux's work covers well the way domestic politics influenced Australia's international presence, little is offered by way of the inverse: how these international conventions and norms were interpreted and utilised domestically. Ravi de Costa's work on indigenous transnationalism, entitled *A Higher Authority*, provides a valuable contribution towards this understanding of how the international was domesticated. De Costa's third chapter, "Human Rights for Indigenous Australians", points to how groups campaigning for Indigenous rights, and Indigenous Australians themselves, could blend their existing ideas "into the new conceptualisation of universal human rights": incorporating rights talk into various organisational constitutions and declarations, protest poetry and appeals for international aid. De Costa presents human rights as a vehicle for local concerns, arguing that it "had not implanted the liberal ideology of rights, but helped local activists to frame their use of that ideology".[31] The present study expands on De Costa's framework, tracking not just how human rights was one amongst many pieces of political clothing worn by various parties, groups and individuals to advance their causes but also how the shifting meanings of rights – from civil and political to economic and cultural – reflected and complemented that of local movements.

---

[29] Marilyn Lake, *Getting Equal: The History of Australian Feminism* (St Leonards, NSW: Allen & Unwin, 1999); Robert Reynolds, *From Camp to Queer: Remaking the Australian Homosexual* (Melbourne: Melbourne University Press, 2002).

[30] Annemarie Devereux, *Australia and the Birth of the International Bill of Human Rights 1946–1966* (Armidale: Federation Press, 2005); for quote, see Simon Kozlina, "Australia and the Birth of the International Bill of Human Rights 1946–1966 by Annemarie Devereux", *Australian Journal of Human Rights* 12, no. 1 (2006), 226.

[31] Ravi de Costa, *A Higher Authority: Indigenous Transnationalism and Australia* (Sydney: UNSW Press, 2006), 84–5.

More recent work has sought to engage with the global explosion of interest in human rights in an Australian context. Dominique Clément's comparative analysis of Canada and Australia concludes that Australia's lack of human rights organisations and long period of almost-uninterrupted conservative rule (1949–83) contributed to the nation's lack of uptake of the political ideas associated with the human rights revolution of the 1970s.[32] Yet, Clément's condensed narrative elides significant individuals and organisations who cleared the way for human rights' advance, while discounting the importance of the brief Whitlam Labor government of 1972–5. Closely focused work by Alison Holland and Jane Lydon draws the attention of historians to the importance of cultural work, in Lydon's case photography, and the work of individual campaigners, such as Indigenous human rights worker Mary Bennett, to Australia's human rights story.[33] Building upon such remarkable contributions, the present study provides significant new insights to the broader story of human rights' uptake in Australia, "a task which has only become more urgent in recent times", as Holland puts it.[34]

Rights before the Declaration

Human rights were not born on 10 December 1948, with the adoption of the UDHR by the conflictual powers of the emerging Cold War era. The phrase "human rights", with an assortment of meanings, in fact appears in relation to some of the earliest political struggles in Australian history. The *Illawarra Mercury* editorialised the 1858 extension of the vote to all white men in the colony of New South Wales as a "human right", arguing for "the universal recognition of all men, as men, to contribute their proper shares to the self-government of the communities of which they are real members".[35] A year earlier, colonial newspapers such as the *Sydney Morning Herald* and Melbourne's *Argus* invoked an idea of human rights to oppose the imposition of anti-Chinese laws in Victoria. The *Herald* commented:

---

[32] Dominique Clément, "The Rights Revolution in Canada and Australia: International Politics, Social Movements, and Domestic Law", in David Goutor and Stephen Heathorn (eds.), *Taking Liberties: A History of Human Rights in Canada* (Oxford: Oxford University Press, 2013), 88–113.

[33] Jane Lydon, *The Flash of Recognition: Photography and the Emergence of Indigenous Rights* (Sydney: NewSouth, 2012); Jane Lydon, *Photography, Humanitarianism, Empire* (London: Bloomsbury, 2016); Alison Holland, *Just Relations: The Story of Mary Bennett's Crusade for Aboriginal Rights* (Crawley, WA: University of Western Australia Press, 2015).

[34] Holland, *Just Relations*, 20.   [35] *Illawarra Mercury*, 14 June 1858, 2.

12   Introduction: Bereft of Words

Englishmen are great admirers of abstract philanthropy. They delight in all those exhibitions of human rights which awaken the profoundest emotions. They can weep over the pain and suffering endured by men of colour, and they warm towards all the inferior races who groan under the power of tyrants. But when these forms of misery and wretchedness come within their own vicinity, and present themselves in the aspect of some barbarian Chinaman, driven from the home of his fathers by an internecine war, and seeking the shadow of institutions said to be founded on the common benefit, all their philanthropy vanishes.[36]

Here we see human rights invoked as a claim of British birthrights, or as a form of colonial humanitarianism, often a poorly masked imperialism. The *Herald* in fact conflated the two in 1860, speaking of how anti-Chinese legislation undermined "the notion of human rights and British freedom" and stating that "in our opinion the defence of rights of a persecuted race is the sacred duty of every enlightened man".[37] This was the central use of human rights as a frame during the pre-1940 period. Without the UDHR, international institutions and the globalised political mindset of the postwar period, human rights could only be deployed as a noble dressing for something else, while some groups began imagining its universalist implications.

While the idea of human rights never featured prominently in white Australian political discussions before 1948, its appearance in movements throughout the nineteenth and early twentieth centuries cannot be ignored. At the outset, however, it is vital to highlight that human rights were overwhelmingly international rather than domestic talking points, often serving alongside humanitarianism as a gloss for imperialism. For Davide Rodongo, Western states used the idea of human rights, and the "right to life" of Christian minorities in the Ottoman Empire in particular, to add a liberal gloss to their desires to carve up the Balkans and Middle East.[38] As early as the 1820s, with the emergence of a strong print culture and the constant movement of people between the "homeland" and the new colony, discourses of humanitarianism began appearing in Australia as well. The campaign to abolish slavery across the British Empire provided a repertoire of ideas, particularly surrounding the dehumanising effects of flogging, which cut across the slave/convict divide.[39] As such, penal reform and ending transportation were early causes, if only adopted by an elite, metropolitan few. The Molesworth report relied on

---

[36] *Sydney Morning Herald*, 13 June 1859, 4.
[37] *Sydney Morning Herald*, 9 October 1860, 4.
[38] David Rodongo, *Against Massacre: Humanitarian Interventions in the Ottoman Empire, 1815–1914* (Princeton, NJ: Princeton University Press, 2012).
[39] On the campaign to abolish slavery as an antecedent to today's human rights language, see Jenny S. Martinez, *The Slave Trade and the International Origins of Human Rights Law* (New York: Oxford University Press, 2011).

humanitarian language to argue against transportation, while Quaker activists from Britain condemned the immoral and unchristian nature of harsh punishments against convicts and Indigenous Australians.[40]

Yet, humanitarianism is not human rights. As Michael Barnett puts it, "Human rights focus on legal discourses and frameworks, whereas humanitarianism shifts attention to moral codes and sentiments."[41] The framework of universal rights was rarely employed by campaigners for these early causes: there was no set of rights of the criminal or Indigenous peoples to appeal to, so instead the activists relied on what Lynn Hunt labels the emotional power of enlightenment values and the sympathetic sentiments these engendered.[42] Such sentiments, as Penelope Edmonds and Hamish Maxwell-Stewart have recently argued, actually had little demonstrable impact on punishment practices in Australia, with these instead evolving in accordance with new forms of less overtly violent but much more controlling and all-powerful punishment and incarceration.[43] Australian Indigenous peoples and their white supporters, however, mixed this moral, emotional rhetoric of humanitarianism with demands for the rights supposedly accorded to them as British subjects. The 1837 Select Committee Report into indigenous peoples across the British Empire spoke of a "humane empire" that was "achievable by extending to Indigenous peoples the civil rights of British subject hood and by protecting those rights in law".[44] While British authorities quickly moved away from the liberal language of Indigenous peoples as "fellow men", born of the anti-slavery moment, and adopted a more utilitarian, pseudo-scientific approach, Indigenous

---

[40] On early activism around transportation and penal violence, see Penelope Edmonds and Hamish Maxwell-Stewart, "'The Whip Is a Very Contagious Kind of Thing': Flogging and Humanitarian Reform in Penal Australia", *Journal of Colonialism and Colonial History* 17, no. 1 (2016), available at https://muse.jhu.edu/article/613283; Penelope Edmonds, "Travelling 'Under Concern': Quakers James Backhouse and George Washington Walker Tour the Antipodean Colonies, 1832–41", *The Journal of Imperial and Commonwealth History* 40, no. 5 (2012), 769–88; Isobelle Barrett-Meyering, "Abolitionism, Settler Violence and the Case against Flogging: A Reassessment of Sir William Molesworth's Contribution to the Transportation Debate", *History Australia* 7, no. 1 (2010), 06.01–06.16; Tim Castle, "Watching Them Hang: Capital Punishment and Public Support in Colonial New South Wales, 1826–1836", *History Australia* 5, no. 2 (2008), 43.01–43.15.

[41] Michael Barnett, *Empire of Humanity: A History of Humanitarianism* (Ithaca, NY: Cornell University Press, 2011), 16.

[42] Lynn Hunt, *Inventing Human Rights: A History* (New York: W. W. Norton & Company, 2007).

[43] Edmonds and Maxwell-Stewart, "The Whip Is a Very Contagious Kind of Thing".

[44] Amanda Nettelbeck, "'We Are Sure of Your Sympathy': Indigenous Uses of the Politics of Protection in Nineteenth-Century Australia and Canada", *Journal of Colonialism and Colonial History* 17, no. 1 (2016), available at https://muse.jhu.edu/article/613284.

14   Introduction: Bereft of Words

Australians continued to employ the Select Committee's rhetoric throughout the nineteenth century and beyond.[45]

Amanda Nettelbeck describes how a deputation of Indigenous Australians – with the assistance of local representatives of the Aborigines Protection Society – presented a gift of weapons to the Queen's representative in Melbourne in 1863, which they saw as a peace offering, and articulated a desire to "live like white men almost".[46] Such an appeal to the Queen – a "higher authority" in de Costa's definition – signalled an awareness of and desire to enjoy the rights that being a subject of the Queen theoretically bestowed.[47] This demand to share in the spoils of British (and later Australian) birthright was to be a constant of Indigenous activism until the end of the assimilation era, but Indigenous peoples rarely spoke of holding inalienable human rights, a concept foreign to the British legal tradition in any case.[48] It was equally to this language of the "rights of the British subject" that activists for self-rule and manhood suffrage turned in the 1840s and 1850s, with any reference to "dangerous" ideas of universality shouted down. Terry Irving discusses how a range of radical ideas permeated New South Wales – the earliest formed and most powerful colony – during this period, including those of a continental European nature that sparked great concern for conservatives. One of the Australian colony's foremost conservative politicians, James Macarthur railed against liberal politician William Macdermott for demanding equal representation – what he termed the "abstract rights of man" – regardless of property qualification in 1842. Macarthur asked whether his liberal opponent was advocating "the rights of Britons or that

---

[45] On activism for Aboriginal rights in the colonial period, see Penelope Edmonds, "Collecting Looerryminer's 'Testimony': Aboriginal Women, Sealers, and Quaker Humanitarian Anti-slavery Thought and Action in the Bass Strait Islands", *Australian Historical Studies* 45, no. 1 (2014), 13–33; Tracey Banivanua Mar, "Imperial Literacy and Indigenous Rights: Tracing Transoceanic Circuits of a Modern Discourse", *Aboriginal History* 37 (2013), 1–28; Zoe Laidlaw, "Indigenous Interlocutors: Networks of Imperial Protest and Humanitarianism in the Mid-nineteenth Century", in Jane Carey and Jane Lydon (eds.), *Indigenous Networks: Mobility, Connections and Exchange* (London: Routledge, 2014), 114–39; Mark McKenna, "Transplanted to Savage Shores: Indigenous Australians and British birthright in the Mid Nineteenth-Century Australian Colonies", *Journal of Colonialism and Colonial History* 13, no. 1 (2012), available at https://muse.jhu.edu/article/475172; Ann Curthoys and Jessie Mitchell, "'Bring this Paper to the Good Governor': Aboriginal Petitioning in Britain's Australian Colonies", in Saliha Belmessous (ed.), *Native Claims: Indigenous Law against Empire, 1500–1920* (Oxford: Oxford University Press, 2012), 182–203; Jessie Mitchell, *In Good Faith? Governing Indigenous Australia through God, Charity and Empire, 1825–1855* (Canberra: ANU E-Press, 2011).
[46] *Goulburn Herald*, 6 June 1863, quoted in Nettelbeck, "We Are Sure of Your Sympathy".
[47] De Costa, *A Higher Authority*.
[48] Such attempts to "redeem" liberalism's promise were also a transnational phenomenon, as discussed in Tim Rowse, "The Indigenous Redemption of Liberal Universalism", *Modern Intellectual History* 12, no. 3 (November 2015), 579–603.

Rights before the Declaration

vile and bastard democracy which has led to so many evil results in different parts of the world. Would they stand for their rights as Britons or follow those abstract rights by which the cannibals of New Zealand ... and the savages of these wild lands would be admitted to a share of government?"[49]

As Irving notes, however, the figure of "abstract rights" appeared as pure shibboleth in these and other debates over the introduction and extension of suffrage: "Macdermott's speech revealed that he thought in a similar way to Macarthur: they were simply demanding their rights as British subjects." Such national-based rights, as Moyn argues, were the "essential crucible" of the rights paradigm. Yet, human rights differ in their "transcending of the state forum": demanding the rights of Britons was demanding inclusion in a very limited horizon of freedoms, not appealing to the universal nature of man, a decidedly unpopular – perhaps even unfathomable – principle in nineteenth-century Australia.[50] These campaigns were, however, the first which involved large numbers of colonists from the soon-to-be dubbed "working class" and, as Sean Scalmer writes, were marked by significant street-based agitation.[51] This was part of a broader debate and gradual reconceptualisation of the meaning of "the rights of Britons". As James Walter writes, the colonial elite – squatters and their political handmaidens – wished for Australians to possess a very restrained version of "British rights". W. C. Wentworth protested at how "[t]he colony of NSW is, I believe, the only one of our possessions exclusively inhabited by Englishmen, in which there is not at least the shadow of a free government, as it possesses neither a council, a house of assembly nor even the privilege of trial by jury ... [t]hose ancient birthrights and bulwarks of the British Constitution".[52] Yet, Wentworth and his ilk's favoured colonial compact was not democracy but one overseen by "men who have been taught to distinguish a rational and well-founded freedom from the disorganizing

---

[49] *Australasian Chronicle*, 1 March 1842, 2–3. Quoted in Terry Irving, *The Southern Tree of Liberty: The Democratic Movement in New South Wales before 1856* (Leichardt, NSW: Federation Press, 2006), 77. Some have criticised Irving's work for overplaying the role of radicals; see Paul Pickering, "From Rifle Club to Reading Room: Sydney's Democratic Vistas, 1848–1856", *Labour History Review* 78, no. 1 (2013), 87–112; Terry Irving and Paul Pickering, "Debate: Terry Irving and Paul Pickering", *Labour History Review* 79, no. 2 (2014), 227–37.

[50] Samuel Moyn, *The Last Utopia: Human Rights in History* (Harvard: Harvard University Press, 2010), 20.

[51] Sean Scalmer, "Containing Contention: A Reinterpretation of Democratic Change and Electoral Reform in the Australian Colonies", *Australian Historical Studies* 42, no. 3 (2011), 337–56; see also Sean Scalmer, *On the Stump: Campaign Oratory and Democracy in the United States, Britain and Australia* (Philadelphia, PA: Temple University Press, 2017).

[52] Walter, *What Were They Thinking*, 43.

16   Introduction: Bereft of Words

doctrines" – and who had the property qualification to prove it. There was thus no contradiction, Walter highlights, "in arguing vigorously for the rights of Englishmen, while advocating a hereditary aristocracy, insisting on the privileges of men of means and opposing democracy".[53]

Yet, it was colonial liberals – that some termed "radicals" – who won the day, with universal (white, male) suffrage and secret ballots introduced across the Australian colonies by the 1860s. Reformers succeeded in shifting the meaning of British rights away from its anti-democratic heritage, stymieing those who wanted to see the "colonial franchise raised so high that the future representation of the colony shall be the same family compact as it has hitherto been and the future colonial constituency be mere horned cattle and pure merinos".[54] This was the climate in which the *Illawara Mercury* could call the granting of universal suffrage a "human right" – demonstrating that "the old corrupt Parliaments of England are not the rule, but the abuse of the British Constitution". That the Australian colonies now "recognise[d] men as members of a community [with] a natural right of access to all the privileges of that community" only granted them the rights – or, as they put it, privileges – that "the British Constitution professes to do".[55] This "popular constitutionalism" also motivated the 1854 Eureka uprising – a rebellion over the high cost of prospecting licences in the Victorian mining town of Ballarat that blossomed into a "radical reinterpretation of the rights of the free born Briton" – but it in no way represented calls for human rights or even republicanism, despite noted interest in American revolutionary thought by some.[56]

Colonial Australia's newly realised democracy was nowhere near as universal as it claimed. Indeed, as Leigh Boucher has recently argued, "racial expulsion and repression was a product of the very ideas concerning self-government and political competency" that birthed the universal franchise in Victoria and other colonies.[57] Perhaps most obvious in their exclusion from the rights of Britons were Chinese, whose arrival in large numbers during the Victorian Gold Rushes was another instigator for the

[53] Walter, *What Were They Thinking*, 45.
[54] *Colonial Observer*, 9 March 1842, quoted in Walter, *What Were They Thinking*, 47.
[55] *Illawarra Mercury*, 14 June 1858, 2.
[56] Paul Pickering, "'Who Are the Traitors?': Rethinking the Eureka Stockade", in David Headon and John Uhr (eds.), *Eureka: Australia's Greatest Story* (Leichardt, NSW: The Federation Press, 2015), 76. On the influence of the American Revolution, see Claire Wright, "'The Next Throb of Outraged Humanity': Australia in a Revolutionary Age", in David Headon and John Uhr (eds.), *Eureka: Australia's Greatest Story* (Leichardt, NSW: The Federation Press, 2015), 44–55.
[57] Leigh Boucher, "Race, Rights and the Re-forming Settler Polity in Mid-nineteenth Century Victoria", *Journal of Australian Colonial History* 15 (2013), 103.

Eureka uprising. While mainstream newspapers of elite opinion called for humanitarianism towards these "inferior races who groan under the power of tyrants", Chinese in Australia relied on the same popular constitutionalism as their white contemporaries.[58] On the Victorian gold fields, Chinese workers collected over 5000 signatures for a petition politely requesting equal treatment, "relying on constitutionalist language and procedures to mediate their plight in a familiar political idiom".[59] Marilyn Lake writes of how this seizure of familiar political idioms continued into the 1880s, with one particular and novel innovation: an appeal to "Common Human Rights". In one of the earliest usages of the term in positive political context in the colonies, resident Chinese used the term "human rights" to argue for their sharing in the privileges bequeathed by British birthright. Works such as *The Chinese Question in Australia* (1879) challenged their relegation to the "uncivilised peoples" of the world, while criticising the racial limits of the rights of Britons.[60] "China had reached a very high stage of civilization when Britain was peopled by naked savages", the pamphlet protested, adding: "It did not matter that Chinese colonists might be British subjects from Hong Kong, Penang, or Singapore ... [H]e differs from the European in the colour of his skin [and] is therefore to be treated as a felon."[61] Yet, Lake also highlights the contradictory nature of this claim, one which "did not emphasize the sanctity 'of the individual'", as human rights advocates did in the postwar context, "but rather the 'equality of races'". This usage of rights, tied firmly into the Darwinian racialised social hierarchy, is represented in the protestations of one Chinese Australian – "is it possible that common human rights accorded to other civilized people are to be denied to us?"[62]

Women were also excluded from the inherent rights of the Englishman. "Colonised", in the controversial words of Anne Summers, from invasion of the continent, women were seen as representing the purity of the nation

---

[58] *Sydney Morning Herald*, 13 June 1859, 4.

[59] Andrew Messner, "Popular Constitutionalism and Chinese Protest on the Victorian Goldfields", *Journal of Australian Colonial History* 2, no. 2 (October 2000), 73. For more on Chinese use of the British legal and constitutional system, see Mark Finnane, "'Habeas Corpus Mongols': Chinese Litigants and the Politics of Immigration in 1888", *Australian Historical Studies* 45, no. 2 (2014), 165–83; Paul Macgregor, "'Before We Came to This Country, We Heard that English Laws Were Good and Kind to Everybody': Chinese Immigrants' Views of Colonial Australia", in Alison Broinowski (ed.), *Double Vision: Asian Accounts of Australia* (Canberra: Pandanus Books, 2004), 41–60.

[60] Marilyn Lake, "Chinese Colonists Assert Their 'Common Human Rights': Cosmopolitanism as Subject and Method of History", *Journal of World History* 21, no. 3 (2010), 383.

[61] Ibid., 385–7.   [62] Ibid., 379.

18 Introduction: Bereft of Words

yet denied any practical social or political stake in it.[63] The language of rights seemed not particularly useful to women, as one scribe for Sydney's feminist journal *The Dawn* wrote in 1897: "We have endless talk, argument and sarcasm about the rights of women. So much, indeed, has been said on this subject that the term has long been used as a sort of reproach, and savors of ridicule."[64] A farce entitled "Rights of Women" graced the theatres of Melbourne, the Victorian colony's capital, in 1854. Featuring as its protagonist "a strong-minded lady who is a Pupil of the New Age and a firm believer in the Rights of Women", this was one of many satirical or dismissive interventions that marked a period that saw Australian women demand access to political rights for the first time.[65] The very notion of women's suffrage was mocked in debates about universal manhood suffrage during this decade, with conservative William Piddington jesting in 1858 that "If the suffrage were a sacred, inalienable, indefeasible right common to human nature, how dared [British law] deprive the fairer half of creation of their indefeasible privilege?"[66] Yet, *The Dawn*'s writer elaborated, that the idea was a source of mirth did not mean that the frame of rights should be abandoned. Rather, it was essential to "establish certain claims that, under the laws of nature, it would seem that women have a right to assert, such as women's natural right "to ... the child that she has borne".[67]

Such a reliance on naturalised womanhood was both a blessing and a curse for early women's rights advocates. The idea of naturalised rights was born of religion, and scripture fired much early feminist activism.[68] In 1900 *The Dawn* reprinted a piece by Frances E. Willard, American Christian suffragist and founder of the Women's Christian Temperance Union, entitled "Human Rights and Social Duties", which argued that the only way that both these principles could be applied was to have "'all ye are brethren' becom[e] the watchword of a holier, happier time."[69]

---

[63] Anne Summers, *Damned Whores and God's Police: The Colonisation of Women in Australia* (Ringwood, VIC: Penguin Australia, 1975).

[64] "Has a Mother Any Right to Her Children?", *The Dawn*, 1 October 1897, 9.

[65] Quoted in Angela Woollacott, *Settler Society in the Australian Colonies: Self-Government and Imperial Culture* (Oxford: Oxford University Press, 2015), 128–9.

[66] "Parliament of New South Wales", *Sydney Morning Herald*, 31 July 1858, 6.

[67] "Has a Mother Any Right to Her Children?", *The Dawn*, 1 October 1897, 9.

[68] For the role of Christianity in the early women's movements, see Ian Tyrell, *Woman's World, Woman's Empire: The Woman's Christian Temperance Union in International Perspective, 1880–1930* (Chapel Hill: University of North Carolina Press, 1991).

[69] Frances E. Willard, "Human Rights and Social Duties", *The Dawn*, 1 July 1900, 23. For more on the intricate connections between Progressive-era campaigners in Australia and the United States, see Marilyn Lake, *Progressive New World: How Settler Colonialism and Transpacific Exchange Shaped American Reform* (Cambridge, MA: Harvard University Press, 2019).

That women in Australia served as "god's police", a discourse utilised by local temperance unions to further their place in the public sphere, is well noted by Summers and others.[70] Women would bring "a new element into political life", feminist Rose Scott wrote in 1903, and their role should be to act as "[t]he moral safeguards of the nation", which the Australian colonies had become only two years earlier.[71] Women's activists understood that the language of British citizenship rights was gender-restrictive. Citizenship was both firmly racialized and gendered, and, as such, the claim for certain maternal rights or a particular female contribution to a racialised conception of nationhood makes sense. Indeed, the labour movement, which emerged at around the same time as women began demanding political equality, oft presented itself as women's champion in the public. One writer to a 1917 issue of Queensland's *Worker* newspaper put this clearly:

[W]oman's equal citizenship and voice in legislation are owing to the ideas and the efforts, the propaganda and the performance of the party that has always stood, as it stands to-day, for human rights, irrespective of sex, the Australian Labor party, the party of the highest ideals of human equality, liberty, and fraternity."[72]

Although many scholars have highlighted the early ALP's lacklustre gender politics, with women's inequality enshrined in the 1907 Harvester judgement that set the foundation for the modern Australian social compact, the movement's articulation of human rights was quite novel.[73]

Calls for state intervention through the universalist language of human rights became more and more common in other areas as well. Women's activists, as part of paternalistic campaigns on behalf of Indigenous women, called on the newly federated Commonwealth to protect them from cultural practices considered abhorrent, such as child marriage. "Australian women had to play a part in securing human rights for their dark sisters", the *Age* reported, in a colourful example of the white woman's burden.[74] It is important to note, finally, the language

---

[70] Summers, *Damned Whores*, chapter 11. For other histories of women's rights claims at this time, see Marilyn Lake, *Getting Equal: A History of Australian Feminism* (St Leonards, NSW: Allen & Unwin, 1999), chapters 1 and 3; Patricia Grimshaw, Marilyn Lake, Ann McGrath and Marian Quartly, *Creating a Nation* (Ringwood, VIC: McPhee Gribble Publishers, 1994), chapter 7; Claire Wright, *You Daughters of Freedom: The Australians Who Won the Vote and Inspired the World* (Melbourne: Text Publishing, 2018).

[71] Rose Scott quoted in Summers, *Damned Whores*, 347.

[72] A. W. Ross, "Women's Co-citizenship", *The Worker*, 6 December 1917, 17.

[73] On the Australian labour movement and the women's movement, see Lake et al., *Creating a Nation*, chapter 8, and Bruce Scates, *A New Australia: Citizenship, Radicalism and the First Republic* (Cambridge: Cambridge University Press, 1999), chapter 6.

[74] *The Age* (Victoria), 7 April 1934, 14.

20 Introduction: Bereft of Words

Indigenous people themselves adopted during this period. The notion of "citizenship rights", employed by the Aborigines Progressives Association and others during the late 1930s, differed to that of human rights. Publications like *The Australian Abo Call* demanded such rights – "the privileges and benefits of civilisation" – in a way that echoed previous articulations of the British subject and "humane empire".[75] Australia's dispossessed and disenfranchised peoples received limited access to the public domain, mostly existed as wards of the state and, perhaps most importantly, were viewed as facing eventual extinction, all of which problematized potential claims to a shared humanity. As Hannah Arendt famously put it, in order to have access to human rights, one must first be a politically and socially recognised member of a nation-state: "humanity was a mark of vulnerability rather than a source of protection" for the effectively stateless.[76]

We then see how the idea of human rights moved from a rarely used, widely condemned or mocked import to a term which entered – if only sparingly – the everyday lexicon of social movement activists. The rights of the British subject, helpful to those demanding manhood suffrage, came to be understood as limited by both gendered and racialised pre-sumptions. One thing remained the same for all of these movements, however: the all-important place of the State – whether colonial or, come 1901, the Australian nation. This supremacy of the nation-state remained at the centre of rights discourse in the 1940s, to which we now turn.

---

[75] J. T. Patten, "Calling all Aborigines: Straight Talk", *The Australian Abo Call*, no. 3 (June 1938), 1; on humane empire see Amanda Nettelbeck, *Indigenous Rights and Colonial Subjecthood: Protection and Reform in the Nineteenth-Century British Empire* (Cambridge, UK: Cambridge University Press, 2019).

[76] Stephanie DeGooyer, Alastair Hunt, Lida Maxwell and Samuel Moyn, *The Right to Have Rights* (London: Verso, 2018), 7–8.

1 Inventing Rights

The modern human rights era is said to have been born in August of 1941. Franklin Roosevelt and Winston Churchill met aboard the American heavy cruiser USS *Augusta*, in what some have called the first ever superpower summit, to author a set of moral principles that would guide a war effort of which America was then not even part.[1] They authored an eight-point statement, less than 400 words in length, quickly dubbed the Atlantic Charter. It "called for self-determination of peoples, freer trade, and several New Deal-style social welfare provisions" and talked of rights not at the level of the nation-state but "to all the men in all the lands".[2] Described by its foremost historian as a New Deal for the world, it was received in such grandiose terminology around the globe, despite the two world leaders later backtracking on many of its more stellar promises. Churchill, in particular, was keen that the Charter not be taken too literally, seeing it as a wartime pact pledging "the deliverance of the oppressed peoples from the Nazi tyranny" rather than a postwar blueprint.[3] Free talk of self-determination or rights – much like Woodrow Wilson's post–World War I fourteen points – would provide ripe fodder for British subjects in India and elsewhere seeking the dismantling of colonial rule.[4] It is perhaps peculiar, then, as Stuart Macintyre points out, that Australian prime minister Robert Gordon Menzies "laid stress on the very aspect that Churchill had resisted".[5] "It is, so to speak, a declaration of human rights", Menzies pronounced in parliament, a document that "sets out in plain language the fundamental aspirations of all the liberty-loving peoples of the

---

[1] Elizabeth Borgwardt, *A New Deal for the World: America's Vision for Human Rights* (Cambridge, MA: Harvard University Press, 2007).

[2] Ibid., 4.   [3] *The West Australian*, 26 August 1941, 5.

[4] On the radical implications of Wilson's 1919 intervention at Versailles, see Erez Manela, *The Wilsonian Moment: Self-Determination and the International Origins of Anticolonial Nationalism* (New York: Oxford University Press, 2007). For a recasting of these events as counter-revolutionary, see Adom Getachew, *Worldmaking after Empire: The Rise and Fall of Self-Determination* (Princeton, NJ: Princeton University Press, 2019), chapter 2.

[5] Stuart Macintyre, *Australia's Boldest Experiment: War and Reconstruction in the 1940s* (Sydney: NewSouth, 2015), 42.

22   Inventing Rights

world". The war was "not merely ... a great struggle in which evil things must be overthrown, but also ... something from which positively good things for men and women must emerge".[6]

Menzies' grand elaboration of the Charter's themes was replicated in Australian reporting. One regional paper welcomed the Charter's "words of good cheer for [the] oppressed", while Melbourne's *The Age* dubbed this non-binding, brief and inconclusive document "the Magna Carta of 1941".[7] Such a flush of emotion, a welcome change from dispiriting news on the battlefront in Europe, shows a populace keen to build a new world in the postwar era: one in which the global war they were engaged in and the economic depression that arguably brought it about could not ever occur again. Interestingly, however, this was not the first declaration of "human rights" to have emerged during wartime – in fact, Australia's Catholic clergy had prepared their own, over a year before Churchill and Roosevelt held their momentous meeting. This chapter is titled "Inventing Rights", and the meaning is very specific. The introductory chapter sought out early usages of rights in Australian political culture, locating an emerging vocabulary that found little use for universality in the face of older, hegemonic notions of "British" rights and duties. Yet, what happened in the 1940s marked as much a departure as a continuation of this heritage – an invention of something new out of composite pieces from around the world. Rights, it seemed, were everywhere in the 1940s. On one register, the term "human rights" appears in Australian newspapers of the time nearly five times more often than in the preceding decade.[8] Yet, the phrase began to carry two sets of distinct meanings. On the one hand, human rights were principles to be enjoyed by individuals, respected by nations and, as the decade drew to a close, enforced internationally. On the other hand, this type of rights talk was heavily contested in the 1940s. Indeed, the dominant reading of the notion of human rights was centred on the state, primarily its responsibility to provide a level of welfare and support to citizens that would stave off another Depression and the war it had birthed. Both "versions" of rights appear starkly in 1940s Australia, demonstrating how "the competition over the meaning of human rights drove its wartime itinerary more than anything else".[9]

---

[6] *CPD* (House) 20 August 1941, 9.
[7] *Goulburn Evening* Post, 25 August 1941, 2; *The Age*, 16 August 1941, 11.
[8] The term appeared 1,953 times between 1930 and 1939, rising to 8,728 from 1940 to 1949. Advanced search for the term "human rights" at www.trove.nla.gov.au/newspaper.
[9] Samuel Moyn, *The Last Utopia: Human Rights in History* (Cambridge, MA: The Belknap Press of Harvard University Press, 2010), 51.

"Fundamental Human Rights"

On the one hand, a progressive Australian Labor Party (ALP) government sought to use the rhetoric of rights as a part of a grab for broader federal government authority in 1944, seeking powers previously residing in individual squabbling states in order to deliver a "cradle to grave" social safety net. The defeat of the constitutional referendum they undertook demonstrates the contested nature of rights talk in the period and was but the first of many ongoing conflicts between Commonwealth authority and state autonomy that have defined Australia's engagement with human rights. Different versions of rights competed for public acceptance: one minimalist and liberal, the other maximalist and social-democratic. This failure had a pronounced effect on Australia's contribution to the drafting of the Universal Declaration of Human Rights in 1948. Equally, though, the 1940s shows that there were those, of the political right and left, who sought to elevate the importance of the human person over that of Labor's social-welfare state. The Catholic Church, in its first ever Social Justice Statement (1940), presented what was dubbed a declaration of "fundamental human rights" that complemented the need of the state to play a greater role in society with a set of stringent safeguards to protect the individual from its inevitably totalitarian machinations. Campaigns led by the wives of Indonesian and Chinese refugees, facing expulsion under the White Australia Policy from 1947 to 1949, show a similar "vernacularising", this time of the idea of individual human rights, at a time when such principles were practically ignored by governments.

"Fundamental Human Rights": Catholicism and the Turn to Rights

Kylie Tennant's novel *The Battlers* (1941) tells the story of four itinerant Australians caught in the midst of the Great Depression in rural Australia. It was one of several fictional works that looked sympathetically on the "vagabonds, failures and criminals" who suffered through the rural agricultural slump of the 1930s, moving from job to job with what was seen as a quintessentially Australian perseverance.[10] Some 30 per cent of the Australian population were unemployed at the time, and shanty settlements multiplied on the outskirts of towns and cities, making poverty an unavoidable spectacle. Compared favourably to John Steinbeck's *The Grapes of Wrath* (1939), Tennant's novel won literary prizes and found favourable reviews in numerous capital city newspapers.[11] Tennant's

---

[10] Kylie Tennant, *The Battlers* (Sydney: Angus & Robertson, 1973 [1941]), vii.

[11] Robert L. Ross, "Departures to the Promised Land: Kylie Tennant's *The Battlers* and John Steinbeck's *The Grapes of Wrath*", in Xavier Pons (ed.), *Departures: How Australia Reinvents Itself* (Carlton: Melbourne University Press, 2002), 37–43.

24 Inventing Rights

work was more than just a literary evocation, however; it was a paean to the downtrodden and an attack on what she perceived as an increasingly bureaucratised, elite capitalist culture. "More and more people are battlers", Tennant pronounces in the introduction to the book's 1945 re-issuing, "not only on the track, but in the suburbs, the factories, the automated living where to be a man or a woman is no longer any claim."[12] Such a defence of the individual man and woman – which put Tennant somewhat outside the class-focused social realism of her fellow communists – was a major concern for numerous Australians in the 1940s from all sides of politics. Yet, Tennant's dual affinities – to the individual human caught in the bureaucratic machine and to the ideal of collective liberation her communism promised – speak to the contested, uneven nature of the uptake of human rights in Australia. In fact, perhaps surprisingly, it was on the reactionary side of Australian political life where human rights received their first sustained wartime attention.

Catholicism in Australia, associated with the Irish and later migrant populations from southern Europe, had a secondary, arguably persecuted, place in an Australia governed largely by Protestants. State aid – provided to the four main Christian denominations during the nineteenth century on the basis of a false equality – saw Catholicism gain a rush of new churches and clergy but only further cemented and embittered sectarian tensions that were only exacerbated by the Irish ancestry of most believers.[13] Members of particular denominations played in the same sporting teams and shopped in the same stores, making it possible to "live just about a whole life within the bosom of the church". Such separateness was furthered in the 1870s, when the introduction of state-based secular education saw the Catholic Church establish a parallel system of schooling which ensured "that Australia's children would grow up in two cultural worlds, Catholic or Protestant".[14] Such divisions manifested in politics, perhaps most vitally during World War I, when sections of the Catholic hierarchy openly campaigned against the introduction of conscription.[15] As the religion of the working class, Catholicism also had a significant sway

---

[12] Tennant, *The Battlers*, cover, vii.

[13] Anne O'Brien, "Religion", in Alison Bashford and Stuart Macintyre (eds.), *The Cambridge History of Australia, Volume 1: Indigenous and Colonial Australia* (Port Melbourne: Cambridge University Press, 2013), 414–37. For more on the history of the Irish in Australia, see Elizabeth Malcolm and Diane Hall, *A New History of the Irish in Australia* (Sydney: NewSouth, 2018).

[14] Graeme Davison, "Religion", in Alison Bashford and Stuart Macintyre (eds.), *The Cambridge History of Australia, Volume 2: The Commonwealth of Australia* (Port Melbourne: Cambridge University Press, 2013), 219.

[15] See Robert Bollard, *In the Shadow of Gallipoli: The Hidden History of Australia in World War I* (Sydney: NewSouth, 2013), chapter 3.

"Fundamental Human Rights" 25

over members of that class' political party, the ALP.[16] By the 1930s, this history had created a deeply sectarian polity, with the Catholic Church wary of state intervention and looking to guard its own interests. The economic depression of the 1930s, as Tennant's books made clear to the reading public, struck the working class hardest – a class amongst which Catholicism was over-represented. Newspapers such as *The Advocate*, a publication of the Catholic Melbourne Archdiocese, understood the Depression as part of modern society's moral failure. Quoting Pope Pius XI's encyclical of 1931, on the reconstruction of the social order, *The Advocate* asked whether it was the "sordid egotism which too often regulates the mutual relations of individuals and society . . . in a word, greed . . . that has brought the world to a pass that we all see and deplore".[17] Man's moral failures were matched by those of the growing bureaucracy, as another article put it: "It would seem that the industrial economic system, like the great machine it is, has got beyond the control of those who guide it."[18]

Such concerns – of secularism as a moral curse and the growth of unaccountable government – led elements of the Catholic Church to flirt with fascism as a solution to the Depression's ills in what historians call the "transwar" era.[19] Fascism, dubbed "a special syndical and corporative organisation" founded on the "peaceful collaboration of the classes [and] repression of Socialist organisations", was a concept *The Advocate* thought in 1932 required "little reflection . . . to perceive the advantages" of.[20] Such conceptions – which James Chappell labels "Paternal Catholic Modernism" – were a way for the Church to accept the reality of secular authority in either democratic or dictatorial dimensions.[21] As *The Advocate* put in 1938:

If the new State, with its huge powers, is not to become a mere tyranny exercised under colour of the "popular will", it must be based on something more than a negative Liberalism. Its power must be founded, not merely on community sovereignty, but on a clear conception of the natural and Divine law, with all that that law involves of human rights, duties and liberties. Where such a law is widely

---

[16] See, for example, Frank Bongiorno and Nick Dyrenfurth, *A Little History of the Australian Labor Party* (Sydney: University of New South Wales Press, 2010), 44.

[17] *The Advocate*, 1 June 1933, 27. [18] *The Advocate*, 23 July 1931, 20.

[19] On the "transwar" era, see Phillip Nord, *France's New Deal: From the 1930s to the Postwar Era* (Princeton, NJ: Princeton University Press, 2012), 12–13; Terrence Renaud, "Human Rights as Radical Anthropology: Protestant Theology and Ecumenism in the Transwar Era", *The Historical Journal* 60, no. 2 (2017), 493–518.

[20] *The Advocate*, 9 June 1932, 6.

[21] James Chappell, *Catholic Modern: The Challenge of Totalitarianism and the Remaking of the Church* (Cambridge, MA: Harvard University Press, 2018), chapter 2. See also Giuliana Chamedes, *A Twentieth-Century Crusade: The Vatican's Battle to Remake Christian Europe* (Cambridge, MA: Harvard University Press, 2019).

26   Inventing Rights

understood and observed as limiting power, freedom can exist even under the political forms of dictatorship: where the sense of it has decayed, the name of "democracy" only serves to veil the reality of arbitrary power and oppression.[22]

Yet, as the 1930s wore on, entertaining such ideas became infeasible. As Samuel Moyn argues, it is at this point – and particularly in the depths of World War II – that Catholics around the world began abandoning authoritarianism and embracing the idea of human rights. The idea of "human dignity" – that had previously referred to groups or traditional social structures such as the family – was reinvented as inalienable individual rights, particularly via the 1937 Irish constitution and the revisionist work of Catholic scholar Jacques Maritain. As Moyn puts it, "the language of rights was extricated from the legacy of the French Revolution, the secularist mantle of which the Soviet leaders were now widely seen to have assumed", and a new form of Christian democracy based on individual rights "became not only palatable but a precious resource for the future of religious values".[23] In the late 1930s, discussion of human rights in Australia became more pronounced. Instances of the term's use in *The Advocate* jump fourfold between the 1920s and the 1930s and over fourfold again in the 1940s.[24] This is reflected in figures from a wide sampling of general Australian newspapers as well; however, usage by *The Advocate* in the 1930s increases much faster than the overall trend.[25]

Human rights, it seemed, provided an antidote to what Catholic author Hillaire Belloc described in *The Servile State* (1912) as the growth of bureaucratic power at the expense of the individual.[26] Belloc was often drawn upon by writers for the Catholic paper, amongst whom was Bartholomew Augustus (B. A.) Santamaria, only then beginning his

---

[22] *The Advocate*, 1 December 1938, 8.

[23] Samuel Moyn, *Christian Human Rights* (Philadelphia: University of Pennsylvania Press, 2015), 9. For a challenge to some of Moyn's argument, see Giuliana Chamedes, "Catholics, Anti-Semitism and the Human Rights Swerve", *The Immanent Frame*, 29 June 2015, available at https://tif.ssrc.org/2015/06/29/catholics-anti-semitism-and-the-human-rights-swerve/.

[24] The term appeared 15 times in the 1920s and 59 times in the 1930s, before exploding to 232 mentions in the 1940s. Advance search for the term "human rights" in *The Advocate*, available at https://trove.nla.gov.au/newspaper/result?q=%22human+rights%22&exactPhrase=&anyWords=&notWords=&requestHandler=&dateFrom=&dateTo=&l-advtitle=792&sortby.

[25] The usage in all newspapers increased by only 25 per cent between the 1920s and the 1930s, to 1,953 mentions from 1,366 mentions. Advanced search for the term "human rights" in Trove, available at https://trove.nla.gov.au/newspaper/result?q=%22human+rights%22&exactPhrase&anyWords&notWords&requestHandler&dateFrom&dateTo&sortby&openFacets=true.

[26] Hillaire Belloc, *The Servile State* (London: T. N. Foulis, 1912).

career as a right-wing lay leader.[27] The "servile state" allowed the Church hierarchy and its popularisers to oppose states of both the political left and right, with Sydney's *Catholic Weekly* arguing in 1938 that "[n]either Capitalism nor Communism is concerned with the ordinary human rights. One would crush them by economic power, the other by revolution."[28] By 1940, *The Advocate* was criticising language of World War II being a "holy war": "We have little patience with much of the prevailing loose talk of 'Christian Civilisation' and a 'New Order' for our capitalist civilisation – 'that lump of damnation', as Mr. Belloc calls it, is not Christian." Materialism and the conditions that capitalism, particularly during the suffering of the 1930s, made widespread were not what Catholics saw the war as being about. Instead, they felt, it concerned "defending the main institutions of our Western order, which spring from the Christian culture upon which it is founded: more especially the conception of human rights and freedom, and the dignity from which such freedom springs".[29]

It is worth noting that such talk was some two years prior to Pope Pius' Christmas Day 1942 statement, which centralised "fundamental personal rights" in postwar Catholic social thought.[30] The specific meaning that the Australian Catholic hierarchy associated with human rights was made clear in 1940, with the drawing up of the first Bishops' Statement on Social Justice, a yearly event "unique on the English-speaking world" that continues to this day.[31] While other documents, like the "Manifesto of the Christian Social Order" produced simultaneously by the Inter-Church Council, were "of a general nature, being a criticism and an exhortation", this one was "a precise statement of first principles" which "not only lays out these principles, but applies them to Australian conditions".[32] The statement was surmised in *The Advocate* to be based on a specific notion of man:

Man is a social being, composed of body and spirit, with a destiny in time and eternity, to be realised through the free service of God. Certain external conditions are essential to the welfare of this being and the achievement of the aim of his existence: they may be called **"Fundamental Human Rights"**.[33]

Predating Roosevelt's 1941 "four freedoms", the hierarchy broke its declaration of rights into four key categories. The "right to life" entailed "not merely social defence measures but also the prevention of evils such

---

[27] On Santamaria, see Ross Fitzgerald, *The Pope's Battalions: Santamaria, Catholicism and the Labor Split* (Brisbane, QLD: University of Queensland Press, 2003).

[28] *The Catholic Weekly*, 8 October 1942, 1.   [29] *The Advocate*, 16 May 1940, 8.

[30] Moyn, *Christian Human Rights*, 2.   [31] *The Advocate*, 9 October 1946, 3.

[32] *The Advocate*, 14 November 1940, 5. Inter-Church Council, *The Movement towards a Christian Social Order* (Melbourne: Manifesto Committee, 1940).

[33] *The Advocate*, 18 April 1940, 8. Bolding in original.

28   Inventing Rights

as contraception and the murder of the unborn", while the "right to live in a human way" cemented the "solidarity of the family" as the centre of social life "without State interference" and "the right to exercise choice in the education of ... children". Catholics had long opposed birth control and demanded government-subsidised religious schooling, but importantly these were reframed as a series of individual rights against the state. The "right to freedom", as it was put, emerged from the fact that "[man] has been endowed with free will and with personal creative faculties whose exercise is of the highest value to his character". A person must have freedom in order to render "free service to God" – a call for the freedom of religion which also worked its way into Roosevelt's four freedoms but was to prove controversial when discussed as part of the UDHR.[34]

The last right, however, sought to provide an answer to Catholicism's opposition to both unrestrained capitalism and the threat of the "servile state". The "right to property" was connected to the earlier right, insofar as it was "the economic basis of freedom". However, such a right to individual property "should not be regarded as the privilege of the few: and the power of the State should be used, where necessary, to prevent abnormal accumulations and unbridled competition, and redistribute wealth to the many".[35] Human rights thus meant not only the freedom to live in a Christian way but also that the state should, and must, step in to curb capitalism's excesses. Indeed, the Bishops' Statement of 1940 was one articulating "an order where the means of decent living are within the reach of all, and where human dignity and freedom are secured by the State's recognition of its own duties and limitations, and of the rights of God as well as man."[36] The idea of human rights, then – even of the limited version encapsulated here – has a long history of being entertained by those of an anti-democratic bent. As Marco Duranti argues in his work on conservative human rights talk in late 1940s Europe, conservative forces used the language of rights as a tool to constrain the ambitions of social democratic political parties.[37] Public reception of the Statement was pronounced yet mixed. *The Advocate* happily reported that in six months the report had sold 51,000 copies, demonstrating its "profound

---

[34] Ibid. On these debates, see Linde Lidkvist, *Religious Freedom and the Universal Declaration of Human Rights* (Cambridge: Cambridge University Press, 2017); Michael Thompson, *For God and Globe: Christian Internationalism in the United States between the Great War and the Cold War* (Ithaca, NY: Cornell University Press, 2015).

[35] *The Advocate*, 18 April 1940, 8.   [36] Ibid.

[37] Marco Duranti, "Curbing Labour's Totalitarian Temptation: European Human Rights Law and British Postwar Politics", *Humanity* 3, no. 3 (2012); Marco Duranti, *The Conservative Human Rights Revolution: European Identity, Transnational Politics and the Origins of the European Convention* (Oxford: Oxford University Press, 2016).

"Fundamental Human Rights"

and widespread influence on the community".[38] The *Catholic Freeman's Journal* reported that a copy had been sent to all Commonwealth parliamentarians, sparking "much favourable discussion".[39] *The West Australian* reported favourably on the statement and a subsequent sermon delivered for "Social Justice Sunday" on 5 May 1940. The "growing tendency towards revolutionary methods of coping with post-war conditions", the newspaper warned, made it "important to recall some fundamental notions concerning human rights ... when we are faced with a well-defined tendency to submerge the human personality into mass movements of various kinds".[40] Despite dubbing them "radical suggestions", Melbourne's *Age* also reported favourably, giving significant space to verbatim quotes of the Statement, while Adelaide's *Southern Cross* labelled its call for a family wage a "charter of rights for workers".[41]

Others doubted the Catholic hierarchy's agenda in publishing the document. Brisbane's *Telegraph* admired the Church's "zeal for improved social conditions" but noted with "pity" the text's ingrained social conservatism, particularly in relation to divorce, that contradicted its defence of individual human rights. "Every proper thing should be done to make the status of family life wholesome, happy and secure", one editorial read, "but to decree that the most horrible mistakes of marriage are never to be corrected is to adopt an intolerable standard of inhumanity which no modern society is likely to sanction".[42] This highlighted the Church's main objective in their particular invention of human rights that was to become a constant of conservative usages over the coming decades: the defence of traditional social values via a global language that espoused individual liberty. Another letter writer to Perth's *Daily News* asked whether the hierarchy realised that the choice of the term "social justice" mirrored the language of Father Coughlin, an American Catholic leader, "admitted admirer of fascism" and head of the "League of Social Justice".[43] Some Australian Catholics had certainly looked kindly on fascism in the past, with Santamaria writing glowingly of Spanish dictator Franco in his honours thesis at the University of Melbourne.[44] However, rather than embracing corporatist dictatorship – politically dubious at best during a war being framed as one of freedom against tyranny – *The Advocate*'s writers looked to a perhaps surprising idol: the United States of America. While Catholics had historically had even less access to political

---

[38] *The Advocate*, 14 November 1940, 5.
[39] *Catholic Freeman's Journal*, 27 June 1940, 26.   [40] *The West Australian*, 6 May 1940, 9.
[41] *The Age*, 15 April 1940, 10; *Southern Cross*, 29 March 1940, 1.
[42] *The Telegraph* (Brisbane), 15 April 1940, 12.
[43] *The Daily News* (Perth), 9 April 1940, 4.   [44] Fitzgerald, *The Pope's Battalions*, 26–8.

30   Inventing Rights

power in the United States than in Australia, a push by the Commonwealth government to insert limited individual rights protections into the Australian constitution in 1944 saw *The Advocate*'s writers propose an American-style bill of rights as part of a heated national debate.

Labor and the Wartime Rights Imagination

In 1944, the wartime Department of Information produced 250,000 copies of a pamphlet entitled *For This We Fight*. It was part of a run of over 1.5 million publications produced by the short-lived department, founded in 1941 and wound up nine years later, with such titles as "Fighting Men Speak" and "We Can Do Better".[45] This was part of a transnational circulation of ideas during and immediately after World War II, with Or Rosenboim commenting how "the Second World War created a unique opportunity to establish a new world order to promote peace and social welfare alike" across the Western world, enthusiasms which complemented the contemporaneous explosion in rights talk.[46] Subtitled "the Story of Australia's Growth to Nationhood", *For This We Fight* presented Australian history as the heroic achievement of freedoms and rights, "of principles and ideals, not of barricades and charging cavalry". Australia's Federation in 1901 – a protracted, indeed frustrating, process of bringing six conflicting colonies together – became "a spirit moving amongst the people themselves that transformed residents of the Colonies into free citizens with the right to elect their own leaders".[47] While such heroic rhetoric and abstract idealism made sense at a time of war, Australia was demobilising by 1944. The relentless US-led pushback of Japanese forces across the Pacific had an ever-increasing tempo, and Australia's fighting men and women were returning home. What was on the mind of the Curtin Labor government in 1944 – as it was in all Allied nations after over a decade of economic depression and conflict – was postwar reconstruction and particularly the need for the Commonwealth government to maintain and extend its wartime powers over prices, industry and a host of other areas.[48] As it was put in the pamphlet's

---

[45] *The Courier-Mail*, 22 July 1944, 3.

[46] Or Rosenboim, "Barbara Wootton, Friedrich Hayek and the Debate on Democratic Federalism in the 1940s", *The International History Review*, 36, no. 5 (2014), 894–918. For a more thorough articulation of these ideas, see Or Rosenboim, *The Emergence of Globalism: Visions of World Order in Britain and the United States, 1939–1950* (Princeton, NJ: Princeton University Press, 2017).

[47] Department of Information, *For This We Fight: The Story of Australia's Growth to Nationhood* (Canberra: Commonwealth of Australia, 1944), 4.

[48] Macintyre, *Australia's Boldest Experiment*.

closing lines, "[T]he freedom for which we fight includes pre-eminently the freedom from fear and want – jobs, homes and economic security – and freedom to think and talk and live our own lives."[49] This sentence encapsulates the contradictions that lay at the core of the ALP's "rights talk" in 1940s Australia.

The rhetoric of Roosevelt's "four freedoms", alongside negative liberal notions of thought and expression, was marshalled to support of what constituted a massive expansion of governmental power. The fourteen powers, as they were referred to in a perhaps unconscious homage to Woodrow Wilson's 1919 declaration of American postwar principles, proposed government control over prices, wages and housing as well as monopolies, corporations and foreign investment. These extended powers were necessary, the pamphlet argued, to deliver "a new, a greater and an enduring prosperity".[50] Owing to Australia's "Washminster" political system, a constitutional referendum requiring the endorsement of both a majority of people and states was necessary and was to be framed around "the human aspects of constitutional reform" or, to quote Macintyre, "translating the Atlantic Charter in terms of jobs, homes and prices".[51] To counterweigh any concerns of over-centralisation or the fears of totalitarianism held by Catholics and others, the referendum also proposed inserting freedom of speech and religion into Australia's founding document. The eventual failure of the progressive Labor government in gaining access to these greater powers had direct flow on effects to the policies and agendas it brought to deliberations over the Universal Declaration of Human Rights. Such rhetoric of "our" rights and privileges also reveals the purposeful blindness of much 1940s rights rhetoric to those it excluded – refugees and immigrants in particular.

The ALP had, since its inception as a series of colonial parties in the 1880s, sought to use the levers of elected office to create a loosely defined form of socialism.[52] The labour movement alongside the concurrent, interconnected land nationalisation and single tax movements were the first Australian political movements to make a sustained use of the language of human rights in a way which differed to that of the rights of the Briton subject. The labour movement, much like that for women's rights, emerged in the 1850s but gained significant national traction from the 1880s

---

[49] Department of Information, *For This We Fight*, 13.   [50] Ibid., 13.

[51] On the Australian constitution's peculiar mixture of American and British models, see Elaine Thompson, "The 'Washminster' Mutation", *Australian Journal of Political Science* 15, no. 2 (1980), 32–40; Macintyre, *Australia's Boldest Experiment*, 259.

[52] On the history of the formation of the Australian Labor Party, see Robin Gollan, *Radical and Working Class Politics: A Study of Eastern Australia, 1850–1910* (Melbourne: Melbourne University Press, 1960); Verity Burgmann, *'In Our Time': Socialism and the Rise of Labor, 1885–1905* (Sydney: Allen & Unwin, 1985).

32   Inventing Rights

onwards. Australian followers of the American radical economist and journalist Henry George, who believed that a single tax on land would solve the increasing problems of inequality and misery, used the idea of human rights rather frequently.[53] "A Song of the Single Tax", appearing in the *Goulburn Evening Penny Post* in 1890, spoke to the term's emerging power:

> The day is dawning in the east,
> And human rights are near;
> No more at hunger's board to feast
> Or labour under fear[54]

The Sydney *Telegraph* reported a lecture given by an A. Gough of the Land Nationalisation League a year earlier, entitled "Contempt for Human Rights", in which the speaker "contrasted the ... abject poverty and degradation" of the poor "to the gorgeous sumptuousness of the millionaire landlords".[55]

But why did this term begin appearing with more regularity? As James Walter writes of this period, the relationship that existed between liberal colonial politicians – "New Liberals" who recognised the need for social reform – and the working class began to disintegrate in the late nineteenth century.[56] Workers began realising that they had their own interests, distinct from those of the wealthy, and that the latter's interests were protected by the sacrosanct nature of "property rights". The idea of "property rights" is one of the oldest and most clearly defined, inbuilt via the Magna Carta and the 1689 British Bill of Rights into the notion of the rights of the freeborn Briton to which activists of earlier causes had appealed. This rearticulation of "property rights" was a transnational phenomenon, as Neil Stammers argues, with "understandings of privilege, power and property ... ubiquitous in the emerging workers' and socialist movement".[57] Thus, human rights were marshalled to the worker's cause, one they increasingly came to call "socialism", if of a non-doctrinal nature. As one writer put it in *The Worker* in 1898: "Socialism! That bete noir! What is it? Simply the equality of human rights – the right to live – justice and equity to all."[58]

---

[53] For more on George's theories, see Frank Stillwell and Kirrilly Jordan, "The Political Economy of Land: Putting Henry George in his place", *Journal of Australian Political Economy* 54 (December 2004), 119–34. George was also a prominent supporter of Australian progressivism, see Marilyn Lake, *Progressive New World: How Settler Colonialism and Transpacific Exchange Shaped American Reform* (Cambridge, MA: Harvard University Press, 2019), 81–2.

[54] *Goulburn Evening Penny Post*, 19 July 1890, 6.   [55] *Telegraph*, 27 June 1889, 2.

[56] Walter, *What Were They Thinking*, chapter 3.

[57] Neil Stammers, *Human Rights and Social Movements* (London: Pluto Press, 2009), 80.

[58] *The Worker*, 16 April 1898, 7.

Such egalitarian sentiment should not be surprising: class was, after all, not a particularly popular form of political rhetoric or understanding in colonial Australia. As Nick Dyrenfurth writes, "however much social class had become a material reality ... by the 1880s ... it most definitely did not define the commonsense political identity of most working Australians".[59] Catholicism, the religion of most Labor members, disavowed the language of "class" entirely as an impediment to the Church's "human family".[60] Humphrey McQueen's biting arguments in *A New Britannia* articulate well how the dream of Australian working-class advocates was one of a middle-class, white man's paradise.[61] Human rights, then, was arguably one of the ways that the Australian working class made sense of its position without recourse to class-based formulations. One scribe in the radical journal *Tocsin* wrote in 1897 that the reason for the working man's continued suffering, despite education and electoral reform, was that

[i]nstead of having Government by the people for the people we have Government by property for its own power and privileges. Human rights are unimportant as matters for legislation, but are very useful for purpose of platform claptrap with which to cajole the votes of the masses.[62]

Human rights, then, could only be realised by the party of the workers, the Australian Labor Party. Such thinking continued into the early twentieth-century, despite the growing popularity of class identity and the rise of Bolshevism. A 1918 poem, entitled "Human Rights" and published in the *Labour News*, *The Worker* and *The International Socialist*, articulated the term's continued importance in the era when critiques of capitalism and class society were becoming ascendant:

> How long, ye clods of human clay,
> Shall capital oppress you?
> A span of mules! How long shall they
> In earning power surpass you?
>
> Will ye stay down beneath the brute
> To property a slave?
> Will ye still, stand with voices mute?
> Look! Yonder waits a grave!

---

[59] Nick Dyrenfurth, *Heroes and Villains: The Rise and Fall of the Early Australian Labor Party* (North Melbourne, VIC: Australian Scholarly Press: 2011), 17.

[60] *The Catholic Press*, 2 May 1935, 6.

[61] Humphrey McQueen, *A New Britannia: An Argument Concerning the Social Origins of Australian Radicalism and Nationalism* (Ringwood, VIC: Penguin Books, 1970).

[62] *Tocsin*, 9 December 1897, 5.

34   Inventing Rights

> Will ye not rise with mighty hand,
> To banish this foul dream?
> Let every eye throughout the land
> See human rights supreme.[63]

Another poem published two months later in the *Westralian Worker* displayed similar sentiments, as well as articulating the more internationalised nature of the post–World War I workers' movement:

> They scorn the socialistic scheme.
> Inured to long misrule
> They call it all a silly dream –
> The socialist a fool.
>
> The flutter of an old red rag
> That stands for human rights –
> The workers' universal Flag –
> Their enmity excites.[64]

Such international interest was exhibited by the movement's positive appraisals of the USA and particularly the thought of President Woodrow Wilson, whose contributions to the Paris Peace Conference in 1919 arguably first cemented human rights in the international arena.[65] Wilson was quoted in one 1914 article in the *Worker* as saying, "Why am I interested in having the government more concerned about human rights than about property rights? Because property is an instrument of humanity; humanity is not an instrument of property."[66]

In keeping with the Australian labour movement's focus on controlling the state, human rights rhetoric also came to colour demands for greater state provision of services and welfare, pointing towards the involvement of Australian labour movement activists in the foundation of the United Nations in the 1940s.[67] Prominent labour activist and journalist Frank Cotton wrote an article entitled "Human Rights and Pauper Doles" for the *Australian Worker* in 1925 in defence of the Maternity Bonus Act, one of the first social welfare provisions ever provided by the Australian state. Cotton put it to his readers that human rights was the best tool through which to argue for this provision: "The only effectual answer ... is to uphold both State aid to mothers and State provision for the aged as human rights. Once, we depart from that standpoint, and treat such State

---

[63] *The International Socialist*, 20 July 1918, 4.
[64] *Westralian Worker*, 13 September 1918, 3.   [65] Manela, *The Wilsonian Moment*, 209.
[66] *Worker*, 19 February 1914, 6.
[67] For a general history of social provision in Australia, see John Murphy, *A Decent Provision: Australian Welfare Policy, 1870–1949* (Farnham, UK: Ashgate, 2011).

Labor and the Wartime Rights Imagination 35

payments as doles to mendicants, we give our whole case away."[68] The onset of the 1930s Depression saw the further extension of such language, with unemployment at all-time highs and calls for state aid more resolute. "[U]nemployment is a curse to the workless", the *Westralian Worker* editorialised in 1934, "depriving them of their human rights and making them mere chattels to be thrown on the scrap heap when no longer needed".[69] Two years earlier, the same paper published the reflections of a jobless worker, who made evocative and important use of rights language in an article entitled "The Demand of the Workless: His Human Rights Considered":

My right to live exists in the fact that I was born, and am now here, 5 feet 9 inches of flesh, and bone, and sinew, and muscle, and brain, capable of earning a living ... I did not ask to come. I did not ask to be born the son of a citizen of the British State. But being born, here or anywhere, I have a right to live. That right inheres in me, not through the British State, but as a gift or responsibility conferred by the Creator.[70]

Explicitly rejecting the restrictive language of "British rights" – most Australians still identified as British prior to World War II – the author argues not only that he holds "universal" human rights implicit in his humanity but that it is the state's responsibility to meet his needs. "The whole of the citizens of the State should bear their share of the suffering [unemployment] entails", he protested.[71] The *Australian Worker* in 1936 called the new "Stalin" constitution of the Soviet Union, then the most democratic constitution ever written, "a charter of human rights": "Where else but in Russia are the toilers guaranteed the full right to work, to rest and to leisure, to every conceivable form of free social service, and an old age free from care?"[72]

For the ALP, then, the achievement of what was increasingly termed "human rights" was a matter of winning control of the state machinery. Rights were not merely negative – protection from their extinguishment by others, as was the basis of British rights – but needed to be positive and life-giving, supported by a strong egalitarian government. However, Labor's agenda had been stymied by internal division and competing ideas on what the party stood for when elected nationally in the 1900s and 1910s and briefly again at the end of the 1920s. In 1921, Federal Parliamentary Labor's policy was finally concretised into what was known as the "socialist objective", which called for "the nationalisation of banking and all principle industries".[73] The labour movement had been early supporters of federation, yet Australia's constitution was highly limiting in the powers granted to

---

[68] *The Australian Worker*, 18 March 1925, 7. [69] *Westralian Worker*, 11 May 1934, 1.
[70] *Westralian Worker*, 26 August 1932, 3. [71] Ibid., 3.
[72] *The Australian Worker*, 12 August 1936, 8.
[73] Bongiorno and Dyrenfurth, *A Little History of the Australian Labor Party*, 69.

36 Inventing Rights

federal governments, with responsibilities for health, education and economic affairs – including taxation – handled at the level of individual states. The breakout of the Second World War provided an opportunity for the Labor movement – united, unlike during the previous war – to gain the powers needed to deliver on its program.[74] Labor sold the war as an opportunity not for national glory on the battlefield – hardly a popular proposition after the nation lost some 60,000 men only two decades before – but for postwar reconstruction. Responsible for the defence of the nation, the Federal Government took on greater powers after Australia's declaration of war against Germany in August 1939, and ALP Federal leader John Curtin made it a central point of his 1940 election campaign that these powers "will be necessary for the Commonwealth to possess in dealing with post-war reconstruction".[75]

Curtin made this call in the context of a broader claim for rights: "Unless the rights of the people are respected; unless the interests of all the people are made paramount over those vested interests [and] profit makers ... we may well win the war but lose the peace." Curtin envisaged "a new social order based upon democracy and the rights of all men and women to enjoy the fruits of honest toil". Here, the "rights of the people" can be seen to have departed completely from earlier ideals of individualism and became the rights of a collective mass of individuals against their enemies: profiteers and capitalists. "There must be no hesitation to assume control of the means of production", Curtin concluded, "where that is essential in the public interest".[76] Rights had been an infrequent way of framing Labor's policy in the 1937 election – around access to state entitlements such as pensions or unemployment benefits – but by 1940 a full array of newly minted, if poorly articulated, intrinsic, collective rights were at the centre of the party's program.[77] Menzies' United Australia Party (UAP), a pro-business, free trade group, won that contest; however, their loss of vital support from independent parliamentarians in October 1941 saw Curtin and the ALP take the helm of a nation which, only two months later, would be fighting not a distant conflict in Europe but a war for national survival. Wartime controls were easy enough to achieve, particularly after Japan's dramatic entrance into the war seemingly imperilled Australia's security.[78] Despite lacking control of either

---

[74] On Labor's approach to federation and wartime disunity, see Dyrenfurth, *Heroes and Villains*, particularly chapters 3 and 6.

[75] *Illawarra Mercury*, 30 August 1940, 2.   [76] Ibid., 2.

[77] For the 1937 platform, see John Curtin, *To Build and Defend a Happy and Self-Reliant Australia: Policy Speech of the Australian Labor Party* (Sydney: Australian Labor Party, 1937).

[78] See Peter Stanley, *Invading Australia: Japan and the Battle for Australia*, 1942 (Camberwell, VIC: Viking, 2008).

house of parliament, Curtin was able to work with state governments – as the individual colonies became post-federation – to transfer most necessary powers to the Commonwealth for the duration of the conflict. It was the extension of significant powers after the war that sparked the need for a constitutional referendum.

As Macintyre explains in his recent contribution on postwar reconstruction, the need for a referendum was clear from an early stage, but Curtin appears to have been reluctant to push ahead with a vote, despite prodding from Evatt and others in cabinet keen on beginning planning to "win the peace".[79] Evatt was vocal in his support for further government powers, commenting in a significant August 1941 broadcast on the Australian Broadcasting Commission (ABC) entitled "Planning for Reconstruction" that government should seek nothing less than "a new world order". He lauded Churchill and Roosevelt's Atlantic Charter, which had been issued only a week earlier, as a "dramatic declaration [of] eight major principles upon which they base their hopes for a better world". Of the eight, Evatt particularly focused on points five and six, those that spoke of "improved labour standards, economic advancement and social security" and "that all men in all lands may live out their lives in freedom from fear and want".[80] Evatt's translation of the Charter into Australian circumstances focused on its social democratic aspects, rather than those speaking of national liberation or minority rights, translating the "freedom from want" to mean not just "abolishing poverty" but "guaranteeing and assuring to every citizen a reasonable standard of living for themselves and their families".[81] Evatt relied on the previous work of Australian Catholics in vernacularising human rights to make further meaning of this reasonable standard of living. While at pains to state that he was "not" a Catholic, Evatt felt "a special duty to pay tribute to the value of this study", entitled "Justice Now" and distributed by the group Catholic Action. Evatt quoted the report at length, remarking that "it is barely conceivable that the working class as a whole can enjoy that independence to which their rights as human beings entitle them if they remain simply wage-earners and are divorced from the ownership of property". It was the ordinary man's lack of ownership of property that had seen "totalitarian ideas ... gain ground and ... invade the inviolable rights of human personality".[82]

This melding – or in some instances clashing – of progressive calls for greater state involvement in the economy and society with conservative

---

[79] Macintyre, *Australia's Boldest Experiment*, 254–5.
[80] Herbert Vere Evatt, "Planning for Reconstruction", in National Archives of Australia (henceforth NAA): A9816, 1943/765 PART 1.
[81] Ibid.   [82] Ibid. Underlining in original.

38   Inventing Rights

ones for the sanctity of property and the individual coloured the dynamic, democratic discussion engendered by the 1944 referendum. One focus of this discussion was an ABC series on the nature of postwar reconstruction, tuned in to by hundreds of "listening groups" across the nation who heard experts and ordinary people discuss the theme of "After the war, then what?" Hundreds of groups were formed – 468 by July 1944, with an average membership of eight to ten and a roughly even geographic distribution – and many sent back reports noting their points of agreement and contention.[83] Well-known editor and journalist Brian Penton recorded an introductory session to one 1944 series of talks, in which an array of speakers reflected on the postwar possibilities of industrial workers, farmers and small-business people, to name but a few. While Australia's geographic isolation rendered it somewhat distant from the world, Penton wrote how the Depression and resulting war forced open Australia's outlook to the world. "The depression and the war have taught us that the world is a single unit and its standards are indivisible", Penton wrote, adding:

A famine in India jolts through the whole complicated mosh of international trade till a banker in New York or a cotton farmer in Texas puts a bullet through his brain and an Australian motor mechanic loses his job . . . The intricate machine of world production and exchange dictates a world organisation of our effort – a equal opportunity for the sharing of all resources on the planet.[84]

Such a global frame spoke to the newfound significance of world affairs, while Penton's discussion of the "indivisible" nature of "standards" was very much the topic of discussion. Various authors debated the referendum's key concerns – full employment, housing and other large-scale government interventions in the economy – in terms of freedom, liberty and rights.

One broadcast debate got to the core of this issue, in which two prominent speakers argued against the conservative case that full employment would undermine "freedom" by questioning the term's seemingly indivisible nature. The notion of freedom of contract or government control was

not by any means typical of the outlook of great numbers of people on low incomes. They value freedom too, but assess it in a different way. For example, a woman who can know that she can begin to have a child with reasonable confidence that in nine months-time her husband won't be out of employment

---

[83] "Australian Broadcasting Commission – Listing Groups Bulletin, July 1944", NAA: A989, 1944/735/710/9.
[84] Brian Penton, "The Problem Is Stated", in NAA: A989, 1944/735/710/9.

at the time she need him most regards that confidence as freedom. It means more to her than merely not having to fill in forms."[85]

Another unnamed ABC scribe put this in explicitly personal terms, telling the story of "Mrs Jones of Slumville". Mrs Jones, an archetype of the city housewife, "has a husband fighting in New Guinea, but her battle is at home", with "four children living with her in two rooms. They have no bathroom, no playground except the street and . . . a backyard coated with the grime of city smoke." What did freedom – or rights, for that matter – mean to someone like this? It was to this imagined Australian worker and his family – not the liberal individual, or Indigenous or colonised people – that the 1940s rights imagination appealed, seeking to deliver freedom from hunger and despondency instead. "Only by co-operation to cement goodwill and check ill-will can we seek to create communities of good living", the author finished.[86] Such commentary was emblematic of the government's broader, if cumbersome and ineffective, media campaign surrounding the referendum. *For this we fight* featured an illustration of slouching black silhouettes outside a factory gate, adorned with the words "NO HANDS WANTED". This "grim shadow of depression, unemployment, poverty [and] starvation", the caption explained, was emblematic of Australia's wartime struggle: "When we say to-day, 'this must not happen again', we mean it."[87]

Yet, the government's detractors took a very different interpretation of the wartime rights zeitgeist – accusing it of, amongst other things, replicating the practices of its fascist opponents. Much as in the United States, where a proposal by New Deal agency the National Resources Planning Board sought the continuation of state control over sections of the economy to ensure the delivery of a "decent standard of living", the plans met stern elite resistance and public apathy.[88] The proposal – despite editorial support from most major daily newspapers – failed to gain popular traction. Of sixty-eight letters concerning the referendum published in the *Sydney Morning Herald*, only thirteen supported the proposed changes.[89] Dissenters highlighted the bill's threat to freedoms in Australia, as one writer to Melbourne's *Age* put it, drawing on then-popular American

---

[85] Frank Louat and F. A. Bland, "What of the Future?", NAA: A989, 1944/735/710/9.

[86] Anonymous, "Housing", in NAA: A9816, 1943/765 PART 1.

[87] Department of Information, *For This We Fight*, 9.

[88] On the similarly timed push for social rights in America, see Samuel Moyn, *Not Enough: Human Rights in an Unequal World* (Cambridge, MA: Harvard University Press, 2018), chapter 2.

[89] Bridget Griffen-Foley, "Dr H. V. Evatt and Letters to the Press in the 1944 Referendum Campaign", *The Hummer* 2, no. 1 (1994), available at http://asslh.org.au/hummer/vol-2-no-1/evatt-and-letters/.

40   Inventing Rights

rights talk: "The equal right of every individual to 'life, liberty, and the pursuit of happiness' is ignored in the scramble to make everyone subservient to the whims of passing political parties."[90] As Moyn argues of the contemporaneous push for social rights in America, that Australians had "been exposed to the want of depression but not the ravages of war" made them less amenable to European-style state welfarism, the arrival of which was to take a further four decades.[91] Such commentary, of the government's supposed threat to freedom that echoed events in Europe, sat alongside another, contradictory, form of rights claim-making that discounted the need for the referendum's so-called two freedoms: specifically, of the press and of religion. Presented by government writers as a long overdue addition to Australia's legal system – having been in the American constitution since 1791 – others looked askance. The Australian Constitutional League, who ran a vigorous campaign against the government's plans in defence of "our right to freedom", asked why such laws were necessary, given that "[u]ntil quite recently these ancient rights of the British people were not thought to be in jeopardy in Australia".[92] Legal precedent and loyalty to the British way of life were enough to ensure freedom, the League insisted. Others, however, took an opposing approach, asking not for fewer official freedoms but for more. Australian Catholics, historically antagonistic to the American revolutionary ethos, expressed hope that the wartime alliance between the USA and Australia would "lead many Australians to read the text of Jefferson's famous manifesto, with its noble appeal to Divine Justice, and its clear statement of the basic human liberties". Though "a deist and a disciple of Rousseau", Jefferson was recuperated as an unwitting propagator of the Church's version of human rights.[93] The "'American idea' in which democratic majority rule is a means of safeguarding the human rights of all" was one Australia could mimic, with *The Advocate* hoping that the 1944 constitutional referendum would "provide ... a clear statement of certain essential principles of freedom", just as the American constitution did.[94]

Yet, perhaps the most significant challenge to Labor's collective rights rhetoric was that of its foremost political opponent. Having lost the leadership of the UAP in 1941 in the aftermath of Curtin's formation of a minority government, Menzies had pause for thought. The UAP he headed was widely perceived as beholden to the big businesses and monopolies that had brought about the Great Depression, and the need for reinvention sparked Menzies to deliver a series of radio talks that have

[90] *The Age*, 18 August 1944, 2.   [91] Moyn, *Not Enough*, 86.
[92] Australian Constitutional League, *The Referendum Issues Analysed* (Melbourne:, The Speciality Press Pty Ltd, 1944), 16.
[93] *The Advocate*, 2 July 1942, 8   [94] *The Advocate*, 5 July 1944, 8

come to known as *The Forgotten People*.[95] Delivered from May to November 1942, Menzies offered a counterpoint to the government's calls for guaranteed work and increasing standards of living. Famously, he opened the series with a defence of the middle class caught between "the rich and powerful" – the UAP's support base – and "the officialdom of the organised masses" that the ALP represented.[96] "The real life of this nation", Menzies intoned, "is to be found in the homes of people who are nameless and unadvertised", for the "home is the foundation of sanity and sobriety; it is the indispensable condition for its continuity; its health determines the health of society as a whole".[97] Placing the home and the comfortable middle class – "salary earners, shopkeepers, skilled artisans, professional men and women, farmers" – at the centre of his political thought meant Menzies could challenge the ALP's collective rhetoric with that of the free citizen, arguing not so much for inalienable rights as the requirement of individual responsibility. Discussing Roosevelt's "Freedom from want", Menzies dismissed "fashionable" talk of a postwar "golden age of long life, reduced effort, high incomes and great comfort": such fortune could not be delivered by the state but needed to "to be earned, to be merited". It would not "fall, like manna, from heaven." Rather than "a fixed and guaranteed state", Roosevelt's freedom from want should be read as "just reward for the good citizen[:] it is not part of a gospel of ease, but calls us to action."[98] Menzies' preference for negative over positive liberties, of creating a society of individuals "quick to discharge our duties and modest about our rights", framed not only the party he launched in December 1942 – the Liberal Party of Australia – but his seventeen years in government (1949–66).[99]

The referendum, held on 19 August 1944, was soundly defeated. The ALP was forced over its next four years in government to pass piecemeal legislation and seek often difficult accommodations with the states to deliver Roosevelt's four freedoms to Australians. A raft of benefits from

---

[95] For more on the importance of these speeches to modern Australian conservatism, see Judith Brett, *Robert Menzies' Forgotten People* (Chippendale, NSW: Pan Macmillan, 1992); Judith Brett, *Australian Liberals and the Moral Middle Class: From Alfred Deakin to John Howard* (Port Melbourne, VIC: Cambridge University Press, 2003).

[96] Robert Gordon Menzies, *The Forgotten People: A Broadcast Address by the Rt. Hon. R. G. Menzies K.C. M.P.* (Melbourne: Robert and Mullens Ltd, 1942), 3, 5.

[97] Ibid., 4–5.

[98] Robert Gordon Menzies, "The Four Freedoms: Freedom from Want", 10 July 1942, available at https://menziesvirtualmuseum.org.au/transcripts/the-forgotten-people/63-chapter-5-freedom-from-want.

[99] Robert Gordon Menzies, "The Nature of Democracy", 23 October 1942, available at https://menziesvirtualmuseum.org.au/transcripts/the-forgotten-people/91-chapter-33-the-nature-of-democracy.

42   Inventing Rights

widow's pensions, unemployment and sickness benefits were rolled into the Social Services Consolidated Act 1947, while plans to nationalise the banking system on a model borrowed from Labour in the United Kingdom were dismissed by the High Court of Australia.[100] Evatt, however, did not lose sight of a more sweeping set of guarantees against Depression and war. Instead, he took these dreams to a global stage. The United Nations came to exist on 1 December 1942 as a formal agreement that "built explicitly on the earlier Atlantic charter" and was signed by twenty-six nations, including Australia. From the outset, Evatt wanted to ensure that Australia had a vocal place in this emerging body, taking as his rhetorical foundation the ambiguous Atlantic Charter and a demand for full employment, as well as a desire to restrict the powers of large states in the new body.[101] Speaking at Colombia University, a few days prior to the foundation conference of the United Nations in April 1945, Evatt called the Atlantic Charter "vital" to the conference's deliberations. Australia's "adherence to the economic objectives of the Atlantic Charter" was premised on "the supreme goal of full employment and increased consumption" – articles Evatt wanted inserted into both the UN Charter and, later, the UDHR. The UN, as Evatt put it, should be a body that "will do its utmost to assure to the peoples of the world a full opportunity for living in freedom from want as well as freedom from external aggression". This statement encapsulated his preference for a body formalising national responsibility to provide social services as well as capable of ameliorating international disputes.[102] Evatt was happy to pronounce, upon his return, that the words "the United Nations shall promote . . . high standards of living, full employment and conditions of economic and social progress and development" were "now written into the United Nations Charter and the obligation will bind fifty nations".[103]

Yet, Australia's other key demand at the United Nations conference was to cement specific protections against these very universal standards: to ensure that what Evatt called "domestic jurisdiction" would be a central pillar of the organisation. "One of the objectives of the Australian delegation at San Francisco", Evatt remarked, "was to make

[100] On Labor's attempts to construct a social welfare state in the 1940s, see Murphy, *A Decent Provision*, chapter 9. On the bank nationalisation attempts, see Robert Crawford, "Supporting Banks, Liberals and the Australian Way: The Freelands and the 1949 Election", *History Australia* 2, no. 5 (2005), 84.1–84.23.

[101] John Murphy, *Evatt: A Life* (Sydney: NewSouth, 2016), 200.

[102] Herbert Vere Evatt, "Australia and America: University of California Charter Address, March 1945", in H. V. Evatt (ed.), *Australia in World Affairs* (Sydney: Angus and Robertson, 1946), 14–5.

[103] Herbert Vere Evatt, "Australia and the United Nations Charter", in *Australia in World Affairs*, 49.

sure that the wide powers of discussion, recommendation and action given to the organization could not be used to enable the organization to interfere with matters which, under international law, fall essentially within the domestic jurisdiction of States".[104] "Internal matters such as the migration policy of a state", Evatt happily reported, "will not fall within the scope of the organisation", thanks largely to Australian efforts.[105] The ALP's long support for what was colloquially known as the "White Australia Policy" – practically meaning the use of provisions in the Immigration Restriction Act 1901 as a means of keeping Australia a land for British peoples and their descendants – was not seen by Evatt as contradicting in any way his commitment to universal values in the international sphere.[106] As Natasha Roberts has argued, "Evatt was a defender of the nation-state who used international human rights as a vehicle for the realisation of his national agenda."[107] While unsuccessful in having an article of the UDHR to directly refer to full employment, Evatt returned to Australia in 1949 to sing the Declaration's praises. He delivered numerous speeches upon returning from Paris, asking Australians to give the UDHR a "fair go". Drawing on a phrase of great vernacular import to Australians, one that Labor Prime Minister Ben Chifley was to make central to his 1949 electoral campaign, Evatt elaborated how "that colloquial statement does express the real spirit behind this document".[108] For Evatt, the Universal Declaration was a victory for those like himself, who, unlike the revolutionary Marxists or the idle rich, "never lost their faith in human beings". "For years they have been seeking opportunities to inspire the masses of the people towards ... idealism and reform", Evatt exclaimed, describing opportunities of the type conveniently contained in Labor's social democratic platform.[109]

Labor was not, however, able to entirely capture the language of human rights. The emergence of the Universal Declaration also provided

---

[104] *CPD* (House), 30 August 1945, 5030.   [105] Ibid.

[106] On the establishment of the White Australia Policy, see Sean Brawley, *The White Peril: Foreign Relations and Asian Immigration to Australasia and North America, 1919–1978* (Sydney: University of New South Wales Press, 1995); David Walker, *Anxious Nation: Australia and the Rise of Asia, 1850–1939* (Crawley, WA: UWA Press, 2012); Marilyn Lake and Henry Reynolds, *Drawing the Global Colour Line: White Men's Countries and the Question of Racial Equality* (Melbourne: Melbourne University Press, 2008).

[107] Natasha Roberts, "The Australian Post-War Utopia: Reconsidering Herbert Evatt's Human Rights Contribution in the 1940s" (BA Honours Thesis, University of Sydney, 2012), 8.

[108] Herbert V. Evatt, Untitled draft of a speech concerning the outcomes of the Third General Assembly of the United Nations, available at http://parlinfo.aph.gov.au/parlIn fo/download/media/pressrel/EFMA6/upload_binary/efma61.pdf;fileType=application %2Fpdf#search=%22human%20rights%201940s%20media%22.

[109] Ibid.

44   Inventing Rights

avenues for political point-scoring by their conservative opponents – for whom national, let alone international, state-based programs for securing human freedom appeared threatening. The Liberal Party MHR for Deakin, William Hutchinson, asked the House whether the UDHR protects the "right to full employment of every person, whatever his religious, political or industrial affiliations", and whether "the government will take action to prevent any person or organization from interfering in such a right". A clearly perturbed Prime Minister Chifley responded that this government "stood for full employment for all citizens ... irrespective of their associations", adding that anyone "whose associations are not such that they are entitled to employment should be in jail", a comment seemingly at odds with the UDHR's prohibition of imprisonment on grounds of belief.[110] Labor renegade Jack Lang, formerly populist premier of New South Wales but by then independent member for the federal seat of Reid, attacked the government's plans to establish a subsidised medical scheme by directing his opponents to "recognise the right of the individual to the basic freedoms to which it pays lip service at the united nations [sic]". Studying the UDHR, Lang insisted, would place the government in "complete negation" of its principles.[111] Other Liberal members took it upon themselves to question the government's commitment to human rights in areas as diverse as compulsory unionism and attempts to join the nascent and ultimately unsuccessful International Trade Organization.[112] In the end, the ALP were unable to reconcile seemingly incompatible demands of personal freedom and governmental control, a contradiction readily apparent in the deportation debates of the late 1940s.

Vernacularising Rights: Deportation Debates, 1947–1949

The rhetoric of global rights irrespective of nationality in the Universal Declaration sat at odds with the realities of state-based power: the extension of which, as we have seen, was the central imperative of the document's authors. Leading members of the United Nations had long-standing colonial ties that were seen as unencumbered by the UN's mandate. In Australia's case, the main international point of contention was not its small number of League of Nations mandates but the highly contentious White Australia Policy. Mark Phillip Bradley describes the 1940s as

---

[110] *CPD* (House), 9 March 1949, 1148.   [111] *CPD* (House), 17 March 1949, 1684.
[112] On compulsory unionism, see *CPD* (House), 17 June 1949, 1166; on the International Trade Organization bill, see *CPD HR*, 1 December 1948, 3785.

Vernacularising Rights: Deportation Debates, 1947–1949

a decade in which the "conditions of possibility" for the implementation of human rights were very wide: its meanings were up for debate and the specific obligations it imposed on states unclear at best. As we have seen, activists took advantage of this window to transform human rights from an "exotic aspirational language to an everyday vernacular".[113] While political parties and the Church read the ideals of human rights in collective terms, some took its rhetoric of personal freedoms – specifically the freedom of movement enshrined in Articles 13–14 and elaborated in the Refugee Convention of 1951 – seriously. And these people – Chinese Australians, Chinese refugees and white Australians – sought to integrate the language of global rights into their local struggle against Australia's racialist immigration policy by focusing not on religion or social and economic rights to full employment or housing but on the personal freedoms of movement and citizenship that typify contemporary conceptions of human rights. Australia had accepted some 6,000 wartime refugees from the Asia-Pacific region "who normally would have been refused admission" during World War II on what Immigration Minister Arthur Calwell termed "compassionate grounds".[114] These refugees, including many seamen moored in Australian harbours during the Japanese advance, were given refuge on the understanding, as Calwell put it, that they "would return to their own countries at the conclusion of hostilities". The slogan "populate or perish" framed postwar population anxieties, and Asian refugees, the vast majority of whom left voluntarily, were presented as a "hard core" of malingerers as opposed to the rush of "good refugees, blond and blue-eyed displaced persons, or DPs, from Lithuania, Latvia and Estonia, [who] were welcomed with open arms".[115] The struggle of these refugees, however, became embedded within a longer history of Chinese-Australian activism. Rather than sparking a racial panic, their marriage to white Australian women saw an outpouring of public sympathy at this time of pronounced global awareness.

Drew Cottle has explained well the formation in the late 1930s of an alliance between left-wing Chinese Australians and white Australians around the Sydney waterfront, particularly members of the communist-dominated Seaman's Union of Australia (SUA). This alliance, allowed by

---

[113] Mark Philip Bradley, *The World Reimagined: Americans and Human Rights in the Twentieth Century* (Cambridge: Cambridge University Press, 2016), 3.

[114] *The Herald*, 29 January 1949, 3, NAA: A4968, 25/10/2.

[115] Klaus Neumann, "Remembering Refugees", *Inside Story*, 20 August 2010, available at http://insidestory.org.au/remembering-refugees. For more on Australia's history of engagement with refugees, see Klaus Neumann, *Across the Seas: Australia's Response to Refugees: A History* (Melbourne: Black Inc, 2015).

46   Inventing Rights

the formation of a "popular front" in China between Communist and Nationalist forces, saw children of leading Chinese-Australian merchants form a branch of the Koumintang's (KMT) Chinese Seaman's Union (CSU) in Sydney in 1942, which represented the Chinese wartime refugees in Australia and organised successful campaigns for improved hours and working conditions amongst stranded wartime seamen. CSU members also played significant roles in the struggle for Indonesian independence, helping to enforce a ban on Dutch shipping leaving Australian harbours instigated by Indonesian seamen in 1947.[116] It was at this stage, however, that the Australian government began to make concerted efforts to force the wartime refugees back to their homes, whether Hong Kong or China proper. In that year, the cases of fourteen Malaysian seamen threatened with deportation to Singapore or Malaysia made headlines, owing both to an international outcry the move engendered and to the government's refusal of visas to their Australian wives.[117] The claims of these Malaysians to stay in Australia were framed within a language that privileged fealty to British imperial ties rather than the then-still-emerging global rights order. As one supporter of the deportees, Rev. E. J. Davidson, put it, the decision to deport these men was "an infringement of fundamental human rights, the more so as the husbands are British subjects". The fact of their Commonwealth citizenship ought to have been reason enough for the minister to employ his "discretionary powers and the application of considerations other than those of strict adherence to the letter of the law."[118] A protest letter from the Ministers' Fraternal of Maitland put it similarly: these Malays were "fellow citizens of the British Empire, [who] have shared with us the perils and hardships of recent years".[119] It was not the sailors "humanity" that was at stake but their rights as fellow members of the British Commonwealth and protagonists in the Allied effort.

Marriage, however, seemed to confer a different universal status on the white Australian women wedded to these sailors. Kim Beazley, an ALP Member of Parliament from Western Australia, broke ranks to criticise

[116] Drew Cottle, "Forgotten Foreign Militants: The Chinese Seaman's Union in Australia, 1942–46", in Hal Alexander and Phil Griffiths (eds.), *A Few Rough Reds: Stories of Rank & File Organising* (Canberra, ACT: Australian Society for the Study of Labour History, Canberra Branch, 2003), 135–151; Drew Cottle, "Unbroken Commitment: Fred Wong, China, Australia and a World to Win", *The Hummer: Publication of the Sydney Branch, Australian Society for the Study of Labour History* 3, no. 4 (2000), available at http://asslh.org.au/hummer/vol-3-no-4/unbroken-commitment/.

[117] Gwenda Tavan, *The Long, Slow Death of White Australia* (Melbourne: Scribe, 2005), 51–70.

[118] *Sydney Morning Herald*, 18 November 1947, 2.

[119] *Sydney Morning Herald*, 29 November 1947, 2.

his government's decision on separating these families. Was "the right of a woman to choose whom she will marry ... a fundamental human right, which should not be interfered with by preventing an Australian woman from joining an Asiatic husband, however mistaken the Government may feel that to be?" Beazley asked Calwell. He was, however, quick to clarify that this stance did not entail opposing the deportation of the men, which he "regarded as an application of the White Australia policy".[120] Beazley's remarks presaged more emphatic rhetoric a few years later: in Australian eyes, the idea of universal human rights did not apply equally to all. The year 1949 saw further deportation controversies, including the well-known case of Annie O'Keefe, an Indonesian woman married to an Australian citizen whom the Chifley government sought to have deported. The O'Keefe case, settled early in 1949 when the High Court ruled her deportation illegal, proved a further international embarrassment for Chifley's government as it sought out allies in the Asia-Pacific region.[121] Yet, the decision on O'Keefe's status was made not on the basis of recently codified universal human rights but – much like the case of the Malaysian sailors – her status as a British subject, around which her supporters and the media presented her case. A cartoon, entitled "The-not-too-trusty sword", appeared in the *Sydney Morning Herald* in February 1949, presented Calwell as a jackbooted Nazi confronting O'Keefe, brandishing a blunted sword inscribed with the words: "Bill of Human Rights". "Calwell" remarked: "don't make me laugh lady, or I won't have the strength to throw you out of Australia".[122]

Human rights was clearly seen as having only limited usability as an activist tool, which renders unsurprising the fact that of over 1,100 articles concerning O'Keefe's deportation published in the Australian media in 1949, only 3 per cent even mentioned the newly minted Convention.[123] Further evidence as to why O'Keefe's supporters avoided the frame of human rights is presented by the case of her contemporaries: Chinese sailors married to Australian women who refused to return to their homelands at the behest of Australian authorities. These Chinese sailors did not have the benefit of being British subjects, and they and their supporters were left to vernacularise notions of human rights in a new context. The idea had more salience in 1949, owing not only to the widely

[120] *Kalgoorlie Miner*, 2 May 1947, 1.
[121] Sean Brawley, "Finding Home in White Australia: The O'Keefe Deportation Case of 1949", *History Australia* 11, no. 1 (2014).
[122] *Sydney Morning Herald*, 8 February 1949, 2.
[123] Advanced search of *Trove* newspaper archive (http://trove.nla.gov.au/newspaper/) for words "O'Keefe deportation" in the year 1949 brings up 1,138 digitised entries. Searching the same database for the words "O'Keefe deportation 'human rights'" brings up 30.

48   Inventing Rights

publicised adoption of the UDHR but also to the formalisation of the United Nations Commission on Human Rights as an authority to whom aggrieved parties could – theoretically, at least – appeal against the policies of nations. In July 1949, the Federal Government tabled the *War-time Refugees Removal Bill 1949* in the House of Representatives, and Calwell's reading of the legislation in parliament pulled no punches. Wartime refugees who refused to abide Calwell's dictates were labelled a "recalcitrant minority" only interested in serving "their own selfish ends". Hundreds were tarred with a traitorous brush, yet, as Calwell put it, "the decision of the High Court in the case of the Ambonese woman has, for the time being, restricted the Government's power". Unable to even mention O'Keefe's name, the clearly embittered Calwell railed that "[n]o government could, of course, afford to ignore the impudent challenge to its authority from this hard core of passive resisters".[124] Refugees, their wives and their supporters, however, hoped that invoking the spectre of human rights, and potential action from the new global authority, might curb Calwell's enthusiasm for state-based power.

Wives of the deportees established an organisation – the Wives of Chinese Seamen Association – to counter Calwell's bill, purporting to have fifty members in Sydney alone. Norma Han, the group's organiser, demanded that "our husbands should be allowed to remain in Australia permanently", only having to leave "in their own time".[125] The group's emerging practice of human rights activism took several forms: appeals to the memory of fascism against which human rights were seen as aimed; petitions and letters directly addressed to various UN bodies; and, perhaps most importantly, attempts to drive a wedge between the authoritarian Calwell and the globetrotting, humanitarian Evatt in popular media. In order to make human rights meaningful to Australians, the first step was to cement its position as the polar opposite to what Australians had just fought against; although, as scholars have identified, the most horrid crimes of Nazism were not widely publicised and far from the thoughts of the Declaration's authors.[126] Samuel Wong, prominent Chinese-Australian political activist and member of the CSU, attacked Calwell's Bill as a "Hitler-like law". Wong claimed that "when Hitler hated and persecuted the Jews he made a special law for them to disobey so that he could 'legitimately' punish them" and that Calwell's "Bill is framed for the Asiatics exactly as Hitler's law for the Jews".[127] The Wives

---

[124] *CPD* (House), 9 June 1949, 810–14.   [125] *Courier-Mail*, 24 August 1949, 3.

[126] Marco Duranti, "The Holocaust, the Legacy of 1789 and the Birth of International Human Rights Law: Revisiting the Foundation Myth", *Journal of Genocide Research* 14, no. 2 (2012).

[127] *The Argus*, 7 September 1949, 2.

Association put this even more bluntly, accusing the minister of "having infringed the whole preamble of the United Nations universal declaration of human rights, and so many articles of that great world document as to make us wonder whether he had become a law unto himself". "[W]e fear Mr. Calwell as millions of the world's people feared Hitler and Togo during the last decade," the petition concluded.[128] Media were highly supportive of this drive to vernacularise rights, with Grafton's *Daily Examiner* one of many newspapers to publish critical stories on Calwell, claiming that "The Minister's interpretation of the White Australia policy puts Hitler's racial purity ideas to shame", in an unfortunate turn of phrase clearly indicative of very low levels of Holocaust consciousness globally.[129]

The Wives Association prepared a petition to submit to the United Nations, challenging Calwell's actions, engaging in an emerging global praxis of utilising this new body as a supra-national "higher authority".[130] In so doing, they threatened to rip open an already fractured relationship between Evatt and his government, setting in motion events many feared could see the immigration minister harangued before an international court. As one newspaper put it, "In any International Court of Human Rights Evatt may achieve[,] it seems Calwell would have a tough time proving his innocence."[131] The petition appealed "in the name of humanity" for the United Nations to step in, saving their husbands "from the arbitrary and inhuman actions" of the responsible minister.[132] While Calwell was presented in a highly unflattering light, petitioners appealed to the "learned and beloved Dr Evatt ... a great advocate of human rights" as their saviour.[133] Moreover, when it became obvious that Evatt was limited by both his marginal influence in the ALP and the highly restrictive nature of what could be achieved within the framework of the Universal Declaration, he was transformed into a hypocrite. The Communist *Tribune*, with whom the CSU was allied, took a particularly harsh line on this, with a leader article entitled "Evatt's 'Human Rights' hypocrisy exposed". Systematically moving through different articles of the Declaration, the *Tribune* called out each of the government's breaches, drawing particular attention to Article 1 and imploring human beings "to act towards each other in a spirit of brotherhood".

---

[128] *Barrier Daily Truth*, 5 September 1949, 4.

[129] *Daily Examiner* (Grafton), 6 September 1949, 2. On Holocaust memory in Australia, see Tom Lawson and James Jordan (eds.), *The Memory of the Holocaust in Australia* (Edgware, UK: Mitchell Vallentine, 2007); David Ritter, "Distant Reverberations: Australian Responses to the Trial of Adolf Eichmann", *Holocaust Studies* 13, no. 2–3 (2007), 59–86

[130] De Costa, *A Higher Authority*.   [131] *The Sun* (Sydney), 10 April 1949, 36.

[132] *Barrier Daily Truth*, 5 September 1949, 4.   [133] *The Argus*, 7 September 1949, 2.

50   Inventing Rights

The *Tribune's* scribe questioned rhetorically, "Does Dr. Evatt imagine that Chinese residents in Australia aren't 'human beings' within the meaning of this article; or is his contention that Mr. Calwell, in tearing Chinese away from their wives and families, is 'acting towards them in a spirit of brotherhood'?".[134] Such criticism was widespread, in a media already oppositional to the government and amongst the public. "It's strange to hear Dr. Evatt talk in UNO about human rights, while Mr. Calwell is working against them", commented one recently arrived northern European immigrant in Perth's *Daily News*, who added, in light of such scandal: "I thank god that I am a Dane and I don't want to be called a 'New Australian'."[135]

When the High Court heard a test case brought by the CSU in late 1949, however, rights were read in a highly circumscribed manner. Jurists in the United States had found invocations of the UDHR – "a more prominent authority" than domestic law, in the words of one – reason enough to strike out such incompatible ordinances as the Alien Land Law, denying property rights to non-citizens".[136] The Australian court's final judgement, delivered by Chief Justice J. G. Latham, instead dismissed the Chinese claimants' argument for a universal right to immigrate:

It was frankly said in argument that if a person succeeded in obtaining entry into Australia and established what he intended to be a permanent home in Australia within a week of his entry, he became entitled to stay in Australia permanently as a matter of right so far as Commonwealth immigration law was concerned. If this be so the power to make laws with respect to immigration is reduced to a power to prevent entry into Australia – it does not include a power to prevent the settlement in Australia of any persons who contrive to enter Australia.[137]

Such language – of refugees "contriving" to enter Australia and claiming the universal right to movement to secure residence – reflected the ongoing state-based reading of rights and how little heed was given to the Universal Declaration's individual principles. Similar cases brought in the United States at the time took such readings seriously; however, Australian authorities and courts held strictly to the notion of "domestic jurisdiction" that Robert Menzies' conservative government would uphold well into the 1960s.[138] As Evatt put it when questioning parliament on this issue, "there is no relationship between the Declaration of Human Rights, or any clause of it, that I am aware of and the exercise by

---

[134] *Tribune*, 10 September 1949, 3.   [135] *Daily News* (Perth), 19 September 1949, 6.
[136] Bradley, *The World Reimagined*, 106.
[137] *Koon Wing Lau* v *Calwell* [1949] HCA 65 (21 December 1949).
[138] Jennifer Clark, *Aborigines and Activism: Race, Aborigines and the Coming of the Sixties to Australia* (Crawley, WA: UWA Press, 2008), chapter 1.

a country of its national right, which has always been recognized in every country, to determine the composition of its own people".[139] Thus, a clear legal boundary was drawn through the heart of the UDHR, one that sat at the core of Australia's international relations. On the one hand, the Australian government had obligations to its people in the form of guaranteed employment and a modest welfare state, a requirement that went largely unquestioned under the conservative governments of the 1950s and 1960s. Yet a hierarchy of humanity was enforced on those outside of the nation's border – or, as shall be shown, those Indigenous Australians whose existence proved deeply troubling.

Conclusion

In 1940s Australia, human rights was very much a language undergoing invention, a vocabulary in the process of becoming vernacularised and a set of ideas finding a place within a wide array of older forms of claim making. Globally, as has been argued by many scholars, the 1940s human rights moment was more about state building than individual rights, and this was certainly reflected in Australia. Catholics – long reticent as to the role of the state – found that canonical understanding of the hierarchical relationship between god, man and political authorities fit well with an understanding of human rights as imposing various limitations on the state's power over parts of social life, while welcoming, or at least accommodating to, its intrusion into the economic arena. In so doing, Australian Catholics began a tradition – which continues to this day – of employing the yearly Social Justice Statement to call the state to account for various social, political or religious lapses. For the ALP, on the other hand, rights meant institutional protection from poverty and guarantees to Roosevelt's "freedom from want", although only for those recognised as members of the pre-ordained national community. For non-citizens, the language of universal, global rights that Labor's globe-trotting apostle of universalism Herbert Evatt espoused meant next to nothing. Despite their lack of success, attempts to use newly minted human rights conventions to call national authorities to account presaged the expansion of this tactic in years to come. As Dominique Clément has recently put it, rather than "stand[ing] above politics . . . rights have a 'social life' in that they are a product of our society".[140] And Australian society in the 1940s was one riven with debate and newly found causes – no possibility, it seemed, was

---

[139] *CPD* (House), 7 September 1949, 11.
[140] Dominique Clément, *Human Rights in Canada: A History* (Waterloo, Canada: Wilfred Laurier University Press, 2016), 3.

closed off. Yet, in only a few short years, the career of rights talk would take a dramatic shift. Labor's reaction to activists' deployments of the UDHR's principles showed a reluctance from policy makers to relinquish their national authority that was only to become more visceral, while activists of the left and right began deploying the term in new contexts. Such efforts were soon to become frustrated, with the doors of possibility quickly closing, as rights became weapons in an undeclared Cold War.

2   Cold War Rights

On 4 March 1949, Laurence Louis "Lance" Sharkey made what was later described in the proceedings of the High Court of Australia as a "carefully worded exhortation".[1] Speaking to a Sydney journalist in his capacity as general secretary of the Communist Party of Australia (CPA), Sharkey remarked: "If Soviet forces in pursuit of aggressors entered Australia, Australian workers would welcome them ... as the workers welcomed them throughout Europe when the Red troops liberated the people from the power of the Nazis."[2] Sharkey, who had served as the Party's chairman and general secretary since 1930, was charged some two weeks later with uttering seditious words. A rarely used provision under British law, the Commonwealth Crimes Act 1914 demanded that "any person who, with the intention of causing violence or creating public disorder or a public disturbance, writes, prints, utters or publishes any seditious words shall be guilty of an indictable offence punishable by [i]mprisonment for 3 years".[3] Sedition law had been used by government to target leaders of previous workers' struggles – from the Eureka Stockade to the 1890s shearers' strikes and 1909 Broken Hill dispute – a tradition of disobedience in which Sharkey found himself.[4] Equally, though, Sharkey became a cause célèbre of the small cluster of emerging Australian civil liberties organisations. His trial and subsequent imprisonment provided a novel case of the violation of newly minted "human rights" while also announcing, alongside a particularly vicious miners' strike of that year and the outbreak of hostilities in Korea in 1950, the Cold War's arrival to Australian shores.[5]

---

[1] *R. v Sharkey* [1949] HCA 46 (7 October 1949).

[2] The quote was delivered over the phone to a journalist on Friday, 4 March but by the morning of 5 March was already receiving nationwide coverage. *The Daily News*, 5 March 1949, 1; *Geraldton Guardian*, 5 March 1949, 3.

[3] Crimes Act 1914 (Cth), s 24B, available at www.legislation.gov.au/Details/C2004C03156.

[4] Laurence W. Maher, "The Use and Abuse of Sedition", *Sydney Law Review* 14, no. 3 (September 1992), 287–316.

[5] On the Cold War in Australia, see Ann Curthoys and John Merritt (eds.), *Better Dead than Red: Australia's First Cold War, 1945–1959* (Sydney: Allen & Unwin, 1986); John Murphy,

54   Cold War Rights

The 1950s has not been a focus of the new wave of human rights historiography. The 1970s, and increasingly the 1960s, take centre stage. There is not much to see, it seems, in this most staid of decades. After just a few short years, as Samuel Moyn puts it, the UDHR had moved from a highly vaunted world document to a language "so geographically specific[,] ideologically partisan ... and, most often, linked so inseparably to Christian, Cold War identity" as to render it meaningless to vast swathes of humanity.[6] What became human rights in later decades was the result of an entirely different set of ideological circumstances to those posed by the end of World War II and the ensuing superpower conflict. As the previous chapter's discussion of Catholic rights-claiming demonstrates, it was conservatives who saw in human rights a way of (re) articulating supposedly age-old notions and who were to find in them a potent weapon for domestic Cold War conflict.[7] The conservative victory on rights was not a pre-ordained outcome, however. Celia Donert's recent work highlights how communist-aligned activists within the Women's International Democratic Federation made use of human rights language in their campaigning against "atrocities" in the Korean War, culminating in a highly publicised trial of West German campaigner Lilly Wächter.[8] Jessica Whyte has revealed the significance of Soviet legal argument to the collective rather than individual framing of rights in the UDHR itself, while scholars of the Soviet Union itself highlighted how the freedoms theoretically granted in the "Stalin Constitution" (1936) led to vocal rights discussion in the decade's later half.[9]

This chapter examines human rights' trajectory in Australia during the 1950s. Popularly remembered as an era of comfort and suburban conformity, it was equally framed by the mushroom cloud and the threat of falling dominos to Australia's north. It explores three case studies:

Imagining the Fifties: Private Sentiment and Political Culture in Menzies Australia (Sydney: Pluto Press, 2000).

[6] Samuel Moyn, *The Last Utopia: Human Rights in History* (Cambridge, MA: Harvard University Press, 2010), 47.

[7] On Conservative rights claiming, see Marco Duranti, *The Conservative Human Rights Revolution: European Identity, Transnational Politics, and the Origins of the European Convention* (Oxford: Oxford University Press, 2017); James Chappel, *Catholic Modern: The Challenge of Totalitarianism and the Remaking of the Church* (Cambridge, MA: Harvard University Press, 2018).

[8] Celia Donert, "From Communist Internationalism to Human Rights: Gender, Violence and International Law in the Women's International Democratic Federation Mission to North Korea, 1951", *Contemporary European History* 25, no. 2 (2016): 313–33.

[9] Jessica Whyte, "The Fortunes of Natural Man: Robinson Crusoe, Political Economy and the Universal Declaration of Human Rights", *Humanity: An International Journal of Human Rights, Humanitarianism and Development* 5, no. 3 (2014), 301–21; Benjamin Nathans, "Soviet Rights-Talk in the Post Stalin Era", in Stefan Ludwig-Hoffman (ed.), *Human Rights in the Twentieth Century* (Cambridge: Cambridge University Press, 2011), 166–90.

Sharkey's jailing, the unsuccessful referendum to ban the CPA and subsequent split in the Australian Labor Party along Cold War lines, and finally the formation of Communist-led campaign group the Council for Aboriginal Rights. While these events transpired on a local level, they were part of global Cold War manoeuvres: the Smith Act trial of Communist Party USA leaders in 1949, the coordination of anti-communist efforts across the newly formed Commonwealth of Nations, and attempts by Indigenous and minority peoples, particularly African-Americans and their supporters, to have their claims heard on a global stage.[10] In locating these events in their specific contexts, then, it also contributes to an emerging global picture of the 1950s.

Civil Liberties and the Sharkey Trial

The idea of civil liberties has appeared often in the Australian colonies, entwined as it was with a sense of colonial inheritance. As one letter writer under the moniker "Civil Liberty" put it to the *Geelong Advertiser* in 1853, "complete liberty of conscience is the birthright of every Englishman".[11] The 1850s in particular, as the introduction to this volume has already discussed, saw a previously unknown preponderance of rights discussion around the granting of self-government. Yet, little clarity was evident on what such liberties entailed. Another scribe, this time to the *South Australian Register* in 1857, quoted Henry Hallam's *The Constitutional History of England* to argue that "civil liberties in this kingdom has two direct guarantees" – the right to a fair trial and the right of parliament to scrutinise legislation.[12] In the 1890s, while employers challenged the decade's protracted strike waves as threatening their "freedom of contract", letter writers to the *Sydney Morning Herald* bemoaned how the collective action of trade unions during the strike were undermining liberty.[13] "If this is not an outrage on our civil rights and liberties ... I should very much like to be informed what is," William Mainer of Broken Hill protested in 1892, after striking mine workers briefly seized effective control of the town and denied free movement to its citizens.[14]

---

[10] Scott Martelle, *The Fear Within: Spies, Commies and American Democracy on Trial* (Rutgers, NJ: Rutgers University Press, 2011); Evan Smith, "Policing Communism Across the 'White Man's World': Anti-Communist Co-operation between Australia, South Africa and Britain in the Early Cold War", *Britain and the World* 10, no. 2 (2017), 170–96; Mary L. Dudziak, *Cold War Civil Rights: Race and the Image of American Democracy* (Princeton, NJ: Princeton University Press, 2000).

[11] *Geelong Advertiser and Intelligencer*, 11 March 1853, 1.

[12] *South Australian Register*, 3 October 1857, 2.

[13] On "freedom of contract", see for example *Goulburn Herald* (NSW), 5 January 1891, 4.

[14] *The Sydney Morning Herald*, 13 July 1892, 3.

56 Cold War Rights

The outbreak of World War I saw the formation of a National Council on Civil Liberties in London to oppose the introduction of conscription, a development that was widely reported in Australia, itself undergoing a profound debate and social crisis on the topic. Australia twice voted down conscription in national votes yet still contributed over 400,000 volunteers – nearly one in every ten Australians – 60,000 of whom were never to return. Rejecting conscription was a remarkable achievement, particularly given the existence of the War Precautions Act, a short document that created the legal category of "enemy alien" and "seriously curtailed" freedom of speech for "citizens who contested and challenged government war policy", particularly if the such was "likely to prejudice the recruiting of His Majesty's Forces".[15]

Supporters of conscription saw the deployment of ideas of "civil liberties' to oppose the war as an affront, with the Brisbane *Telegraph* labelling the organisation's members a "little group of busybodies".[16] Australian newspapers variously judged the Council and those who would attend its conference in December 1916 – only months after Australians first voted down conscription – as "peace mongers", "peace prattlers" and "Britain's Peace Party".[17] Such re-definition of "civil liberties" was also present in the Australian anti-conscription movement. The Victorian Political Labour Council (PLC) Conference issued a manifesto just prior to the 1916 vote, asking how a war in which "Australia engaged ... because she so loved civil liberties and loathed tyranny" had now seen "that military tyranny against which she fought imitated by her own rulers".[18] While it was "the duty of Englishmen to bear arms in defence of their homes against the invader", the PLC statement argued that no such invasion had taken place. Instead, Australians were being called upon to serve "at the other end of the world". By 1916, and particularly after the huge loss of life on the Somme, it was increasingly felt that enough blood had been shed. "Conscription is the enemy of civil liberty", the manifesto concluded, and it was up to Australians "in the name of Labor, of Liberty, of Conscience, and of our Common Humanity ... to answer 'NO!'"[19] Under the headline "Prussianising Australia", Brisbane's *Daily Standard* asked for Australians to oppose those "enemies of Labor [who] look with eyes of hatred upon the civil liberties still left to us"

---

[15] Diane Kirkby, "When 'Magna Carta Was Suspended': National Security and the Challenge to Freedom of Speech in Australia", in Catharine MacMillan and Charlotte Smith (eds.), *Challenges to Authority and the Recognition of Rights: From Magna Carta to Modernity* (Cambridge: Cambridge University Press, 2018), 321–2.

[16] *The Telegraph*, 19 December 1916, 4.

[17] *The West Australia,* 6 December 1916, 7; *The Daily News* [Perth], 6 December 1916, 6; *The Argus*, 7 December 1916, 5.

[18] *The Evening Echo* [Ballarat, VIC], 10 October 1916, 3.   [19] Ibid., 3.

Civil Liberties and the Sharkey Trial 57

through "oppos[ing] by all possible means the introduction of conscription".[20] Over 3,500 cases were prosecuted under the War Precautions Act from 1915 to 1919, most related to enemy aliens or trading offences; however, the Act also targeted printers of such critical literature. High Court justice Isaac Isaacs dismissed those seeking to draw parallels between the German and Australian governments, framing the conflict as one against an enemy with a "ruthless and cynical disregard of all human rights and sufferings".[21]

In 1923, the first attempt to found what was then called the Australian Civil Liberties League was announced in an article in Brisbane's *Daily Standard* by socialist Ernie Lane, writing under the pseudonym of fifteenth-century British popular agitator Jack Cade.[22] The group challenged what it called "unwarranted interference with the rights of free speech and liberty by various means" in defence of "citizens' rights".[23] That year was a particularly prominent one for the construction of Australian immigration law, as Mark Finnane has noted, with the highly contentious deportation of two Irish Republican envoys and the exclusion of British socialist Thomas Mann showing "the uses of immigration law to manage political order in Australia".[24] The deportation decision was particularly rancorous, with the arrest of visiting Sinn Fein activists Michael O'Flanagan and John Joseph Kelly in the dying days of the Irish civil war on charges of sedition furthering the deep religious divisions stoked by the World War I. While the sedition charges were quickly abandoned – the "evidence appeared insufficient to ensure successful prosecution" – the use of powers under the Immigration Act to deport the men showed "the sort of freedom that exists today under a reactionary 'Nationalist' administration" of prime minister Stanley Bruce. Claiming a genealogy extending to wartime anti-conscription groups that fought for "individual liberty" against "the heavy haul and boot of military dictatorship", the new League articulated its remit as "challenging th[e] scandalous abuse of power in the interests of … the capitalist class".[25] Such terminological usage as well as the communist-dominated organisations from which it drew membership – the New South Wales Trades and Labor Council, the Women's Workers Organisation and the Russian

[20] *Daily Standard* [Brisbane], 5 September 1916, 5.
[21] *Sickerdick Informant* v *Ashton* [1918] HCA 54 (26 September 1918).
[22] *Daily Standard* [Brisbane], 25 August 1923, 5. For more on Lane, see Jeff Rickertt, *Conscientious Communist: Ernie Lane and the Rise of Australian Socialism* (North Melbourne: Australian Scholarly Publishing, 2016).
[23] *Daily Standard* [Brisbane], 31 August 1923, 5.
[24] Mark Finnane, "Deporting the Irish Envoys: Domestic and National Security in 1920s Australia", *The Journal of Imperial and Commonwealth History* 41, no. 3 (2013), 403.
[25] *Daily Standard* [Brisbane], 25 August 1923, 5.

58   Cold War Rights

Workers Organisation –demonstrates how ideas of rights and liberties were quickly taken up by the Communist Party of Australia after its founding in October 1920. Whether directly informed or not, such 1920s initiatives coincided with similar moves in the United States, where the American Civil Liberties Union (ACLU) was founded in 1920. The ACLU also had its origins in anti-war activism and draft resistance during World War I, was a target of the 1920s "red scare" and its early role of publicising the class and race-based nature of the American legal system was widely reported in the Australian press.[26]

While the 1923 organisation appears to have fizzled out quickly, the 1930s proved more fertile ground. In Britain, a National Council for Civil Liberties (NCCL) – with no obvious connections to the older group of a similar name – was founded in February 1934. The organisation's emergence quickly piqued the interest of the Melbourne-based Book Censorship Abolition League, founded in that same year to contest restrictions on the availability of political literature in Australia.[27] The first meeting of the Australian Council for Civil Liberties (ACCL) was held in December 1935, and much was owed to their British co-thinkers: the founders even put off the ACCL's launch until an official relationship between the two groups was secured.[28] Christopher Moores' work on the NCCL has characterised the group's existence during the 1930s and 1940s as wavering between two poles. Its public appearance of a group of "decent citizens" from all walks of life contrasted with a widely expressed view that its members were agitators under communist influence. This was a key problematic for groups operating in the Popular Front period, when alliances between liberals and socialists were a high priority to challenge global fascism.[29] Such a characterisation is equally fitting of its Australian protégé. Macintyre and Waghorne detail how the organisation's public face and driving force, the historian, journalist and Communist Party fellow traveller Brian Fitzpatrick, clashed with more conservative members, such as Economics History lecturer and ACCL President Henry Burton.[30] A draft

---

[26] On the ACLU, see Laura Weinrib, *The Taming of Free Speech: America's Civil Liberties Compromise* (Cambridge, MA: Harvard University Press, 2016). On the ACLU's Australian reception, see for example *Daily News* [Perth], 18 July 1922, 2; *The Daily Mail* [Brisbane], 19 September 1925, 7; *Daily Herald* [Adelaide], 21 August 1923, 4.

[27] The ACCL is amply covered in the organisational history: Stuart Macintyre and James Waghorne, *Liberty: A History of Civil Liberties in Australia* (Sydney: University of New South Wales Press, 2011).

[28] Ibid., 11.

[29] Christopher Moores, *Civil Liberties and Human Rights in Twentieth-Century Britain* (Cambridge: Cambridge University Press, 2017), 23. For more on the popular front, see David Blaazer, *The Popular Front and the Progressive Tradition: Socialists, Liberals and the Quest for Unity, 1884–1939* (Cambridge: Cambridge University Press, 1992).

[30] Macintyre and Waghorne, *Liberty*, 14–16.

constitution – written by Fitzpatrick – was adopted in May 1936 that defined the Council's role as "assisting in the maintenance of the rights of citizens – especially freedom of speech, press and assembly – and ... advancing measures for the recovery and enlargement of these liberties and for the reform of existing relevant legislation".[31] A key early publication – *Six Acts against Civil Liberties* – was also written by Fitzpatrick and identified the key pieces of legislation passed since the outbreak of World War I that had curtailed liberties and which it was the Council's role to oppose.[32] This wording, closely resembling that of the NCCL, meant the Council's work was information dissemination and public advocacy rather than the legalistic approach of the ACLU.

Despite its formal affiliation with the British organisations, the ACCL maintained connections with its more radically minded American counterpart. Colston Warne, professor of economics at Amherst College, who had headed the Pittsburgh branch of the ACLU, delivered a keynote address at the ACCL's second Annual Meeting in May 1937, as part of a well-publicised three-month tour and inquiry into Australian working conditions.[33] A year later, such connections became part of a broader conflict around the visit of German navalist and Nazi apologist Count Felix Von Luckner.[34] Burton wrote a letter to Melbourne's *The Age* in which he criticised the Conservative federal government for allowing Von Luckner unprecedented access to the airwaves and meeting halls while having denied the same to County Court judge and League of Nations Union President A. W. Foster. Foster's radio programme – ironically entitled "Freedom of Speech" – had been recently censored by the board of the Australian Broadcasting Commission for potentially libellous statements, and the ACCL took the opportunity to reprint the speech in full, quickly selling 10,000 copies. The contrast between the government's treatment of Foster and Von Luckner "is most illuminating to say the least", Burton remarked.[35] A lengthy response to Burton was published two days later, calling the ACCL a "pink body", the meetings of which "are advertised in the official paper of the Victorian section of the

---

[31] ACCL Draft Constitution, adopted 6 May 1936, quoted in Macintyre and Waghorne, *Liberty*, 12.

[32] Macintyre and Waghorne, 12. The chosen legislation were the Crimes, Transport, Workers, Immigration, Customs, Broadcasting and War Precautions Acts.

[33] On Warne's visit, see *The Herald* [Melbourne], 1 May 1937, 3; *The Herald* [Melbourne], 29 April 1937, 42; *The Argus* [Melbourne], 5 May 1937, 13.

[34] On Luckner's visit, see James N. Bale, "Count Felix Von Luckner's 1938 'Propaganda' visit to New Zealand and its Consequences", *New Zealand Journal of History* 35, no. 2 (2001), 221–37; David Bird, *Nazi Dreamtime: Australian Enthusiasts for Hitler's Germany* (Carlton, VIC: Australian Scholarly Publishing, 2012).

[35] *The Age*, 14 June 1938, 8.

Communist party". The scribe also claimed that the ACCL had close affiliations with the ACLU – an organisation which expended "fully 90 per cent of its efforts ... on behalf of communists".[36] Burton's published defence – that the ACLU's political predilections had "no relevance to the Council for Civil Liberties here: we are affiliated with the English Council ... and not the American Union" – did little to stop the organisation's further tarring with an imported anti-communist brush.[37]

While the outbreak of the Second World War saw little of the political turmoil that marked the first, the Communist framing of it as an inter-imperialist conflict in line with Soviet dictates sparked the Party's banning in 1940. This meant that, despite the ACCL's non-party status, more and more of its work turned on supporting communists who had fallen foul of the law. The council sent observers to monitor anti-war meetings, often subject to attack by soldiers, and supported the hunger strike of two CPA members arrested and held without trial for secretly printing communist literature. "They were secretly arrested and secretly interned", the Council protested, and after seventeen days the pair were transferred to a military hospital.[38] Such support saw the ACCL even more roundly criticised for its closeness to pro-Soviet elements. Then attorney general, and formerly prime minister during the conscription debates, long-time enemy of the Left W. M. (Billy) Hughes condemned the group as "the salesmen of communism [who] under the pretext of a passionate concern for civil liberties ... plan to destroy the very foundations of our free institutions".[39] International political events quickly shifted the organisation's perspectives, as the Nazi invasion of the USSR transformed the Communist Party's position, while the fall of Robert Menzies' conservative government and replacement by Curtin's Labor administration saw the ACCL gain "unprecedented influence".[40] Fitzpatrick, who took on a role in the Rationing Commission in 1942 and argued for a conciliatory approach to the new Labor government, was centrally involved in preparing the wording of the ultimately unsuccessful "Powers" referendum of August 1944.[41] The council's close collaboration with government and consequential lack of activity at an organisational level left it weakened at war's end in 1945, and a new star also appeared on the horizon – the United Nations and its newly minted ideal of "human rights".

---

[36] *The Age*, 16 June 1938, 10.   [37] *The Age*, 18 June 1938, 14.
[38] Macintyre and Waghorne, *Liberty*, 43.   [39] Macintyre and Waghorne, *Liberty*, 37.
[40] Macintyre and Waghorne, *Liberty*, 47. For more on Australian communists' response to the Nazi-Soviet pact, see Stuart Macintyre, *The Reds: The Communist Party of Australia from Origins to Illegality* (Sydney: Allen & Uniwin, 1998), 381–411.
[41] Macintyre and Waghorne, *Liberty*, 59.

The Council made an early commitment to share information with ACLU co-founder Roger Baldwin's International League for the Rights of Man in September 1945 but took no steps to directly affiliate. While the ideals of rights and liberties were quickly gaining in global currency, their universal applicability did not coincide with the Council's articulation of civil liberties. As Macintyre and Waghorne put it, "For the Council, rights were not universal; they were always dependent on the balance of interests in the particular circumstances of each case."[42] It was equally true, as Moores said of the NCCL, that "human rights in the immediate postwar era ... belong[ed] in the conference room rather than humanitarian networks". Rather than "rights and liberties as components of a critique of national and international political institutions", the human rights language of the 1940s was "rights for export", lacking in any clear domestic usability.[43] The ACLU, while moving from a critique of the legal system to embracing it as a way of furthering change, looked not to international human rights but instead to a rearticulation of the American Bill of Rights as its starting point.[44] It appears, then, unsurprising that the ACCL "rejected the post-war project by international organisations to reinterpret civil liberties within a framework of international human rights through the United Nations".[45] It was a discourse of the world, not of the individual state or person, and lacked sufficient clarity or applicability to supersede older notions of British rights, which remained the organisation's mainstay through both the Sharkey case and the Communist Party referendum in 1950–1.

Lance Sharkey was served with six summonses on 21 March 1949, three alleging utterances of seditious words and another three the publication thereof. In a move borrowed from a similar case in France, Sharkey and two other communists – Gilbert Burns of Queensland and Kevin Healy of Western Australia – were each accused of uttering similarly seditious sentiments. While sedition charges related to the criminal law, the Communist Party and its supporters began to discuss Sharkey's treatment as a violation of human rights. In a move speaking to the deep global connectedness of the 1940s and the global socialist world, the Communist *Tribune* reported on 20 April 1949 that a Polish delegate to the United Nations had already brought Sharkey's treatment to the attention of the organisation during heated debate on the treatment of

---

[42] Macintyre and Waghorne, *Liberty*, 66.
[43] Moores, *Civil Liberties and Human Rights*, 99.
[44] Laura M. Weinrib, "From Left to Rights: Civil Liberties Lawyering between the World Wars", University of Chicago Public Law & Legal Theory Working Paper No. 571, 2016.
[45] James Waghorne, "Civil Liberties and the Referendum", *Australian Historical Studies* 44, no. 1 (2013), 107.

62   Cold War Rights

religious leaders in Soviet-occupied Europe. "Who is coming to the rescue of alleged Human Rights violations in Hungary", the Polish representative was said to have asked:

> from the Antipodes comes Australia, a country whose ... arrest of labor and trade union leaders [should] be brought to the attention of the [General] Assembly to find out whether a charge of sedition is not a violation of Human Rights.[46]

Sharkey himself had previously written an article on the trial of American communists under the so-called Smith Act. Introduced in 1939, the ordinance banned immigrants who had a history of membership in Communist organisations and made it illegal to "advocate, abet, advice, or teach the duty, necessity, desirability, or propriety of overthrowing any government in the United States by force or violence".[47] Such an egregious stripping of the first amendment, barely discussed at the Act's passing, was of a similarly sweeping nature to sedition law in nations under British legal systems. On 20 July 1948, twelve leaders of the Communist Party of the United States of America were charged under the Smith Act, as one historian has put it, over "the books they read, the political schools they supported, and, in essence, their thoughts".[48] The parallels with Sharkey's charges are striking, but writing several months prior to his own summons, the communist leader limited his criticism to America having "the audacity to talk about 'democracy' and 'human rights'" while "their hands are red with the blood of American workers and lynched Negroes".[49]

This rights turn amongst Communist Party commentators, to be discussed in more detail soon, was reflected in other communist-allied outlets. The *Worker's Star* in Perth reproduced the *Tribune* article describing Sharkey's sedition charge as a violation of human rights.[50] The *Maritime Worker*, newspaper of the communist-controlled Waterside Workers Federation, employed lyrical poetry in Sharkey's defence, which read in part:

> We've put a ban on passports and loud speakers on the Bank,
> We've mucked up demonstrations and processions till we stank
> We even jailed Lance Sharkey, and we've sold you to the Yanks
> And we're gonna disunite the working class.[51]

Yet, when it came time to defend Sharkey's case, Fred Paterson – Communist Party lawyer and Member of Queensland Parliament for the seat of Bowen – adopted a less alien vernacular. Both Paterson's

---

[46] *Tribune*, 20 April 1949, 1.   [47] Martelle, *The Fear Within*, 6.
[48] Martelle, *The Fear Within*, 31.   [49] *Tribune*, 29 January 1949, 8.
[50] *The Workers Star*, 29 April 1949, 2.   [51] *The Maritime Worker*, 11 November 1950, 4.

defence speech and other transcripts of the trials, including an impassioned speech by Sharkey from the dock, were reproduced and distributed by the CPA in an attempt to cast his ordeal as politically motivated. Paterson's defence of Sharkey at the Sydney Federal Court engaged less with the rights of the situation than the technicalities of making a seditious utterance. Had Sharkey made "certain movements with his tongue which caused certain sounds to be uttered or issued from his mouth", or had those words been put there by the right-wing *Daily Telegraph* newspaper, to which he had merely agreed? Had Sharkey published these words, or had that been the role of the mass media, in which case why weren't they and not Sharkey facing charges?[52]

A second pamphlet contained Sharkey's statement, delivered at a sentencing hearing in October 1949, after the High Court had thrown out his last appeal. The author, Sharkey's solicitor Harold Rich, went to some effort to set the scene of Sharkey as the individual sacrificed to the power of the state:

Sharkey [spoke] in a crowded courtroom from the dock, enclosed by iron railings and guarded by officers of the police; on his left were seated, in tiers, a large number of senior members of the police force and some whose main function is to hound progressive peoples. Immediately before and below him seated at the table were the barristers who had prosecuted him ... [O]n his right hand side were the reporters of the Sydney daily press which had been utilised by the Crown in the course of the prosecution. Behind him the Court was crowded with spectators, sympathisers and Communists who came to share Sharkey's burden and to see what sentence would be meted out to the man who spoke in the cause of peace.[53]

While Sharkey is here presented in sympathetic tones as a political prisoner, a victimised individual at the hands of state power, the content of his speech appealed to no international arbiter. Rather, Sharkey spoke of a long tradition of individuals prosecuted for Sedition – from Peter Lalor at the 1854 Eureka Stockade on – and closed with a rousing call for world peace.[54] The ACCL produced a pamphlet on the Sharkey trial in 1950, placing it alongside Burns and Healy's trials in Queensland and Western Australia, as well as proposals for a ban on the Communist Party. Fitzpatrick authored the pamphlet and used the different judgements of the courts to shine a light on the political nature of the trials.

Sir John Dwyer, the presiding judge in the Western Australian Supreme Court, had instructed the jury to view their deliberations on Healy's guilt as "simply a determination of the practical question whether the accused

---

[52] Fred Paterson, *Political Charge against Sharkey* (Sydney: Current Books, 1949), 3.
[53] Harold Rich, *The Story of the Sharkey Trial* (Sydney: Release Sharkey Committee, 1949), 18.
[54] Rich, *The Story of the Sharkey Trial*, 18–21.

64   Cold War Rights

was just expressing opinions or whether he had seditious intent".[55] While
the jury in the Western Australian case were instructed to see this as
a dispassionate test of law, Justice Francis Dwyer of the New South
Wales Supreme Court asked that jurors "draw a distinction between
communists" such as Sharkey, on one hand,

> and on the other hand those who might regard [such utterances] as words alien
> and offensive to ... the love of race and country and tradition which you might
> think is characteristic of a large number who live in this country and are proud to
> call themselves Australians.[56]

Such "tendentious, romantic and passionate language" was "not juridi-
cal, but belongs rather to some school of politically partisan oratory" – and
the ACCL put Sharkey's imprisonment and Healy's freedom down to
such polarising views.[57] The divergent judgements, the ACCL argued,
were part of "a concerted effort ... towards depriving minorities of
common rights – freedom of speech and association, even the right to
vote and to possess ... property" that made use of certain sections of the
Crimes Act to criminalise dissent.[58] The Council's use of the term "common rights" marks a move away from a pure focus on civil liberties, while
discussion of "minorities" also hints at the diversification of its interests in
later years.

Referenda, Religion and Rights

Sharkey's trial and eventual three-year imprisonment were to be only an
opening shot in Australia's Cold War. The Communist Party abandoned
its "popular front" strategy in 1948, taking a radical turn that saw it lead
a wave of industrial strikes, most famously in the coal sector over June–
August 1949.[59] The ALP, which in communist discourse moved almost
overnight from potential allies to representing "the poisonous plant of
social democracy", responded in kind.[60] Prime Minister Ben Chifley sent
troops to break the miners' strike, a significant strategic defeat for the
communists, while a Royal Commission was launched by the conservative Victorian state government to examine the truth of allegations made

---

[55] *West Australian*, 2 November 1949, 2.
[56] Brian Fitzpatrick, *A Public Remonstrance* (Melbourne: Australian Council for Civil
Liberties, 1949), 12–13.
[57] Fitzpatrick, *A Public Remonstrance*, 13   [58] Fitzpatrick, *A Public Remonstrance*, 19.
[59] Phillip Deery, "Chifley, the Army and the 1949 Coal Strike", *Labour History* no. 68 (May
1995), 90–97.
[60] Phillip Deery and Neil Redfern, "No Lasting Peace? Labor, Communism and the
Cominform: Australia and Great Britain, 1945–50", *Labour History* no. 88 (May,
2005): 72.

by a former member of vote tampering in union elections and covert communist coordination of industrial disputes in key industries.[61] It was the ALP government that ordered Sharkey's sedition trial, and Labor Party organisations in various states – particularly Victoria and Queensland – initiated a policy of forming "industrial groups" in communist-controlled trade unions to preserve Labor dominance. The party, which in 1945 had 22,000 members and was able to command national trade union policy, had by the time of Sharkey's trial halved in size and lost significant trade union positions such as the Federated Ironworkers Association. Yet, despite such setbacks, the ALP did not move to ban the CPA. Such a ban did, however, become the policy of Menzies' Liberal Party after a March 1948 party room meeting.[62] This reflected moves in conservative civil society organisations like what was then known as the Returned Soldiers' and Sailors' Imperial League of Australia (RSSILA) to expel "communists or communist sympathisers", as well as a spate of similar bans overseas.[63] Such measures were a priority for the Liberal Party when it won the December 1949 election under Menzies, and the Communist Party Dissolution Act was first tabled in April 1950.[64]

The referendum itself is a widely remembered and studied moment in Australian history. It is presented as a continuation either of the population's rebellious, anti-authoritarian streak or of Australia's conservative record of voting in constitutional referenda. Yet, few scholars have paid close attention to the language that both sides used in their respective campaigns. Prominent Australian political historian Frank Bongiorno finds evidence not of human rights' primacy but of their almost total absence from the campaign's rhetoric. Bongiorno found but one instance wherein human rights champion Herbert Evatt utilised its precepts – during the second reading of the *Constitution Alteration (Powers to Deal with Communists and Communism) Bill* in July 1951.[65] "Recognition of Evatt's contribution to founding a regime of international human rights does not take us very far in understanding his actions in 1951," Bongiorno concludes, drawing a similar conclusion to that of conservative writer John Hirst that the 1950s were a period where the rights of British

---

[61] For more on the Royal Commission, see Vicky Rastrick, "The Victorian Royal Commission on Communism, 1949–50: A Study of Anti-Communism in Australia" (Master's Thesis, Australian National University, 1973).

[62] *The Age*, 12 March 1948, 3.

[63] *The Sydney Morning Herald*, 8 July 1948, 4. It became the Returned Services League in 1964.

[64] On the impact of this referendum, see the special issue of *Australian Historical Studies* 44, no. 1 (2013).

[65] Frank Bongiorno, "Herbert Vere Evatt and British Justice: The Communist Party Referendum of 1951", *Australian Historical Studies* 44, no. 1 (2013), 54–70.

66   Cold War Rights

citizenship remained supreme and human rights a passing fancy.[66] Yet, I want to propose here that on both sides of politics, a strong undercurrent of opinion sought to use ideas of British rights to historicise and vernacularise a more expansive concept of human rights. While human rights was not the dominant form of claim making, forces wider than Evatt made use of its ideas within and alongside older traditions.

While this chapter argues that "human rights" was one way the Australian Communist Party and its supporters responded to Menzies' attacks, one key roadblock to such usages was the CPA's own antagonism towards rights. The party had traditionally held a dismissive view towards individual rights, in keeping with the Marxist-Leninist theory that abstract rights were irrelevant unless accompanied by those of a social and economic nature. Sean Scalmer describes the way that such doctrinaire notions of Marxism operated within the CPA as a "master discourse – a language within which members argued out policies and talked about the world".[67] This was an enclosing language and a self-fulfilling prophecy, with the tools crafted by Marx and Lenin seen as able to predict the laws of history. Yet, such rigidity had not always been the case. The CPA of the 1920s was marked by its heterogeneity; forces as diverse as One Big Union supporters, left trade unionists and anarchists called themselves members. By 1930 the Communist International (Comintern), of which the Australian party was a member, imposed what was termed "Bolshevisation" on the party and forced it to adopt the forms and practice of Stalinist Marxism that Scalmer details.[68] Lenin's concept of democratic centralism became both organising principle and disciplinary procedure ensuring that, to paraphrase Marx, the ideas of the Moscow-centric leadership became the ruling ideas.[69]

For Marxist-Leninists, bourgeois rights were merely a part of capitalism's ideological superstructure: under class society, "[t]he practical application of man's right to liberty is man's right to *private property*", as Marx put it in *On The Jewish Question*.[70] What was the use of rights – to freedom,

---

[66] Bongiorno, "Herbert Vere Evatt and British Justice", 74–5; John Hirst, "From British Rights to Human Rights", *Quadrant* 48, no. 3 (March 2004), 14–15.

[67] Sean Scalmer, "Marxist Ideology inside the Communist Party of Australia 1942–1956", *Journal of Political Ideologies* 3, no. 1 (1998), 47.

[68] Much literature exists exploring this early history, most importantly Macintyre, *The Reds*. See also Alastair Davidson, *The Communist Party of Australia: A Short History* (Stanford, CA: Hoover Institution Press, 1969); Tom O'Lincoln, *Into the Mainstream: The Decline of Australian Communism* (Carlton North, VIC: Red Rag Publications, 2009).

[69] Original quote is "The ideas of the ruling class are in every epoch the ruling ideas." Karl Marx and Frederick Engels, *The German Ideology* (New York: International Publishers, 1970), 64.

[70] Karl Marx, *On The Jewish Question* (1844), available at www.marxists.org/archive/marx/works/1844/jewish-question/. Italics in original.

to life or to expression – without access to the social and economic means to make these abstract principles a concrete reality? Rights, it was argued, could be left until after the revolution. While this was in many ways a misreading of Marx, such notions became central to Soviet legal and political practice after the Bolshevik revolution, particularly embodied in the "Stalin" Constitution of 1936.[71] While civil rights to voting, expression and assembly were guaranteed to citizens, this was on the proviso that their exercise "correspond[ed] to the interest of toilers and the strengthening of the socialist system". The document clearly gave precedence to social rights in the areas of education, employment, aged care and health – for which the Soviets ambitiously labelled their constitution "the most democratic in the world".[72] And while Jenifer Amos highlights the Soviet Union's adoption and use of the Universal Declaration of Human Rights internationally in the postwar years, it was not until Khrushchev's rule that "the Declaration became a part of the domestic politics as well".[73]

The Bolshevised Australian party adopted similar ideas – and the rigid, undemocratic mode of organising that went along with them. At its 1948 conference, the CPA re-affirmed the secondary importance, and reactionary intent, of rights language by arguing that the conservative side of politics upheld "human freedom" only to allow "a handful of parasitical millionaires to continue to exploit and plunder the Australian people". In keeping with Marxist-Leninist notions of subordinating personal freedoms to those of a social and economic nature, it was argued that "the first condition of personal freedom for the great majority of the people is to smash monopoly-capitalist control".[74] While the party called for the defence of "democratic rights", these were usually synonymous with collective Trade Union rights, and the defence of the individual against the predations of the state was rarely if at all mentioned.[75] Yet, within two years Communists had moved from cynicism towards individual rights to what appear at least to be their staunchest champions and articulators. The communist weekly *Tribune* published nearly 100 articles concerned with human rights in 1949 alone, organised commemorative events to mark "Human

---

[71] For a recent reinterpretation of Marx's attitude towards rights see Paul O'Connell, "On the Human Rights Question", *Human Rights Quarterly* 40, No. 4 (November 2018): 962–88.

[72] Nathans, "Soviet Rights-Talk in the Post-Stalin Era", 171–2.

[73] Jennifer Amos, "Embracing and Contesting: The Soviet Union and the Universal Declaration of Human Rights, 1948–1958", in *Human Rights in the Twentieth Century*, 148.

[74] *The Way Forward: Resolutions of the 15th Congress of the Australian Communist Party* (Sydney: Communist Party of Australia, 1948), 9.

[75] See, for instance, "Resolutions of the Queensland State Conference, Communist Party of Australia, 1955", in Papers of Eva and Ted Bacon, UQFL241, Fryer Library, Box 4, Folder "CPA Queensland Branch State Conference".

68   Cold War Rights

Rights Day" on 10 December in 1949 and 1950, and frequently found recourse to quoting from the UDHR on issues of political prisoners, indigenous rights and a slew of international imbroglios.[76] Such a stance was reflected in the Party's trade unions – the *Maritime Worker*, published by the CPA-controlled Waterside Workers Federation, recorded that it had received "many requests" for a copy of the Universal Declaration, and, as it was "impossible to get sufficient printed copies", they printed the "historical document" in its entirety.[77] The powerful Building Workers Industrial Union demanded the Australian Council of Trade Unions support a referendum to "incorporate the principles of the Universal Declaration of Human Rights" into the nation's constitution in 1951, early hints towards more emphatic calls for a bill of rights in later decades.[78]

Outside of the Party itself, human rights were greeted as a continuation of the British – and wider European – rights tradition stretching to the Magna Carta and beyond. This was but part of a much broader interest in the UDHR, which saw the document reprinted in full by newspapers around the country, while questions around immigration and Indigenous welfare were increasingly framed using its language.[79] Evatt's wife, Mary Alice Evatt, remarked to newspapers on the couple's return from New York that "human rights mean women's rights", arguing that "once we get down to discussing human rights most of the rights that women have fought for will fall into place".[80] This teleological notion that human rights were but the latest and final step in human – and particularly British – betterment was reflected in much contemporary commentary. Evatt himself described the Declaration as "a landmark in world history comparable to the Magna Carta and the Bill of Rights in British Commonwealth history".[81] Taking such geneology even further, the *Cootamundra Herald* welcomed the Universal Declaration as "one of the greatest achievements of the liberal mind in this century". "We look back in thanksgiving to the French Declaration of the Rights of Man, 1789; to the English Declaration of 1689; to Magna Carta; and to similar declarations from the Old Testament onward", one editorial extolled.[82] In the northern New South Wales town of Lismore, the *Northern Star*

---

[76] Advanced search at www.trove.nla.gov.au for statistics; on Human Rights Day, see *Tribune*, 14 December 1950, 5; on multiple uses of human rights, see *Tribune*, 26 March 1949, 3; *Tribune*, 30 July 1949, 5.

[77] *Maritime Worker*, 25 November 1950, 1.   [78] *Tribune*, 4 July 1951, 11.

[79] For UDHR reprints, see, for example, *The Courier-Mail* [Brisbane], 24 October 1949, 2; *Shepparton Advertiser* [Victoria], 15 March 1949, 3; *National Advocate* [Bathurst], 10 January 1949, 4.

[80] *The Argus* [Melbourne], 18 January 1949, 8.   [81] *The Sun* [NSW], 23 June 1949, 40.

[82] *Cootamundra Herald* [NSW], 1 February 1949, 2. The *Cairns Post* [QLD], 3 December 1949, 7, made a similar point.

declared the declaration part of "Anglo-Saxon thought, from Magna Carta to the Four Freedoms", which "emphasised the rights of man as a political and moral individual".[83] The *Glen Innes Examiner* saw fit to quote Indian leader Jawaharlal Nehru that "the objectives of the Commonwealth", the newly founded conglomeration of independent or soon-to-be British colonies, "can only be the objectives so nobly stated in the Charter of the United Nations [including] the establishment of human rights all over the world".[84] British Freedom and Human Rights, it seems, were being read as part of the same tradition.

Such lofty language and truncated exhortations were however only part of the story of vernacularising – which after all required moving from a celebration of the document to understanding its individual articles in a national context. Given the nature of the referendum question – asking whether Australians had the right to identify as communists and seek membership in an avowedly communist organisation – Article 20 of the Declaration seemed particularly relevant. Indeed, this was the only section of the UDHR to be mentioned in a High Court judgement during this period – it would not be until 1975 that its phrasings would again be cited in a decision of the nation's highest judicial body. Sir John Latham, who served as Chief Justice from 1935 to 1952 after a career as a conservative politician and aspiring prime minister, is a controversial figure whose "extra-judicial advising" on such matters as increasing government powers during World War II and party political matters of his former allies became well known after his death. Particularly, though, Latham is charged with having advised Menzies on how best to alter the Constitution so as to override his own court's decision (on which he was the only dissenter) in the *Communist Party Case* (1951).[85] His political dalliances aside, Latham's adopted a "strictly legal approach" to his position on the High Court, adhering to the letter of the Constitution, and "left the law much as he found it" upon retirement.[86] This is why his decision to cite the Universal Declaration, in a decision regarding union compulsion in the clerical industry, is so remarkable. The Federated Clerks Union, headed by noted Communist Jack Hughes, had filed in 1949 for a variation of its industrial agreement with the Employers' Association of Wool Selling Brokers "which provided that no one should

---

[83] *Northern Star* [NSW], 24 May 1947, 8.

[84] *Glen Innes Examiner* [NSW], 14 March 1949, 3.

[85] Fiona Wheeler, "Sir John Latham's Extra-Judicial Advising", *Melbourne University Law Review* 35 (2011), 651–76.

[86] Stuart Macintyre, "Latham, Sir John Greig (1877–1964)", *Australian Dictionary of Biography Vol. 10*, available at http://adb.anu.edu.au/biography/latham-sir-john-greig-7104/text12251, published first in hardcopy 1986.

70 Cold War Rights

be employed in the employers' industries unless he were a member of the union."[87] While "not part of the law of Australia", Latham quoted in his final judgement Article 20 of the UDHR in full: "(1) Everyone has the right to freedom of peaceful assembly and association. (2) No-one may be compelled to belong to an association." As Latham put it, "the signatory nations specified certain human rights and fundamental freedoms", enshrining understandings that "had been the subject of much controversy for many centuries".[88] To Latham, the Declaration then provided added moral legitimacy to his otherwise strictly constitutional arguments on a matter of seemingly only industrial significance.

The Union's claim and eventual disallowance gained significant media attention at the time, serving to further demonise illiberal communism and provide precedent for the struggle over Menzies' referendum. Tabled in April 1950, the *Communist Party Dissolution Act* passed the House of Representatives in November of that year, with the ALP supporting it as a way to counter Menzies' "false and slanderous allegations" that the Opposition was soft on communism.[89] The Communist Party and ten industrial unions successfully challenged the Act's constitutional validity, with Evatt breaking his party's position to represent the Waterside Workers Federation. The former attorney general, who would become opposition leader in June 1951, took little time in bringing Latham to account for his previous deployments of rights language. On 17 November 1950 Evatt told the court that "it is difficult to imagine a more serious infringement of what is called the right to association" than Menzies' Act, "a right to which the Chief Justice referred recently when he quoted the Declaration of Human Rights to which Australia is a party".[90] Evatt's representation proved successful, with the court ruling Menzies' Bill unconstitutional in March 1951, sparking a flurry of discussion and debate. "Would banning of Communists contradict the UN Declaration of Human Rights", Sydney's *Catholic Weekly* asked its readers, to which the paper's writers gave a firm "No" – for while "a government has not the right to suppress all liberties, it has the right to suppress some" – in a novel reading of the UN's domestic jurisdiction provisions. "The same Declaration demands freedom of conscience and worship, freedom of movement and residence, and freedom to own property", so "[w]hen communists are prepared to grant these it will be time enough for them to claim other freedoms".[91]

---

[87] *The Sun* [Sydney], 4 August 1949, 13.   [88] *R. v Wallis* [1949] HCA 30 (4 August 1949).
[89] George Winterton, "The Significance of the Communist Party Case", *Melbourne University Law Review* 18 (1992), 647.
[90] *The Sun* [Sydney], 17 November 1950, 11.
[91] *Catholic Weekly* [Sydney], 26 October 1950, 2.

Communists, as we have seen, began experimenting with human rights as a continuation of a broader tradition of struggle for what they tended to call "democratic rights". The tabling of the Dissolution Act was met with a thundering front-page denunciation in the *Tribune:* "Smash this Rotten Bill – Gross Abuse of Human Rights – Don't let Menzies become Dictator". The bill was dubbed a "gross and impudent violation of human rights and civil liberties … on behalf of Collins House, BHP and the other monopolies".[92] That the relatively fresh idea of human rights could sit alongside much older traditions of British civil liberties shows that the Communists at least hoped the Universal Declaration had begun entering the public consciousness. The Party held an Australian People's Assembly for Human Rights in September of 1950, organised by the Communist-affiliated Democratic Rights Council in Victoria, which attracted some 700 attendees to discuss a proposed Australian Charter for Freedom.[93] Just weeks before the vote, the *Tribune* published a detailed, annotated list of each article of the Declaration Menzies' proposed laws denied – from freedom of opinion and freedom of assembly to the right to a free trial and to own property.[94] The ACCL, for its part, played only a limited role in the heated referendum debates. As Macintyre and Waghorne write: "It seemed … that policy would no longer be determined by rational debate and informed judgement; instead it would run the inflamed gauntlet of public opinion."[95] When the question of a ban had been one left to parliament, the ACCL produced no fewer than five pamphlets addressed largely to elected representatives, but when it became a public campaign only one publication appeared. "The council was acutely conscious of its limited influence in such a setting", and many council members saw what seemed like overwhelming popular support for the bill as "incomprehensible".[96] Smarting from the High Court verdict, Menzies called a constitutional referendum to empower his government to circumvent their decision, held in September 1951. When the "No" campaign won the day, by only 52,000 votes nationally, the only solace ACCL head Fitzpatrick could muster was that "half-plus of our people" had seen through the Cold War's dark shadows.[97]

The Referendum had not only cleaved national opinion: it also had dramatic effects on the Labor Party itself. While Catholic human rights thought in Australia in the 1930s and 1940s had seen capitalism and Marxism as equally threatening of totalitarianism, the Cold War saw a pronounced sharpening of focus by organs of Catholic opinion on the

---

[92] *Tribune*, 29 April 1950, 1.
[93] *Tribune*, 19 July 1950, 6; *Tribune*, 2 September 1950, 2; *Tribune*, 15 September 1950, 7.
[94] *Tribune*, 22 August 1951, 4.   [95] Macintyre and Waghorne, *Liberty*, 95.   [96] Ibid., 96.
[97] Ibid., 97.

72   Cold War Rights

latter. That Evatt had seemingly taken the side of communists during the referendum only exacerbated tensions between conservative Catholics – particularly in the Party's Victorian branch – and the federal party. The Industrial Groups, launched by the party to undermine Communist control in trade unions, quickly became battlegrounds, as Catholics secretly organised in the Catholic Social Studies Movement (colloquially known as the "Movement") under B. A. Santamaria's leadership to exert control over the Federal Party. Such moves had the vernacular support of Australia's bishops via their yearly Social Justice Statements.[98] The 1948 Bishops' Statement dealt with the topic of "Socialisation", a key ALP platform and subject to a referendum in that year specifically concerning the banking sector.[99] In 1943 the *Catholic Weekly* condemned the "perversity of capitalism", but the 1948 statement tempered such language.[100] While "definitely opposed to the system of industrial capitalism which the community experiences today", the Statement placed "a strong emphasis upon the private ownership, control and operation of productive property".[101] Only under a system of private ownership, with minimal but necessary state intervention, could "the human person be free, and secure in the enjoyment of his inviolable rights".[102] The threat of communism, as in other parts of the world, drove Catholics to a compromise with both the state and capital.

Open ideological warfare broke out between Catholics and Evatt's supporters in 1954, amidst an election campaign during which Evatt was judged to have taken a soft line on the Red menace, exacerbated by his controversial appearance at the Petrov Royal Commission, investigating allegations of communist spying in Australia.[103] The Catholic press presented this struggle as one for human rights. Dismissing those who labelled Catholic opposition to communism as "fanatical", the *Advocate* used an editorial to opine that "it is not that the Christian anti-Communist is

---

[98] Monetarily, the Movement was also supported by the Church hierarchy; see Robert Murray, *Split: Australian Labor in the 1950s* (Melbourne: Cheshire, 1970), 44–65.

[99] While the ALP "Socialisation" platform was reinterpreted in 1953 to only require wholesale national ownership of industry "to the extent necessary to eliminate exploitation and other anti-social features of industry", this failed to cool tensions. Australian Labor Party, *ALP Official Report of Proceedings of the 19th Triennial Conference, March 1951*, 43.

[100] *Catholic Weekly*, 15 April 1943, 11.

[101] The Archbishops and Bishops of the Catholic Church of Australia, *Social Justice Statement 1948: Socialisation* (Carnegie, VIC: Renown Press, 1948), 5.

[102] Ibid., 3.

[103] Sean Scalmer, "The Affluent Worker or the Divided Party? Explaining the Transformation of the ALP in the 1950s", *Australian Journal of Political Science* 32, no. 3 (1997), 410.

'illiberal' ... or that he denies the human right to freedom ... [W]hat he stands for is the right of men and communities to establish and preserve a way of life based on the Truth."[104] Much as Catholics in Europe were establishing Christian Democratic parties, the *Advocate* told its readers, "It is not enough ... for the Catholic in public affairs to keep his Christianity and his politics in separate compartments ... He has to be, not merely a Christian and a politician, but a Christian politician."[105] As "politics encroaches more and more on human personality, on the family, on basic human rights", it was incumbent upon Catholics to have their own political voice outside of the ALP.[106] Amongst the most significant issues associated with this debate was the perennial topic of schooling. The 1949 Social Justice Statement informed readers that the UDHR granted a "priority right" allowing parents to "chose the kind of education to be given to their children" and that the state's funding of secular public education attacked the rights of Catholics who sought religious instruction. "It is contrary to every principle of freedom that a majority should trample on a minority", the statement fulminated in language redolent with postwar meaning, "that a powerful nation should smash a small one, that giant monopolies should destroy small owners on the ground that might is right ... The same principle surely applies to education."[107] Labor's unwillingness to support what was known as "State Aid" to religious schools was a key concern of what would become the Democratic Labor Party, formed after the entire executive of the rebellious Victorian ALP was declared vacant in late 1954.[108] The Party won concessions from Menzies' government in exchange for its support in crucial marginal seats, helping to keep Labor out of federal power until 1972. Newly politicised Catholics, who had been amongst the first to argue publicly for human rights in the war years, continued to find in them a significant vehicle for conservative politics. Yet such deployments were not the limit of the term's usability.

"A Contradiction in Terms": Civil Libertarians and Indigenous Rights

In 1946, a recently demobilised British journalist by the name of Geoffrey Parsons penned a book, *Black Chattels: The Story of the Australian*

---

[104] *Advocate*, 18 November 1954, 6.
[105] *Advocate*, 16 December 1954, 6. On the foundations of Christian Democracy, see Chappel, *Catholic Modern*, chapter 4.
[106] Ibid.
[107] The Archbishops and Bishops of the Catholic Church of Australia, *Social Justice Statement 1949: Christian Education in a Democratic Community* (Carnegie, VIC: Renown Press, 1949), 13.
[108] Scalmer, "The Affluent Worker or the Divided Party", 413–15.

74   Cold War Rights

Aborigines, published in London by the NCCL. Having served in the Royal Air Force in the Pacific theatre, Parsons returned with a trove of information regarding Indigenous Australians: "reports, cuttings, correspondence, newspaper clippings and other materials".[109] The publication was part of broader attempts by the NCCL to shift from a purely domestic to an international focus. A "Sub-Committee on the New World" was established in 1945, and the organisation launched an International Consultative Conference on Human Rights in 1947. The NCCL wished to add "a new dimension to civil liberties stretching beyond the rights of a citizen into a broader notion of human rights for humanity", as the organisation's 1946–7 Annual Report intoned.[110] Parsons' book contributed to this goal, opening with a quotation from Evatt that "human rights and fundamental freedoms" applied "without distinction of race, sex, language or religion". Such sentiments sat oddly besides a quotation from geographer and historian Archibald Grenfell Price that Australia's native policies were "the most backwards and meanest of the English-speaking countries", demonstrating the continued relevance of driving a wedge between the worldly Evatt and the policies of his government.[111] Parsons' narrative opens with a surprisingly nuanced understanding of Indigenous pre-contact customs, before reporting the "appalling" realities of European invasion. Of an estimated 300,000 Indigenous peoples in 1788, only 50,000 remained "and are still diminishing each year".[112] Parsons judged that "the words 'Aborigine' and 'civil liberty' form a contradiction in terms", such was their denial of even the most basic rights and privileges:

The aborigine is not mentioned in the Australian constitution, does not figure in the Commonwealth Census of population, returns no representative to Parliament; his property rights are not respected, his labour neither free nor adequately recompensed; his children not his own.[113]

Of plans to use Indigenous Reserves for the testing of new rocket weapons, Parsons said only that "there would appear to be some lack of coordination between the … Minister for Defence and … Dr Evatt, who is so eloquent a champion of national minorities" in international fora.[114]

---

[109] *The Argus* [Victoria], 17 February 1947, 5.
[110] Moore, *From Civil Liberties to Human Rights*, 78.
[111] Geoffrey Parsons, *Black Chattels: The Story of the Australian Aborigines* (London: National Council for Civil Liberties, 1946), 6.
[112] Ibid., 11. This last claim was incorrect: the population had been increasing since at least the 1930s. See Russell McGregor, *Indifferent Inclusion: Aboriginal People and the Australian Nation* (Canberra: Aboriginal Studies Press, 2011), 1.
[113] Ibid., 34.   [114] Ibid., 45.

"A Contradiction in Terms" 75

Parsons concluded his book with a discussion of a photo exhibition, entitled "Meet Australia", held in Australia House, London. Indigenous peoples were pictured only twice: as a noble savage – "courageous, honest [and] with a simple dignity" – and on the receiving end of a colonialist's bullet. There appeared to be "no contradiction between the first picture and the second, no reason to explain why the 'simple dignity' of the stone-aged man should be answered with bullets". That such images could sit alongside model homes and examples of export produce in an exhibition "whose centrepiece cited Australia as a land where the Four Freedoms of the Atlantic Charter were enjoyed be all" was deeply disconcerting.[115] The way forward, Parsons hoped, was for emerging voices of international opinion to "let the Commonwealth Government know that they cannot accept this claim to be regarded as a spokesman for democracy until it accords human rights to the natives of its own country".[116] Melbourne's *The Argus*, while questioning whether Parson had "taken isolated incidents of cruelty and presented them as a general picture", noted that the "important fact is that thousands of people in Britain will see this indictment" and "it will be eagerly seized on by foreign propagandists". Whatever the truth of Parsons' tale, he had made "some kind of case, and it will need to be answered".[117]

Parsons' publication formed part of a significantly broader global discussion around the applications of those rights and liberties that framed Allied war aims to Indigenous peoples of the Pacific and other colonised regions. A group of West African journalists issued a memorandum on "The Atlantic Charter and West Africa", while the Phelps-Stokes Fund in the United States published a report on "The Atlantic Charter and Africa from an American Standpoint", co-authored by W. E. B. Du Bois.[118] Mohandas Gandhi wrote to Roosevelt himself to say that that claims the Allies were "fighting to make the world safe for . . . the individual and for democracy" as spelt out in the Charter "sounds hollow, so long as India, and for that matter, Africa are exploited".[119] In Australia, previous generations of humanitarians and colonial reformers had attempted to make the cause of Indigenous peoples a global one, but it was only in the

---

[115] Ibid., 47. Many Australian states protested at the exhibition's "libellous" depiction of their produce and attractions, yet none cited the indigenous imagery as problematic. *Warwick Daily News* [Queensland], 4 April 1946, 5; *The Advertiser* [Adelaide], 5 April 1946, 8; *Barrier Miner* [NSW], 4 April 1946, 1.
[116] Parsons, *Black Chattels*, 49.   [117] *The Argus* [Victoria], 17 February 1947, 5.
[118] Bonny Ibhawoh, "Testing the Atlantic Charter: Linking Anti-colonialism, Self-Determination and Universal Human Rights", *The International Journal of Human Rights* 18, no. 7 (2014), 843, 856.
[119] Quoted in Elizabeth Borgwardt, *A New Deal for the World: America's Vision for Human Rights* (Cambridge, MA: Harvard University Press, 2007), 8–9.

76   Cold War Rights

postwar era that such enterprises gained considerable success. Since 1925, the British Commonwealth League, a feminist organisation that sought to use the ties of empire to improve conditions for women and colonised peoples, had served as fertile ground for internationally minded women humanitarians. This forum allowed for the discussion of the fate of Indigenous women – either bartered or sold on the fringes of white settlement – and the position of colonised peoples as "subjects" and not "citizens" within the Commonwealth, but it had limited functionality beyond a conduit for information and debate.[120] Equally, attempts to utilise the League of Nations system to shine light on Australia proved negligible. Its position as a dominion within the British Commonwealth of Nations meant Australia lacked much by way of an independent foreign policy or treaty-making capacity – the 1931 Statute of Westminster granting such powers to Australia was not ratified until 1942 – sat alongside the League's own varied failings.[121] Susan Pedersen's study of women who worked on the League's Mandates Commission found that their commitment to "well-ordered, benevolent rule" meant that, despite "assiduously defending inhabitants' formal rights of petition", they accepted "at face value even the most implausible and self-interested responses offered by the mandatory power".[122] And in any case, Indigenous Australians were not considered part of a Mandate territory, and while feminists in the organisation campaigned strongly against sexual trafficking, this practice within nations was not within the organisation's purview. The deficiencies of these international organisations were starkly revealed by the advent of yet another world war, and the Atlantic Charter was welcomed around the world as a genuine attempt to create a new world order that might realise the League's unfulfilled prerogative. This was explicitly seen as a new order that must include what were termed the "native peoples of the South-West Pacific" in acknowledgement of the "valuable part they have played in helping us as carriers, labourers and stretcher bearers" in the Pacific theatre.[123]

Little time was wasted in seeking to apply Charter principles to Indigenous Australians and peoples of the Pacific in general. Less than

---

[120] See, in particular, Fiona Paisley, "Citizens of Their World: Australian Feminism and Indigenous Rights in the International Context, 1920s and 1930s", *Feminist Review*, no. 58 (Spring 1998), 66–84.

[121] On the implications of the Statute and its delayed ratification, see Paul R. Bartrop, "The Holocaust, the Aborigines, and the Bureaucracy of Destruction: An Australian Dimension of Genocide", *Journal of Genocide Research* 3, no. 1 (2001), 75–6.

[122] Susan Pedersen, "Metaphors of the Schoolroom: Women Working the Mandates System of the League of Nations", *History Workshop Journal* 66 (2008), 196.

[123] A. P. Elkin, *Reconstruction and the Peoples of the South-West Pacific* (Sydney: Association for the Protection of Native Races, 1943), 1.

"A Contradiction in Terms" 77

a year after the Charter's promulgation, a Methodist minister residing in Sydney, J. W. Burton, wrote a book entitled *The Atlantic Charter and the Pacific Races*, which was quickly followed by Anglican clergyman and professor of anthropology A. P. Elkin's *Wanted: A Charter for the Native Peoples of the South-West Pacific*. The religious tonality of these statements ought not to be surprising: religious orders ran many of the "missions" onto which Indigenous Australians were forced after the closing of the frontier wars.[124] War service by the peoples of the South Pacific was seen as legitimating the application of Charter principles to them: these "unoffending peoples" were not only "our administrative responsibility", as Elkin put it, but "have provided us with indispensable service in holding and driving the enemy back".[125] Thus, while Churchill and Roosevelt "were probably not thinking specifically about the backward and primitive peoples of the world nor of Colonial policies when they framed the Atlantic Charter", the fact that the war had dramatically expanded contact with "native" races meant that "we cannot restrict its application to some groups only". That the war had "drawn into its orbit many of the primitive and backward peoples of the world", including tribal populations in northern Australia whom the authors imagined to be untouched by foreign influences, should be reason enough to "bring them within the sphere of application of the beneficent principles of the ... Charter".[126] H. V. Evatt echoed such ideas, stating in September 1942 to the House of Representatives that, while "security comes first", Australia's commitment to the Atlantic Charter meant that "the peoples of South-Eastern Asia and the South-West Pacific ... shall be able to live their lives in freedom from want as well as freedom from fear".[127] Even conservative organisations such as the RSSILA Western Australia branch proposed in 1947 that a "Charter of Liberty" reflecting Atlantic Charter principles replace that state's Aborigines Act and that all those who served in the armed forces during WWII be granted full citizenship rights "retrospective to the date of discharge".[128] Yet the Charter's aims were limited: it was a wartime document designed to express only a minimalist programme. The language these pamphlets used – of bringing natives into the "sphere" of the charter, and Evatt's evocation of the "doctrine of

---

[124] In particular, see Jessie Mitchell, *In Good Faith? Governing Indigenous Australians through God, Charity and Empire, 1825–1855* (Canberra, ACT: Australian National University Press, 2011).

[125] A. P. Elkin, *Wanted: A Charter for the Native Peoples of the South-West Pacific* (Sydney: Australasian Publishing Co, 1943), 7.

[126] Ibid., 12.   [127] *Gippsland Times* [Victoria], 2 December 1943, 4.

[128] *The West Australian*, 6 October 1947, 9.

78   Cold War Rights

trusteeship" – echoed the hollow internationalism of the League of Nations rather than a genuinely universal document.[129]

Applying the Atlantic Charter to Australian Indigenous people was, however, a more difficult task than in the case of colonies or former mandate territories in the region. As Western Australian socialist and Christian humanitarian Mary Bennett wrote to British Labour MP Arthur Creech Jones in 1943, while Australia had signed numerous League of Nations covenants prohibiting forced labour and protecting Indigenous rights, "application ... was limited to Mandated Territories".[130] The signing of the Charter of the United Nations in 1945 provided a more promising outlook and was soon being utilised for the Indigenous cause. The Australian government's 1946 decision to use outback South Australia as a test site for British long-range rockets – a predecessor to its use as a nuclear test site – however provided "Aboriginal activists ... a wider public platform than ever before" and allowed for the first use of that Charter's new vocabulary of human rights.[131] Though it was dubbed "uninhabited wasteland" when first reported in July 1946, Charles Duguid – campaigner, doctor and founder of the progressive Ernabella Mission in rural South Australia – learned that the huge piece of land in fact included a large Indigenous reserve.[132] As the Adelaide *News* wryly asked, "has the safety of human beings in the area been considered?"[133] Doris Blackburn – the second woman ever to be elected to Australia's House of Representatives after winning the Victorian seat of Bourke as an independent socialist in 1946 – moved a protest motion in March 1947 against the rocket tests. Therein, Blackburn labelled them an "act of injustice to a weaker people" and a "betrayal of our responsibility to guard the human rights of those who could not defend themselves".[134] Blackburn claimed that the "basis of the United Nations Charter was sentimentality", and as such "the government should have regard for the rights of the black man from whom we had taken Australia".[135] Yet, Blackburn's concerns – "the desecration of

---

[129] On the possibilities and failings of the League in general, the key text is Susan Pedersen, *The Guardians: The League of Nations and the Crisis of Empire* (Oxford: Oxford University Press, 2015).

[130] Mary M. Bennett to A. Creech Jones Esq. MP, 27 April 1943, Anti-Slavery Society (ASS) Papers, Mss Brit Emp S22 G700, Bodleian Library, Oxford (BL). For more on Bennett, see Allison Holland, *Just Relations: The Story of Mary Bennett's Crusade for Aboriginal Rights* (Crawley, WA: University of Western Australia Press, 2015).

[131] Macintyre and Waghorne, *Liberty*, 74.   [132] *Courier-Mail* [Brisbane], 11 July 1946, 2.

[133] *News* [Adelaide], 26 July 1946, 2.

[134] *Mercury* [Tasmania], 7 March 1947, 20. For more on Blackburn, see Carolyn Rasmussen, *The Blackburns: Private Lives, Public Ambition* (Melbourne: Melbourne University Press, 2019).

[135] *Kalgoorlie Miner* [Western Australia], 2 May 1947, 4.

"A Contradiction in Terms" 79

sacred native preserves; the interference with native women; and the ruin of lives" – did not easily reconcile with Charter principles, and her claim that "fine and clean native lives were possible only in areas where the white man had not penetrated" spoke more of primitivism and the "noble savage" than that of equal rights.[136]

Perhaps due to the unclear nature of exactly which rights or liberties were being violated by the rocket range, the ACCL distanced itself from these protests: "Aboriginal concerns did not fit easily within the Council's understanding of democratic rights", as Macintyre and Waghorne put it.[137] Unlike their British counterparts, the ACCL took little interest in "native affairs" at this time, judging that Indigenous people did not require "special treatment", and it took the government's case for the range at face value.[138] Despite convening a Sub-Committee on Aboriginal Civil Liberties, onto which were invited respected Indigenous activists such as Bill Onus and Doug Nicholls, Fitzpatrick commented in a report to the NCCL's International Human Rights Conference in 1947 that Indigenous Australians did not encounter "discrimination".[139] It was not until 1952 that the Council properly entered the fray of Indigenous politics, when Committee member Yvonne Nicholls wrote a pamphlet entitled *Not Slaves, Not Citizens*, exploring the position of Indigenous people in the Northern Territory.[140] Therein, Nicholls was blunt as to the potential applications of the UDHR. Quoting Grenfell Price's labelling of Australia "the most backward and meanest of the English-speaking countries", she asked whether Australia could "afford either the situation or the odium it brings" in newly established international forums.[141] Nicholls' seemingly unbiased authorial position, indicative of ACCL publications during the period, meant that she appealed less to humanitarian empathy and more to the possibility of Australia's international embarrassment. The emergence of what Nicholls termed a "world court of appeal" in the form of the United Nations Commission on Human Rights meant that unless Australia "domestically and quietly tidies up its house in the Northern Territory", the possibility was that "these natives will somehow take their entire case to the United Nations". Nicholls found the Commonwealth to deny all but one of the 30 Articles in the UDHR to Indigenous peoples in the Northern Territory – the only significant body of land under direct Federal control and hence potentially subject to treaty provisions –

---

[136] *Mercury* [Tasmania], 7 March 1947, 20.   [137] Macintyre and Waghorne, *Liberty*, 71.
[138] Ibid., 71, 74–5.   [139] Ibid., 75.
[140] Yvette Nicholls, *Not Slaves, Not Citizens: Conditions of the Australian Aborigines in the Northern Territory* (Melbourne: Australian Council for Civil Liberties, 1952).
[141] Ibid., 3.

80   Cold War Rights

a situation requiring immediate attention to "save our face and conscience" from being put "before the councils of the world".[142]

Duguid delivered a similar message in that same year to over 1,000 people at the Melbourne Town Hall, at a gathering sponsored by the newly founded Council for Aboriginal Rights (CAR). He found that Indigenous Australians were not accorded the basic rights inherent in the majority of the UDHR's Articles and added a similarly globalised conclusion. Australia's recent decision to vote against a UN motion censuring South African apartheid, the only British Commonwealth nation to do so, was widely noted abroad, and Duguid pointed to the similarities of the two nations' policies. "Common honesty demands no less" than the full realisation of the UDHR for indigenous Australians, Duguid concluded, "and Asia is looking on".[143] The mention of Australia's near neighbours – made all the more sinister by Mao's victory in China and the nationalist regime in Indonesia – marked an early use of what was to become a vital tactic of shaming Australia abroad. Duguid made even stronger criticisms a year later. When a group of Indigenous men were arrested on the outskirts of a white settlement in Western Australia, he commented: "any law that discriminates [against] the human rights of the natives will have to be reconsidered soon". "It is a good thing for Australians to learn that the apartheid which exists in South Africa is not confined to that country alone," Duguid said, adding, "We have the same thing here."[144] The CAR, which hosted Duguid's speech, made it their prerogative to deliver on his agenda, stating in their founding constitution a commitment "to help the aborigines to win for themselves the liberties envisaged for all people by the Universal Declaration of Human Rights".[145] The Council was born out of this period of rights experimentation, sharing membership with both the CPA and the ACCL, and its foundation can be traced to the communist-sponsored Australian People's Assembly for Human Rights, held in September 1950. This conference was organised by the Democratic Rights Council (DRC), which had been founded in 1949 with involvement from but no direct connection to the ACCL and originally concerned itself with the anti-democratic legislation of Victoria's state government.[146]

---

[142] Ibid., 12–13.
[143] Charles Duguid, "The Universal Declaration of Human Rights as it relates to the Aborigines of Australia", Council for Aboriginal Rights (CAR) Papers, Box 8, Folder 4, State Library of Victoria (SLV).
[144] *News* [Adelaide], 29 April 1953, 9.
[145] "Council for Aboriginal Rights – Constitution", CAR Papers, Box 5, Folder 6, SLV.
[146] *The Argus*, 21 September 1949, 5.

"A Contradiction in Terms" 81

In April 1950, the DRC held a Conference for Democratic Rights, where a "Charter of Freedom" was adopted through which the Council hoped to force the "full application in Australia" of the UDHR's principles so as to "guard and strengthen our democratic heritage".[147] "Human Rights" was but another way of expressing the "deeply-rooted love of our people for freedom", of framing the populace's long struggle "against convict slavery, against colonial subjugation, against militarism, fascism and all forms of tyranny".[148] The document listed six key freedoms – of speech, of publication, of organisation, of science and culture, of the person, and from racial and religious persecution – and so demonstrated the group's willingness to accept a "minimalist" or negative reading of rights without calls for the broader social and economic rights of the 1918 and 1936 Soviet constitutions or even the "full employment" championed by Evatt and Chifley.[149] Yet, in many ways, the Charter aped the CPA's long-held disdain for rights language. Jessie Street, independent socialist and key proponent of the UDHR's including principles regarding women, provided the Charter's section on the Declarations applicability to Australia, asserting:

In Australia the only people that enjoy the Human Rights set out in these articles are the "Big Boys" who own or control the public halls, private halls, churches, theatres, sports grounds and other meeting places, who own or control the press and radio and other organs of publicity and propaganda, who have assumed power to themselves over public gardens, parks, thoroughfares and water ways to permit or forbid the use of loud speakers.[150]

This mirrored the CPA's traditional ambivalence to personal liberty, which was after all "the freedom of private property" in Marx's formulation. Street also used her paper to exhort the DRC to stand up for the "Human Rights of the little people", particularly women's right to equal pay.[151] Few people were more "little" in Australia than Indigenous people, who were acknowledged in the Charter as "our deeply wronged forerunners in this country" – subject to "inhuman practices such as flogging and chaining by the neck", who needed to receive a "guarantee to … full economic, social and political rights", as well as the "strict preservation of their remaining tribal lands".[152] The Charter became a centrepiece of September's Assembly, which despite being overshadowed by government bans of many key speakers – including African American performer Paul Robeson – drew together trade unionists,

---

[147] Democratic Rights Council, *A Charter of Freedom: Report of a Conference for Democratic Rights Held in the Lower Melbourne Town Hall, Sat. April 22, 1950* (Melbourne: Victorian Democratic Rights Council, 1950), 3.
[148] Ibid., 3.   [149] Ibid., 3–5.   [150] Ibid., 10.   [151] Ibid., 10.   [152] Ibid., 5.

82   Cold War Rights

actors, teachers and the churches as well as a small delegation of Indigenous Australians from the Northern Territory.[153]

The Assembly consisted of numerous "Commissions" into different areas of concern, and the final resolution of the "Aborigines and Mixed Bloods" commission extended on the Charter's freedoms, declaring "the Australian native race is denied the most elementary human rights, and is one of the most oppressed sections of the world's population". The resolution demanded "tribal aborigines" be given their land "with security of tenure [and] absolute legal ownership", while those of "mixed European and Aborigine blood" received "full equality in all respects with other citizens, full human rights, equal education and opportunities for employment and full social benefits".[154] While those who would go on to form the CAR first saw the need for such a group at this Assembly, a strike amongst Northern Territory Indigenous workers provided the practical impetus. Inspired by another strike in the Pilbara region of Western Australia from 1946 to 1949, on which communist Don McLeod had significant influence, in late November 1950 some 300 Indigenous men and women walked off the Berrimah Aboriginal Reserve on the outskirts of Darwin to demand better wages and equal laws with whites.[155] Murray Norris, president of the North Australian Workers Union, went on a speaking tour of southern states in February 1951 to raise the strikers' cause, regaling crowds of the "callous policy of slavery which is in defiance of the Universal Declaration of Human Rights to which Australia is a signatory". Why, he asked, did white Australians "pay so much attention to minorities in Yugoslavia or Bulgaria" only to "smother up what we are doing to minorities in this country"?[156]

In keeping with this emerging tradition of rights claiming, CAR's founding constitution described the group's functions as "to help the aborigines to win for themselves the liberties envisaged for all people by the Universal Declaration of Human Rights and the conditions for advancement necessary for their very survival".[157] Initially the Declaration was used as an appeal to government, as a part of the group's

---

[153] *The Courier-Mail*, 9 August 1950, 3.
[154] "Democratic Rights Council – Australian People's Assembly for Human Rights – Commission on Aborigines and Mixed Bloods – Resolution", CAR papers, Box 9, Folder 6, SLV.
[155] On the Pilbara strike, see Anne Scrimgeour, "'We Only Want Our Rights and Freedoms': The Pilbara Pastoral Workers Strike, 1946–1949", *History Australia* 11, no. 2 (2014), 101–24.
[156] "Address by Murray Norris, President of the North Australian Workers Union, 12.2.51", CAR Records, Box 9, Folder 6, SLV.
[157] Henry Wardlaw, promotional letter, 22 May 1951, CAR Records, Box 5, Folder 6, SLV.

letter writing campaigns. As a signatory to the Declaration, CAR protested in a letter to the Minister for Territories, Indigenous affairs in their present state left "the Australian government open to justifiable charges of hypocrisy".[158] Shirley Andrews, then CAR secretary, wrote to the responsible minister Paul Hasluck that Australia's Indigenous policies, "laid down very many years ago", were "quite contrary to the ideas of the times, particularly those laid out in the Universal Declaration".[159] Yet, the nature of the rights and liberties the UDHR promised were a topic of some debate and disquiet. CAR sent its draft constitution to numerous individuals with some experience working in Indigenous politics seeking guidance. Tom Wright, communist, secretary of the Sheet Metal Workers Union and author of *New Deal for the Aborigines* (1939), felt that the talk of liberties and advancement was deeply problematic. Wright sought to weaponise the pseudo-scientific distinction of "full blood" and "half castes", theorising that struggles for "tribal autonomy" suited the former and "workers' rights" the latter, in line with long-standing communist policy.[160] For "full bloods" a policy of rights-giving, the "gradual election of the individual aborigine to citizenship", would lead to the "destruction of tribal life ... and means the extermination of the aboriginal native race". Rather than assess Indigenous people as individuals in need of liberties and rights, the "tribe can be identified as a collective unit to treat with them as such", ideas that were only to grow in prominence in later decades.[161]

Yet the seeming mandate that human rights gave activists proved largely illusory. Protests around human rights were fobbed off or met with disdain by Hasluck and his department. While the wartime Labor government saw an international rights order as a potential vehicle for their social democratic policies, conservatives of the 1950s and 1960s chose either to ignore the United Nations – bar participation in the

---

[158] Henry Wardlaw to Paul Hasluck, Minister for Territories, 28 August 1951, CAR Records, Box 1, Folder 2, SLV.

[159] Shirley Andrews to Paul Hasluck, Minister for Territories, 9 March 1953, CAR Records, Box 1, Folder 6, SLV.

[160] For a close analysis of Wright's thoughts on this, see Tim Rowse, *Indigenous and Other Australians since 1901* (Sydney: UNSW Press, 2017), 76–8; Bob Boughton, "The Communist Party of Australia's Involvement in the Struggle for Aboriginal and Torres Strait Islander People's Rights, 1920–1970", in Ray Markey (ed.), *Labour and Community: Historical Essays* (Wollongong, NSW: University of Wollongong Press, 2001), particularly 265–6. On the CPA's indigenous policy more generally, and its close links to that of American communists, see Drew Cottle, "The Colour-Line and the Third Period: A Comparative Analysis of American and Australian Communism and the Question of Race, 1928–1934", *American Communist History* 10, no. 2 (2011), 126–31.

[161] Tom Wright to Henry Wardlaw, 20 September 1951, CAR Records, Box 1, Folder 2, SLV.

84 Cold War Rights

Korean War – or stonewall "imaginative rights" like racial equality or economic justice that moved beyond a very narrow conception of "legal rights".[162] Domestically, the 1953 Northern Territory Welfare Ordinance was designed to comply with the wording, if not the spirit, of this emerging rights consciousness. Rather than being focused on the "protection" of Indigenous Australians, it was subtitled "an ordinance to provide for the care and assistance of certain persons".[163] Hasluck's 1952 response to one of Andrews's many letters announced that the "old system whereby aborigines are under special legislation" would be superseded by a "new system under which they will be regarded as having full exercise of their rights unless they are specifically committed to the care of the State because of their own need for care and assistance".[164] Such rhetorical gestures were rarely backed by perceivable change in practice, and the rights chorus continued. Hasluck used the launch of an Anti-Slavery Society report on the treatment of Indigenous Australians to attack those who sought an "easy and showy way out of their responsibilities by asking someone else to carry pious resolutions".[165] "[T]hose sympathisers with aborigines who insist strongly on his 'right to be an aborigine'" were mere impediments to the state's task of assimilating Indigenous Australians into citizens with the same rights and duties as others.[166] Hasluck was able to use international rhetoric of equality between races to sidestep demands for Indigenous cultural or social rights, a point on which his government was to be resisted in later decades. Equally, the usability of international institutions proved to be decidedly limited: the United Nations followed in its predecessor's steps by adhering "rather strictly" to a definition of its mandate that excluded indigenous minorities in nation states, problematizing the taking of Indigenous cases before the Trusteeship Commission.[167] Thus, when the first national organisation for Indigenous rights – the Federal Council for Aboriginal Advancement – was founded in 1958, it sought not to take the Indigenous case before the United Nations but instead to launch a campaign for a referendum to change the nation's Constitution.

---

[162] Annemarie Devereux, *Australia and the Birth of the International Bill of Human Rights: 1946–1966* (Annandale, NSW: The Federation Press, 2005), 234.

[163] McGregor, *Indifferent Inclusion*, 82–3.

[164] Paul Hasluck MP to Shirley Andrews, 4 March 1952, in CAR papers, Box 1, Folder 6, SLV.

[165] "Anti-Slavery Society Annual Report – Statement by the Minister for Territories, The Hon. Paul Hasluck", 13 July 1956, ASS Papers, MSS Brit Emp S22 G828, BL.

[166] "Some Problems of Assimilation – Address to Section F of the Australian and New Zealand Association for the Advancement of Science in Perth, Western Australia", 28 August 1959, ASS Papers, MSS Brit Emp S22 G828, BL.

[167] Shirley Andrews to Jessie Street, 3 March 1963, CAR Records, Box 8, Folder 4, SLV.

Conclusion

The Cold War had a deep impact on Australian society, closing a period of wartime experimentation and hope as friends became enemies and the nation's near-neighbours moved from wartime allies to dangerous threats. Yet, rights still found a hearing in these years. This chapter has shown how a long tradition of nationally sanctioned civil liberties became entwined with global processes of rights articulation and how this process was one the former's champions often looked askance at. For human rights, more so than seemingly "apolitical" notions of liberties – became a plaything in a global superpower conflict. Human rights became synonymous in the eyes of conservatives with concepts of European (or increasingly, Western) identity, read as either a minimalist program of negative freedoms – from being forced to join a trade union, for example – or as protectors and guarantors of private religiosity unencumbered by the totalitarian state. The defence of human rights from communism was a cause for which many freedoms could be sacrificed, it seemed. For the left, human rights provided a new way to dress up old ideas. Long considered "bourgeois", the newly sacrosanct international nature of individual rights came to sit alongside longer-term communist defences of trade union and other collective rights in the postwar period. Equally, human rights were "vernacularised" within and alongside older traditions of British rights and privileges that Australians already understood.

Indigenous Australians, while appearing largely as mute victims in white activist discourse of the decade, were a significant focus of much rights talk. It was an opinion often expressed that if Australia claimed to be a defender of national minorities abroad, it should start locally first. Human rights, and an international organisation at which disputes could be arbitrated, seemed a novel way in which to give the Indigenous cause a global airing. The limitations of such an approach soon became readily apparent, as the threat of international condemnation saw Australia engage in window dressing rather than substantive reform, at least in the short term. Equally, human rights and civil liberties, as exhibited in state constitutions and global charters, elided the specific reality of indigenous injustice – namely the central importance of land as a collective unit. If, as Marx put it, new ideas come garbed in the "time-honoured disguise and borrowed language" of the past, it is equally apparent that old ideas can dress up as new.[168] It was not until the 1960s that the true novelty of rights came to be realised.

---

[168] Karl Marx, "The Eighteenth Brumaire of Louis Napoleon", in Robert C. Tucker (ed.), *The Marx-Engels Reader* (New York: W. W. Norton, 1978), 595.

3 Experimental Rights

The 1960s, and in particular the epochal year of 1968, is rightly seen as a decade of revolt and disruption. The decade's temporal boundaries have been extended by employing the concept of a "long 1960s" to encompass events from the mid-1950s until well into the 1970s. It was also inherently global.[1] "Paris, New York, Berkeley, Rome, Prague, Rio, Mexico City, Warsaw – those were the places of a revolt that stretched all around the globe and captured the hearts and dreams of a whole generation," as French-German radical Daniel Cohn-Bendit reminisced.[2] Something of a cottage industry of both popular and academic works has reconceptualised the scope of the decade's profound changes – political as well as cultural, economic and personal – while also significantly widening its geographical scope beyond the well-known locales listed by Cohn-Bendit. The global and long Sixties had as profound an impact in cities like Kuala Lumpur, Dar es Salaam and Sydney as it did in the global metropole.[3] As well as the "Year of the Barricades", 1968 was declared the "Year of the Heroic Guerrilla" by the Cuban government and, perhaps surprisingly, the International Year of Human Rights by the United Nations.[4]

---

[1] Numerous volumes exist exploring the "global" nature of the decade, but see in particular Karen Dubinsky, Katherine Krull, Susan Lord, Sean Mills and Scott Rutherford (eds.), *New World Coming: The Sixties and the Shaping of Global Consciousness* (Toronto: Between the Lines Press, 2009); George Katsiaficas, *The Imagination of the New Left: A Global Analysis of 1968* (Boston, MA: South End Press, 1987); Carole Fink, Phillip Gassert and Detlef Junker (eds.), *1968: The World Transformed* (Cambridge: Cambridge University Press, 1998); Chen Jian, Martin Klimke, Masha Kirasirova, Mary Nolan, Marilyn Young and Joanna Waley-Cohen (eds.), *The Routledge Handbook of the Global Sixties: Between Protest and Nation-Building* (Abingdon: Routledge, 2018).

[2] Quoted in Martin Klimke, *The Other Alliance: Student Protest in West Germany & The United States in the Global 1960s* (Princeton: Princeton University Press, 2010), 1.

[3] For each in turn, see Meredith L. Weiss, *Student Activism in Malaysia: Crucible, Mirror, Sideshow* (Ithaca, NY: Cornell Southeast Asia Program Publications, 2011); Andrew Ivaska, *Cultured States: Youth, Gender, and Modern Style in 1960s Dar Es Salaam* (Durham, NC: Duke University Press, 2011); Jon Piccini, *Transnational Protest, Australia and the 1960s: Global Radicals* (Basingstoke, UK: Palgrave Macmillan, 2016).

[4] For the role of Cuba in the events of 1968, see Anne Garland Mahler, *From the Tricontinental to the Global South: Race, Radicalism and Transnational Solidarity* (Durham, NC: Duke University Press, 2018).

Experimental Rights

At the suggestion of Jamaica, the United Nations General Assembly voted in December 1963 to endorse a motion that the twenty-year anniversary of the passage of the Universal Declaration of Human Rights (UDHR) made 1968 an ideal year for "intensified national and international efforts and undertakings in the field of human rights, and also . . . an international review of achievements in the field".[5] The opening to signature of the "twin covenants" that sought to transform the UDHR from declaration to enforceable international law in 1966 added a further dimension to the year's activities: "that states become parties to the existing human rights conventions and . . . hasten the conclusion of other such instruments".[6] The year was, however, to fall short of such expectations. Roland Burke has documented how the drafters of the UDHR looked on in horror as their noble internationalism gave way to "a new intellectual and ideological milieu, which exalted the power of the State and the primacy of economic development", led by figures from third-world states such as Iran, host of the First International Conference on Human Rights.[7]

A briefing document prepared for Australia's diplomatic delegation to the Tehran gathering, convened during April and May 1968, captured the sense of frustration evident in Western government circles. While "ostensibly concerned with the whole range of Political, Civil, Social and Economic rights . . . the field of human rights tends to be one of the main battlegrounds on which racial and anti-colonial issues are fought out". With Australia particularly culpable on these fronts owing to the White Australia Policy and continued discrimination against Indigenous people, the document concluded that "countries like Australia have little to gain from prominent participation in more emotionally charged aspects of human rights discussions".[8] External Affairs Minister Paul Hasluck used the opportunity of a human rights seminar in Perth to harangue the UN's focus on such racial issues, happily reminiscing that "he could look back on a time when there had been no racial issue in any United Nations debate". While "lip service to human rights and freedoms had not lessened" in the years since Hasluck's postwar involvement

---

[5] General Assembly resolution 1961(XVIII), *Designation of 1968 as International Year of Human Rights*, A/RES/67/97 (12 December 1963), available at http://legal.un.org/avl/pdf/ha/fatchr/A%205493.pdf.

[6] "30 Questions on Human Rights", *The UNESCO Courier*, January 1968, 12.

[7] Roland Burke, "'How Time Flies': Celebrating the Universal Declaration of Human Rights in the 1960s", *The International History Review* 38, no. 3 (2015), 398. It could equally be argued, however, that their statism was in fact the logical conclusion of the UDHR's focus on social and economic rights. See Antony Anghie, "Whose Utopia?: Human Rights, Development, and the Third World", *Qui Parle: Critical Humanities and Social Sciences* 22, no. 1 (Fall/Winter 2013), 63–80.

[8] "Draft Instructions to the Australian Delegation to the International Conference on Human Rights, Tehran, 22nd April–13th May, 1968", National Archives of Australia (Henceforth NAA), A1838, 929/1/5 PART 4.

88   Experimental Rights

(1946–7), "their denial in some of the emerging nations had been savage and brutal". On the other hand, "controversy" over their granting in developed nations "had stirred up anger and resentment" – an unsubtle reference to ongoing civil rights struggles in the United States.[9] Aese Lionaes, the Norwegian chair of the Nobel Peace Prize Committee, could only describe 1968 as "so bitter a year for human rights".[10]

Such a pessimistic view, however, elides those admittedly few proponents human rights had and how they sought to utilise local contexts. "Human Rights have their own 1968 story", Steven Jensen remarks in his exploration of the decade's debates, and "while it was a peripheral one … it was not absent" from the concerns of activists, government and bureaucrats.[11] Jensen focuses on the way newly decolonised nations such as Jamaica embarked on human rights–focused foreign policies in the decade, and this chapter highlights some equally peripheral players in the Australian context. Moving on from traditional civil liberties organisation, it follows three organisations – the Communist Party of Australia (CPA), the Ex-Services' Human Rights Association of Australia (ESHRAA) and emerging sections of London-based Amnesty International (AI). How these groups engaged in considered, well-informed and practically driven attempts to make human rights meaningful in a domestic context where other ideas held significantly more sway is examined. In a decade so redolent with causes – conscientious objection from service in the Vietnam War most centrally – it is important to heed Barbara Keys' reminder that "not every struggle for justice and freedom is a human rights movement" and "nor is every cause fought under [its] flag recognizable as such today".[12] The questions that underpin this chapter are, then, why did these groups – one that was undergoing reinvention, another establishing an old tradition anew, and the last cultivating a new type of politics altogether – attach themselves to an idea with seemingly little real-world life beyond the halls of the United Nations? How did global shifts in the meanings of human rights make such rhetorical investments worthwhile yet, in the end, ephemeral? How, in short, did reinvigorated rights discussion assist in challenging ageing socialist and religious doctrines while disassembling what one activist dubbed "the rotten framework of cold war politics"?[13]

---

[9] *The Canberra Times*, 9 September 1968, 3.
[10] Quoted in Steven L. B. Jensen, *The Making of International Human Rights: The 1960s, Decolonisation and the Reconstruction of Global Values* (Cambridge: Cambridge University Press, 2016), 174.
[11] Ibid., 175.
[12] Barbara Keys, *Reclaiming American Virtue: The Human Rights Revolution of the 1970s* (Cambridge, MA: Harvard University Press, 2014), 5.
[13] Dan O'Neill, "The Rise and Fall of Student Consciousness", *Semper Floreat*, 20 May 1976, 10.

Communist Human Rights in the Long 1960s

Late in the night of 20 August 1968, tanks and armoured personnel carriers rolled from their positions in the wooded borderlands of the Czechoslovak People's Republic towards the socialist nation's restive capital, Prague. The elevation of the mild-mannered 46-year-old Slovak Alexander Dubcek to first secretary of the Communist Party of Czechoslovakia began a period remembered as the "Prague Spring", when the nation's principal guiding philosophy moved from dictatorship of the proletariat to "socialism with a human face".[14] When news reached Sydney, the CPA's National Executive Committee quickly convened an extraordinary meeting and declared their opposition "with a heavy heart, but without hesitation, on principle, on the issues themselves". "We cannot agree to the pre-emptive occupation of a country," the Party protested, and unprecedented calls were made for an immediate withdrawal of troops.[15] The CPA, which had so closely followed the Soviet line for decades, finally broke asunder. Yet this was not an action without precedent. The twenty-first Congress of the CPA in 1967 saw the emergence of a slim document entitled the *Charter of Democratic Rights*. Prepared by the party's Political Committee, its opening pages declared "the indivisibility of human rights" to be "more than an abstract principle" and demanded "a new social system that will strengthen and expand democracy by elevating the rights of the individual and creat[e] institutions of government designed exclusively to serve the people and fully answerable to them."[16] As one communist rank and file union member put it:

[W]hen we talk of democracy that's what we've got to mean. If an author writes a book we don't like or people refuse to toe our political line, that's too bad. When we talk about bloody democracy that's what we've got to mean – democracy – it's as simple as that.[17]

Issues of democracy and individual rights had not always been, as previous chapters have demonstrated, so simple for the party. The CPA's cautious, particular embrace of human rights rhetoric in the 1940s and

---

[14] For more on the Prague Spring and its international consequences, see Gunter Bischof, Stefan Karner and Peter Ruggenthaler (eds.), *The Prague Spring and the Warsaw Pact Invasion of Czechoslovakia in 1968* (Lanham, MD: Rowman and Littlefield, 2010); M. Mark Stolarik (ed.), *The Prague Spring and the Warsaw Pact Invasion of Czechoslovakia, 1968: Forty Years Later* (Mundelein, IL: Bolchazy-Carduci Publishers, 2010).

[15] *Tribune*, 28 August 1968, 1.

[16] *Charter of Democratic Rights* (Sydney, NSW: Communist Party of Australia, 1967), 1.

[17] John Sendy, "Socialism and Democracy", *Australian Left Review* 3 (June–July 1968), 8–9.

90   Experimental Rights

early 1950s was very much framed by their usability within an emerging Cold War battleground. The principled stance of 1968 can be read as the party's emergence from the long shadow of 1956. The year delivered dual shocks for the global communist movement. In February, Soviet leader Nikita Khrushchev delivered an unprecedented speech to the twentieth Communist Party of the Soviet Union (CPSU) Congress denouncing Stalin and castigating the cult of personality his long reign had fostered. In November, Warsaw Pact troops invaded restive Hungary to demonstrate that such openness had dramatic limitations.

In an Australian party acclimatised to clear, if often quickly changing, messaging from Moscow, confusion was the order of the day. While an uneasy period of questioning followed the CPSU Congress, with criticism encouraged at the branch level and within the party newspaper *Tribune*, by late 1956 a reversion to dogmatism was apparent. A *Tribune* report from July of 1956 indicates how little ground had shifted after the secret speech in relation to rights: "Freedom to criticise does not ... mean freedom to propagate anti Party or disruptive views through the Party or through the press."[18] Even Eric Aarons, who had argued for greater transparency and debate in early 1956, wrote in November that "it would be ridiculous to think [that] freedom means freedom to disseminate slanders more appropriate to the capitalist gutter press or to propagate ideas opposed to the basic principles we have voluntarily combined in the Party to give effect to".[19] The return to Stalinist dogmatism was, however, only to be brief. The 1961 CPSU party program removed mention of the "dictatorship of the proletariat", replacing it with the notion of an "all-people's state" which was to wither away in classical Marxist terms and be replaced by "mass organisations". This new approach was imagined by reformist communists as "the basis for change in the whole political system according to democratic principles," while lessening the state's role was anathema to the country's conservative bureaucrats.[20] This theoretical, at least, freeing-up of democracy was a part of a general turn in rights discourse under Khrushchev's rule. During the post-Stalin years "it became increasingly possible to talk meaningfully of a general system of rights, or at least aspects of such a system".[21]

---

[18] *Tribune*, 25 July 1956, 2, quoted in Rachel Calkin, "'Cracking the Stalinist Crust': The Impact of 1956 on the Communist Party of Australia" (Master's Thesis, Victoria University, 2006), 82.

[19] Eric Aarons, "Democratic Centralism", *Communist Review*, December 1956, 369.

[20] Alexander Titov, "The 1961 Party Programme and the Fate of Khrushchev's reforms", in Melanie Ilic and Jeremy Smith (eds.), *Soviet State and Society under Nikita Khrushchev* (New York: Routledge, 2009), 16.

[21] Mark B. Smith, "Khrushchev's promise to eliminate the urban housing shortage: Rights, rationality and the communist future", in *Soviet State and Society under Nikita Khrushchev*, 27.

Communist Human Rights in the Long 1960s

Literary censorship was largely lifted, and works long suppressed began to appear, while criticism of government was more vocal and the foundations of a dissident politics were laid. As Soviet dissident Valery Chalidze presciently remarked, the "Communist movement for human rights was begun by Nikita Khrushchev", though this was far from his intention.[22] Melbourne cadre Bernie Taft was hopeful:

> The labour camps had been emptied, and inmates were returning with horrifying stories about life in the camps ... People were now talking about things they dared to mention before. I desperately wanted to believe that the Soviet Union was now heading in the right direction and that the problems of the past ... were now behind them.[23]

This slackening of political control was reflected in the CPA, and emerging leaders found further evidence of the benefit of liberalisation in China and Italy.

Many younger cadres like Melbourne lawyer and functionary Rex Mortimer, Melbourne organiser Bernie Taft, and Eric and Laurie Aarons – soon to be respectively the Party's key theorist and its general secretary – were encouraged by Mao's 1950s rhetoric of letting "one-hundred flowers bloom" and allowing local conditions rather than stale dogma to drive political action. Such ideas were inculcated in many of these individuals during Party schools in Beijing in the early to mid-1950s.[24] Others saw hope in the Italian Communist Party's *Partito Nuevo* (New Party) concept that massified its appeal, developed independence within a national framework, and accepted Western norms of rights and democracy while maintaining Soviet support.[25] Taft recalled a meeting with Togliatti in Moscow during 1961, where he was particularly impressed with the Italians' "open and much more self-critical" attitude.[26]Laurie Aarons' late 1964 trip to Italy and France, only months before he was to take on the top position of general secretary of the CPA, cemented the Party's new leadership's interest in moving beyond rigid Soviet domination. While he saw "it [as] quite impossible to transplant mechanically the experience of other Parties", Italian ideas like a plurality of political ideas and forces under a socialist state and the democratisation

---

[22] Valery Chalidze, quoted in Samuel Moyn, *The Last Utopia: Human Rights in History* (Harvard, MA: The Belknap Press of Harvard University, 2010), 133.

[23] Bernie Taft, *Crossing the Party Line: Memoirs of Bernie Taft* (Newham, VIC: Scribe Publications, 1994), 121.

[24] For more on this, see Jon Piccini, "'Light from the East': Travel to China and Australian Activism in the Long Sixties", *The Sixties* 6, no. 1 (June 2013), 25–44.

[25] Donald Sassoon, "Reflections on a Death Foretold: The Life and Times of the Italian Communist Party", in Robert Leonardi and Marcello Fedele (eds.), *Italy: Politics and Policy, Volume 2* (Aldershot: Ashgate, 2003), 41.

[26] Taft, *Crossing the Party Line*, 114.

92 Experimental Rights

of party processes could be employed locally.[27] Implementing these new, experimental ideas required shifts in the Party's long-entrenched Stalinist leadership caste.

The first of these occurred in 1963, when Edward 'Ted' Hill and others particularly enamoured with Mao's later guise as a neo-Stalinist split from the CPA to form a Beijing-aligned organisation, freeing the Party of many hard-liners.[28] The second was in 1965, when a generational shift saw Lance Sharkey (1948–65) replaced by Laurie Aarons (1965–76) in the position of general secretary. Changes at the top reflected those in society: the leadership style of the austere 1930s had little appeal in the affluent nation of the 1960s, a sense only exacerbated by Sharkey's "incompetent and shifty" performance on his first television interview in 1965.[29] Additionally, while the Party maintained a strong position in "blue collar" construction and transport unions, membership was in a steady decline, and new "white collar" or middle-class workers – what the Melbourne-based new left Marxist journal *Arena* called the "intellectual class" – proved more difficult to organise.[30] Thus, when Khrushchev was deposed by Leonid Brezhnev in a bloodless 1964 coup, the CPA's Political Committee was able to publish a closely worded statement – labelled "wishy-washy" by Aarons in a private communication – entitled "Changes in the Soviet Union." Therein, the Australians expressed their hopes that "the basic policies pursued over the past decade", responsible for "big advances towards correcting serious mistakes of the past ... will remain unchanged."[31] The statement raised eyebrows in the CPSU's International Bureau, as well as amongst less critically minded Australians.[32]

The publication of an anti-semitic tract in the Union of Soviet Socialist Republics (USSR), *Judaism without Embellishment*, sparked further recriminations. As Philip Mendes argues in his work on this topic, the international outcry that emerged after this book's publication "provided an

---

[27] Laurie Aarons, "Party Building and the Path to a Mass Party", Papers of Eva and Ted Bacon, UQFL241, Box 3, Folder "CPA National Committee, National Executive", Fryer Library, The University of Queensland.

[28] For more on this, and the political nature of Hill's Communist Party of Australia (Marxist-Leninist), see Justus M. van Der Kroef, "Australia's Maoists", *Journal of Commonwealth Political Studies* 8, no. 2 (1970), 87–116.

[29] Mark Aarons, *The Family File* (Melbourne: Black Inc, 2010), 207.

[30] The *"Arena* Thesis", as it was known, is spelled out in two key articles; see Geoff Sharp and David White, "Features of the Intellectually Trained", *Arena* no. 15 (1968), 30–33; Geoff Sharp, "A Revolutionary Culture", *Arena*, no. 16 (1968), 2–11.

[31] Political Committee, "Changes in the Soviet Union", *Communist Review* 276 (December 1964), 369. A similar carefully worded criticism can be found in J. Moss, "Some Aspects of Soviet Democracy", *Communist Review* 281 (June 1965), 141.

[32] Aarons, *The Family File*, 205–6.

opportunity for the CPA's new openness to be put to the test."[33] Taft and the Aaronses were of Jewish extraction and bore the brunt of anti-semitism within the Party. Sharkey was a known anti-semite, while records of the Australian Security Intelligence Organisation (ASIO) – a domestic spy agency established in 1949 and modelled on Britain's MI5 – indicate that some Central Committee members referred to the Aaronses in similar ways. Mendes tells of how Taft and Rex Mortimer, the latter editor of the Victorian CPA's weekly *Guardian* newspaper, began meeting with Melbourne Jewish leader and prominent campaigner Isi Leibler in late 1964. They both issued statements criticising the USSR, part of their plans of "testing the limits of party democracy", while also assisting Leibler's aims of breaking monolithic Communist Party thought on the issue.[34] After his discussions with Taft and Mortimer, Leibler published a pamphlet entitled *Soviet Jewry and Human Rights* in early 1965 – to which the CPA Political Committee issued a prevaricating reply. While "mistakes were made on the national question in the Soviet Union" and Soviet Jews "suffered from these acts", it was claimed that Jews held significant social and economic rights and were dramatically over-represented in all field of endeavour. The pamphlet ended with a condemnation of those who use "the whole question of Soviet Jewry ... to engage in anti-Soviet and anti-Communist propaganda, interests in no way concerned with the well-being of the Jewish people anywhere."[35] Not content with this reply, Leibler wrote to Laurie Aarons personally in August of 1965, encouraging the CPA to adopt an overt position that was "principled, based on evidence and not connected with Cold War polemics" against the USSR's Jewish policies.[36] "The Soviet authorities will surely be influenced if their friends in the West insist that human rights are indivisible and that they are prepared to speak out against the deprivations of equal rights to groups in socialist countries as well as in the West," Leibler concluded.[37]

Such exhortations coincided with the new leadership's desire to express its independence. Not only did Aarons raise these concerns with Soviet officialdom but, when interviewed for Tribune in December 1965, he

[33] Philip Mendes, "A Convergence of Political Interests: Isi Leibler, the Communist Party of Australia and Soviet Anti-Semitism, 1964–66", *Australian Journal of Politics and History* 55, no. 2 (2009), 162.

[34] Ibid., 163.

[35] Political Committee, CPA, "Soviet Jewry: A Reply to I. Leibler", in Sam Lipski (ed.), *Soviet Jewry and the Australian Communist Party* (Caulfield, VIC: Human Rights Research Publications, 1966), 29–30.

[36] Isi Leibler to Laurie Aarons, 9 August 1965, in *Soviet Jewry and the Australian Communist Party*, 33.

[37] Ibid., 36.

94   Experimental Rights

responded to Soviet attempts at having Zionism and Nazism linked in a UN resolution on racism by commenting that "it is certainly wrong to link Zionism and Nazism in this connection". He argued, contrary to many decades of excusing Soviet actions as responding to capitalist imperialism, that "[t]he fact that the USA has been attacking the Soviet Union in pursuance of the cold war does not alter the fact that the formulation was wrong".[38] Aarons' raising of these criticisms, implying that an action can be subjectively amiss despite objective conditions, marked a significant turning point. This also evidences the view of many contemporary scholars that the idea of universal and global Human Rights emerged as the "long-term connection of rights and state sovereignty" was rendered invalid.[39] As the CPA saw international and domestic politics as intricately linked, it is no surprise that these criticisms of the previously unassailable Soviet Union using a new form of universalist discourse saw similar changes in party operation and policies in Australia. This period marked the start of a delayed thaw that changed the direction of Communist policies in Australia, which aimed to save the Party from what well known member and writer Dorothy Hewett called its destiny as a "a shrinking, conservative, ingrown sect".[40] Leading Communist Party member Bill Brown noted in the July issue of *Communist Review* how the idea of democratic centralism, while "emerg[ing] from the basic, material and universal experience of ... the working class against capitalism in all countries", need not be applied the same way everywhere.[41] "What is necessary is to remove all clogs from our Party's arteries; to allow lively fresh blood to continually course through the whole process of Party thought and action," Brown remarked, adding, "Democratic centralism, *properly applied*, provides the method to ensure this."[42]

Conservatives were equally aware of the local effects of global political commentary, like that which the Party had levelled at the CPSU. Longtime CPA member Ernie Thornton, former head of the Federated Ironworkers' Association wrote in December 1965 that the newfound taste for questioning and criticism was "excessive". Thornton mused that the "pre-occupation with mistakes of the past to the exclusion of proper examination of the problems of the present" by the current crop of

---

[38] Interview with Laurie Aarons, *Tribune*, 15 December 1965. Reproduced in *Soviet Jewry and the Australian Communist Party*, 54–5.
[39] Moyn, *The Last Utopia*, 52.
[40] Dorothy Hewett, "Communists and Individual Responsibility", *Discussion Journal* 4 (May 1967), 63.
[41] W. J. Brown, "Party Organisation and Methods of Leadership", *Communist Review* 282 (July 1965), 195–6.
[42] Brown, "Party Organisation and Methods of Leadership", 197. My italics.

Communist Human Rights in the Long 1960s 95

reformers was "sterile and useless".[43] Similar questions exploded to the fore during the preparation for the twenty-first Congress of the CPA.[44] The foundations of the Congress' *Charter of Democratic Rights* were laid out in the Party's new broad left journal the *Australian Left Review* (ALR) in late 1966.[45] Victorian John Sendy's "Democracy and the Communist Party" recommended that "the dust should be shaken off the textbooks" and that "lubrication must be provided for minds clogged with the formulas of yesteryear". This would require the "free discussion of ideas ... the rights of dissenters, and an end to attitudes of suspicion, and gestures of retaliation against members who feel constrained to disagree or challenge majority viewpoints".[46] Moving beyond the Party itself, Eric Aarons pointed out that Australians "are deeply attached to the measure of actual freedom they have, and will vigorously defend it; they are not moved by abstract discourses on the superiority of socialist over bourgeois democracy."[47] The rhetorical toolkit of the 1930s proved less pertinent in the prosperous 1960s.

The Charter itself was released for circulation in early 1967, followed by a formalised version a year later. A new draft Constitution was also released, which controversially removed all reference to democratic centralism and the dictatorship of the proletariat, while proposing that socialism in Australia could arrive via a coalition of the left and expand on what were previously branded "bourgeois" freedoms. As one *Tribune* columnist put it, "the struggle for human rights is one which must be waged under socialist conditions as well", adding that while the attainment of socialist economic relations was "essential to these rights, [it] is far from guaranteeing them of itself".[48] The release of these documents "sparked off a wide discussion unique in our 47 year history", as long standing member Sam Aarons put it.[49] Debate in publications like *Discussion Journal*, the first intensive and public form of pre-conference discussion in CPA history, speaks to the openness and transparency of

---

[43] Ernie Thornton, "The Application of Theory to Practice", *Communist Review* 287 (December 1965), 349.

[44] Taft, *Crossing the Party Line*, 152.

[45] *Australian Left Review* replaced the *Communist Review* in June 1966. It followed in the footsteps of the recently established (1963) *Arena* journal in welcoming contributions from non-Party members, including those from the new social movements of the 1960s, as a means of jettisoning the *CR*'s narrow and uninteresting focus.

[46] John Sendy, "Democracy and the Communist Party", *Australian Left Review* 1 (June–July 1966), 37.

[47] Eric Aarons, "Socialism: only one party?", *Australian Left Review* 4 (December 1966–January 1967), 36.

[48] *Tribune*, 4 December 1968, 9.

[49] Sam Aarons, "The Communist Party Will Live and Work", *Discussion Journal* 3 (May 1967), 84.

96   Experimental Rights

this debate.[50] Covering "372 large pages" in which "[e]verything submitted was printed", *Discussion Journal* was where the main issues percolating amongst the membership were for the first time publicly and thoroughly debated. The gap between the party's public profile and private intrigues almost entirely dissolved, an openness that sparked interest and comment from many outside the party.[51] Melbourne's *Age* asked, "[A]re Australian Communists going soft?", while Taft recalled that *Discussion Journal* reached a wide readership in the Labor Party and other progressive circles.[52] The ALP itself was undergoing a significant leadership and structural change at just the same moment. Arthur Calwell – who had assumed leadership of the parliamentary party in 1960 after Evatt's eventual exit – was replaced by a young, reforming lawyer named Gough Whitlam in 1967. Whitlam promised not just a fresh face but also a new agenda. Long-term support for White Australia was reversed, the Party's relationship with the trade unions that formed it was modernised to give the former greater power and a series of policies – on expanded health care, urban renewal and law modernisation – appealed to the progressive sensibilities of the decade.[53]

CPA youth leader Mavis Robertson summed up the feelings of many contributors to *Discussion Journal* when she argued that policy needed to "derive from attitudes, traditions and experiences of Australians" and not from "foreign forms of organization [sic]"[54] – statements which only years earlier could have seen her expelled. Betty Lockwood concurred, explaining, "Democracy is strong in Australia's heritage, and lack of it in our Party ... has been the main reason for waning enthusiasm and drop in activity" among local branches.[55] Others argued that this turn was in fact reflected the Party's history of fighting for social and economic rights. One correspondent pointed out that communists "have been in the forefront of the struggles for democratic rights" and as these freedoms were now regarded as "an attribute of our society ... [w]e have to be able to demonstrate that we will extend such freedom".[56] Australia, much like

---

[50] Jim Henderson, "Memoirs of a Communist", unpublished manuscript, Papers of Jim Henderson, UQFL267, Fryer Library, chapter 23.

[51] Sendy, *Comrades Come Rally*, 164. Indeed, Aarons notes that the CPSU itself was upset with the openness of *Discussion Journal* – as "[t]hings previously unsaid in communist publications could be said about them as well as us". Eric Aarons, "As I Saw the Sixties", *Australian Left Review* 27 (October–November 1970), 71.

[52] *The Age*, 6 June 1968, 4; Taft, *Crossing the Party Line*, 152.

[53] See Frank Bongiorno and Nick Dyrenfurth, *A Little History of the Australian Labor Party* (Sydney: UNSW Press, 2010), 119–27.

[54] Mavis Robertson, "Seeking Australian Solutions", *Discussion Journal* 4 (May 1967), 27.

[55] Betty Lockwood, "Price of Dogmatism and Democratic Discussion", *Discussion Journal* 4 (May 1967), 66.

[56] Yvonne Smith, "Program and Organisational Changes to Help Party Forward", *Discussion Journal* 3 (May 1967), 9.

the rest of the Western world, experienced significant economic growth and rising prosperity after the end of World War II, and a resulting baby boom saw university enrolments rise from 29,000 in 1956 to 101,000 in 1968.[57] New universities flourished, such as Monash University on Melbourne's suburban outskirts. Growing from 300 enrolments in 1963 to 7,000 in 1967, Monash's radical student culture soon saw it dubbed "Australia's Nanterre".[58] These radicalising youth saw the party as "stodgy and conservative . . . a stern disciplinarian against dissent in its own ranks, and chastising with Old Testament zeal those intellectuals who may question our Ten Commandments on the graven tablets", as Queensland Communist Party member and journalist Pete Thomas put it.[59] Yet, Hewett felt that the reforms didn't go far enough, venturing that the program "keep[s] the idea intact, just dressed up a little".[60] Changing the organisation's long-established practices and structures was much less simple than altering phraseology. Opponents on the conservative side of the debate were just as vocal: Douglas Price questioned why the existing constitution needed to be changed at all, describing its proposed replacement as one "that would be equally suitable for a left social democratic party as for the Communist Party".[61]

Jack Hughes condemned the new approach to rights, describing Australian democracy as a form of class rule and insisting that the Party return to its position of "seeking . . . unity to end the present democratic system of inequalities".[62] Another critic argued that the CPA's new democratic approach posed internal dangers as well, with the new upswell of criticism needing to be "restrained" by Party leaders. Such "deficiencies of discipline", as the author presented them, "need to be corrected by Centralist leadership".[63] Yet, despite this criticism, reformers felt that much had been gained with relatively little cost. Taft insisted that "[w]e

---

[57] Compare Australian Bureau of Statistics, *Year Book Australia 1956* (Canberra: Australian Bureau of Statistics, 1969), 480, with Australian Bureau of Statistics, *Year Book Australia 1969* (Canberra: Australian Bureau of Statistics, 1969), 510.

[58] On Monash, see Graeme Davison and Kate Murphy, *University Unlimited: The Monash Story* (St Leonards, NSW: Allen & Unwin, 2012). For the student movement in general, see Robin Gerster and Jan Bassett, *Seizures of Youth: The Sixties and Australia* (South Yarra, VIC: Hyland House, 1991); Piccini, *Transnational Protest*, particularly chapters 3 and 4. For the postwar development of the Australian university sector, see Hannah Forsyth, *A History of the Modern Australian University* (Sydney: NewSouth Publishing, 2014).

[59] Pete Thomas, "Labor Movement and Progressive Intellectuals", *Discussion Journal* 3 (May 1967), 77.

[60] Hewett, "Communists and Individual Responsibility", 63.

[61] Douglas C. Price, "The ALP and Unity", *Discussion Journal* 1 (March 1967), 84.

[62] J Hughes, "Communist Policy on Democratic Rights", *Discussion* 2, no. 3 (August 1968), 3.

[63] Jayeff, "General Agreement – and Some Views", *Discussion Journal* 3 (May 1967), 34.

98   Experimental Rights

were living in an exciting atmosphere, and felt that we were travelling on a new road towards a model of socialism that was pluralist, open, democratic and humane".[64] The effect of Czechoslovakia in this climate was pronounced. The Czech Party developed an Action Plan for reform, published around the world, which was met with great support amongst party members in Australia. Eric Aarons, by now Australian communism's key theoretical mind, described it as a document of "world significance" that "faces questions as they actually present themselves" and did not "seek to shift the ground by raising other questions which ... are not really at issue".[65] Trade unionist Jack Mundey remarked that policies adopted at the Party's 1967 Congress were similar "in more than a few ways" to those of their Czech counterparts.[66] In a similar vein, Laurie Aarons declared that "the Czech renaissance lights a way for us," with Dubcek's reforms "showing that ideas ... advanced at our 21st Congress and developed in the draft Charter for Democratic Rights ... are neither a dream nor a manoeuvre".[67]

Thus, even before the invasion, Czechoslovakia had become a prism through which Party members could debate these new democratic and rights-based policies. Seaman Max Wood, from the conservative waterside branch of the Party, attacked the Czech's attitude towards free speech for the bourgeoisie and the existence of capitalist political parties. Drawing on what were seen as examples of "capitalist roading" and right-wing revanchism in Czechoslovakia, he argued that "the old order still is prepared to raise its putrefied head, under cover of the new democratic improvements now being tried out", setting a dangerous precedent for Australia.[68] Such debates became only more heated after the Soviet intervention. Mark Aarons relates how Moscow began exerting significant pressure on leading CPA members to reverse their heresy, and these manoeuvres are evidenced by increasingly heated exchanges within Party publications. Aarons described censorship in a late 1968 article for *ALR* as "wrong in itself", sparking the ire of conservatives who saw such a universal claim as ignoring the importance of "class struggle", particularly the need to repress bourgeois ideas in a post-revolutionary environment.[69] Equally, on the principle of self-determination, Ted Bacon argued that the right to self-determination applied equally in the

---

[64] Taft, *Crossing the Party Line*, 153.   [65] Ibid., 8.
[66] Jack Mundey, quoted in Lani Russell, "Today the Students, Tomorrow the Workers! Radical Student Politics and the Australian Labour Movement, 1960–1972" (PhD Thesis, The University of Technology Sydney, 1999), 271.
[67] Aarons, *The Family File*, 222.
[68] Max Wood, "Further Comment on the Charter", *Discussion* 2, no. 3 (August 1968), 13.
[69] Analyst, "Revisionism", *Australian Left Review* 6 (December 1968), 28.

socialist and capitalist worlds. The "basic faults in Soviet democracy cannot be excused merely by reference to the difficulties of the historical development of the USSR," Bacon argued: in fact, "the defects of Soviet democracy are not just the internal affair of the Soviet Union. They are the affair of all communists, for they affect the whole present and future of the world socialist movement."[70] This sort of rhetoric, speaking to the importance the "right to self-determination" held in global rights discussions, was the last straw for many. Such utterances "reek[ed] with right opportunism and revisionism", in the opinion of one writer, while others opined that "[o]ld formulas of self-determination" were no longer relevant in a "period of ever greater integration", and a clear divide was exposed.[71].

The fracture between reformists and conservatives was now almost complete, and by 1970 a Stalinist grouping around Henderson and trade union leader Pat Clancy were publishing their own newspaper – the *Australian Socialist* – and were finally expelled the next year, establishing the Socialist Party of Australia with Soviet aid.[72] For those who remained, experimentation on human rights and the Australian conditions soon gave way to that of the student New Left and, later, the pronounced influence of Eurocommunism. For the CPA, a new utopia was needed, one that allowed international ties to be challenged and local practice re-founded. Perhaps the new and seemingly unchallengeable notion of rights – human and democratic – was the utopia they needed at the time, but one that could just as easily be abandoned. Human rights proved to be an effective way of questioning old ideas and assumptions beyond the CPA as well, connecting to a new wave of radicalisation based on individual conscience.

Human Rights, Conscience and the Anzac Tradition

The Australian Broadcasting Commission's (ABC) flagship current affairs program *Four Corners* aired a startling exposé on Saturday evening, 31 August 1963, of an organisation that sat at the core of Australian life. The Returned Services League of Australia (RSL), as the Returned Sailors, Soldiers and Airmen's League of Australia officially became

---

[70] Ted Bacon, "On Self Determination", *Australian Left Review* 5 (October–November 1968), 44–5.

[71] Analyst, "Revisionism", 28; Jim Henderson, "The Principle of Self-Determination", *Australian Left Review* 6 (December 1968), 22–3.

[72] For more on this, see David McKnight, "Breaking with Moscow: The Communist Party of Australia's New Road to Socialism", in Evan Smith, Jon Piccini and Matthew Worley (eds.), *The Far Left in Australia since 1945* (Abingdon: Routledge, 2018), 59–76.

100   Experimental Rights

known in 1965, had been established in the wake of World War I to ensure that veterans received benefits and recognition commensurate with their sacrifice for the nation. Since then, it had also become perhaps the most vocal and important "pressure group" in Australian politics.[73] Custodians of the "Anzac tradition", their spirit of mateship and egalitarianism was supposedly born on the cliffs of Gallipoli in 1915; Donald Horne opened his 1964 book *The Lucky* Country with a scene from one of the organisation's many clubhouses: a suburban sporting, cultural and social hub patronised by people "of only average earnings". Horne, whose book at once became a standard text, imagined such venues to "represent the Australian version of the old ideals of equality and the pursuit of happiness: that everyone has the right to a good time".[74] Yet, the 250,000-strong organisation had a dark side, with its political sway on issues such as anti-communism and non-white immigration increasingly gaining attention. Television was first introduced to Australia in 1956 to a rapturous reception, and one of the new medium's rising stars, young journalist Allan Ashbolt, presented the ABC's controversial programme.[75] It portrayed an ageing organisation whose ideas were divorced from the new postwar generation, a gulf that was dramatised by the interview of 24-year-old Peter Wilenski, a migrant of Polish-Jewish extraction who would go on to be a prominent public servant.[76] Wilenski protested that the RSL's policy towards matters of political contention was to "ban it, outlaw it or suppress it ... in a way that causes an infringement on individual liberties". This approach demonstrated a "somewhat tenuous belief in democratic principles" and that "too often the RSL is ready to give up the civil liberties they fought so hard to retain during the war".[77] Australia was one of the world's most censorious nations at this time, rivalled only by South Africa and Ireland in restrictions on the consumption of suspect literature of a sexual or political nature, and the RSL was one of the regime's most ardent

---

[73] G. L. Kristianson, *The Politics of Patriotism: The Pressure Group Activities of the Returned Servicemen's League* (Canberra: Australian National University Press, 1966).

[74] Donald Horne, *The Lucky Country: Australia in the Sixties* (Ringwood, VIC: Penguin, 1964), 19.

[75] While only 1 per cent owned a set in 1956, over 90 per cent did only nine years later. Michelle Arrow, *Friday on our Minds: Popular Culture in Australia since 1945* (Sydney: UNSW Press, 2009), 29.

[76] For more on Wilenski and his career, see Gareth Evans, "The World after Wilenski: An Australian Who Mattered", Inaugural Peter Wilenski Memorial Lecture, Canberra, 22 June 1995, available at https://foreignminister.gov.au/speeches/1995/gewilens.html.

[77] Allan Ashbolt (Executive Producer, Reporter), Michael Charlton (Presenter), "Returned Servicemen's League" (Sydney: Australian Broadcasting Commission, 1963), first aired 31 August 1963, available at www.abc.net.au/4corners/rsl–1963/2833754.

protagonists.[78] The RSL condemned the program's portrayal of a "false image" of the organisation, but protest focused on Ashbolt himself, who was labelled a communist and castigated by then-Minister for the Army Malcolm Fraser for allowing another communist – *Tribune* editor Alec Robertson – uninterrupted air time, concluding that "the ABC should be ashamed of this program".[79] Ashbolt was quickly fired from his position as editor of *Four Corners*.[80]

Ashbolt's was but one criticism of the power wielded by this group of ex-soldiers. In 1958, 31-year-old Alan Seymour wrote a play entitled *The One Day of the Year* which presented similar generational tensions and incomprehension between a young university student and his veteran father. Due to its salacious content, it did not professionally premiere until 1961. Seymour's play was in turn based on a series of controversial articles in Sydney University's *Honi Soit*.[81] Anzac Day – an annual holiday on 25 April commemorating the botched landing of Dominion troops on the shores of Gallipoli, Turkey, in 1915 – was castigated as an exemplar of rank hypocrisy. "The people who stand solemnly in silent prayer at the cenotaphs at dawn, do not feel obliged to continue their weeping in the afternoon, and head with as much reverence towards the racecourses as they did towards the memorials in the morning". This "yearly pageant of national necrophilia" was less about remembering the horrors of war than "a festival of hero-adulation unequalled anywhere in the world".[82] Participation in yearly Anzac Day parades, huge during the 1940s and early 1950s, had dropped so far by the time of Ashbolt's broadcast as to become a matter of public comment, if not concern. Such criticism was not limited to public broadcasters or university students – who could be easily brushed aside – but came from within the RSL itself. Leslie Waddington – a 45-year-old Sydney-based leather goods manufacturer, ALP member and Second World War veteran – announced in November 1966 the formation of a new organisation to challenge the RSL's policy on conscription and the unfolding Vietnam War, the Ex Services Human Rights Association of Australia (ESHRAA). While the acronym hardly rolled off the tongue, and its membership was only 150 strong, Waddington and an associate were subsequently expelled from

---

[78] Nicole Moore, *The Censor's Library: Uncovering the Long History of Australia's Banned Books* (Brisbane: University of Queensland Press, 2012),

[79] Malcolm Fraser, "Draft – ABC Television Programme *Four Corners* and the RSL", 17 September 1963, Malcolm Fraser Radio Talks Transcripts, 2007.0023.0121, University of Melbourne Archives.

[80] G. L. Kristianson, "The RSL and 'Four Corners'", *The Australian Quarterly* 36, no. 1 (March 1964), 20–30. Ashbolt quietly returned his position several months later.

[81] Alan Seymour, *The One Day of the Year* (Sydney: Angus and Robertson, 1962 [1958]).

[82] *Honi Soit*, 24 April 1958, 4.

102   Experimental Rights

the RSL's New South Wales branch for "conduct ... subversive to the objects and policy of the League".[83]

Australia entered the war in Vietnam in 1962, sending a thirty-man training contingent to aid the South Vietnamese government in containing communist rebels. In 1964, the Menzies government augmented an existing National Service scheme to allow for potential overseas deployments, and in April 1965 Australia joined America in committing ground troops – including twenty-year-olds conscripted via a lottery system – to the conflict for the first time.[84] Vietnam and the National Service scheme – soon labelled "the Draft" following American nomenclature – became inseparable, inescapable issues during the late 1960s and from early on encountered a small but growing number of protesters.[85] Leslie Waddington was one of them. Waddington originally came of interest to ASIO in 1964 owing to his membership of the Australia-Indonesia Association of New South Wales and role as director of an Indigenous co-operative organisation.[86] Waddington was not a typical radical – one agent commented how he "wears an RSL badge" when in public – and he was not known to be a member of the CPA.[87] A founding meeting of what would become ESHRAA was held on 16 October 1966, and no attendee – aside from the group's president, Allan Ashbolt – had previously received "adverse attention" from the domestic security agency. The group's first newsletter, entitled *Conscience* and dated the same day as this foundational gathering, set out a series of aims, including to "promote individual liberties and democratic rights", "recognise the right of dissent as an integral part of a truly democratic society" and "assist in the abolition of war as a way of settling international disputes". The group was to only "consist of Ex-servicemen and women", a categorisation that would be "liberally defined".[88]

Resistance to war by ex-servicemen has a long history in Australia. The RSL was established alongside numerous other ex-service organisations,

---

[83] *The Australian*, 2 June 1967, 3.

[84] For more on Australia's Vietnam War, see John Murphy, *Harvest of Fear: A History of Australia's Vietnam War* (St Leonards, NSW: Allen & Unwin, 1993); Peter Edwards, *Australia and the Vietnam War* (Sydney: NewSouth Publishing, 2014).

[85] While troops were first deployed in 1965, it was not until a year later that the first draftees were dispatched. Chris Dixon and Jon Piccini, "The Anti-Vietnam War Movement: International Activism and the Search for World Peace", in William Knoblauch, Michael Loedenthal and Christian Peterson, *The Routledge History of World Peace since 1750* (New York: Routledge, 2018), 371–81.

[86] "Australia Indonesia Association of New South Wales", 1 May 1964, in Waddington, Martin Leslie Volume 1, NAA: A6119/6398; "Tranby Co-operative for Aborigines Ltd", 5 August 1966, in NAA: A6119/6398.

[87] "Leslie Waddington", 6 May 1965, NAA: A6119/6398.

[88] *Conscience*, no. 1, 16 October 1966, 1.

such as the Returned Sailors' and Soldiers' Labour League, while dissent from ex-servicemen was particularly pronounced as the clouds of war gathered in the late 1930s. Communist ex-serviceman Len Fox published a pamphlet entitled *The Truth About Anzac* in 1936, which called out the militaristic jingoism of such commemorations, while the postwar Democratic Rights Council's *A Charter for Freedom* included a section composed by veterans declaring "our determination to honour in peace the liberties for which we fought".[89] The emergence of ESHRAA was, however, novel – dissent had previously either occurred from outside the RSL or been contained within it – and equally so was its focus on human rights. Nick Irving's study of the broader anti-conscription campaign, particularly two key organisations, Youth Campaign Against Conscription and the Draft Resistance Movement, finds little resonance of human rights language, despite the government seemingly breaching numerous articles of the UDHR in its forcible requisitioning of manpower. Instead, young activists relied on ideas of citizenship, appealing to national traditions of anti-war resistance, and later ideas of liberal individualism derived from the United States.[90] ESHRAA's older age cohort, however, drew on the toolkit of the 1940s "people's war" rather than that of the growing youth counter-culture. The third issue of *Conscience* provides a detailed list of the organisation's objectives, including "to promote the civil and political liberties of individuals traditional in British societies" as well as to "uphold and disseminate the high ideals and aspirations of the peoples of the world as they are expressed in the United Nations Charter".[91]

The group originally started in 1966 as simply the Ex Services' Association of Australia, electing a 15-person steering committee including figures such as Francis James, head of the Anglican Press Ltd, and the secretary of the Miscellaneous Workers Union, D. Hancock.[92] The addition of "Human Rights" was proposed in early 1967, and the group's statement of aims was concretised as defending "individual liberties [that] are being eroded through the world ... and to uphold and promote the

---

[89] L. P. Fox, *The Truth about Anzac* (Melbourne: Victorian Council against War and Fascism, 1936); Democratic Rights Council, *A Charter of Freedom: Report of a Conference for Democratic Rights Held in the Lower Melbourne Town Hall, Sat. April 22, 1950* (Melbourne: Victorian Democratic Rights Council, 1950), 20.

[90] Nick Irving, "Anti-conscription Protest, Liberal Individualism and the Limits of National Myths in the Global 1960s", *History Australia* 14, no. 2 (2017), 187–201. See also Nick Irving, "Global Thought, Local Action: A Transnational Reassessment of the Australian Anti-War Movement, 1959–1972" (PhD Thesis, The University of Sydney, 2017).

[91] *Conscience*, no. 3, 25 November 1966, 1.

[92] *Sydney Morning Herald*, 14 October 1966, 5.

104   Experimental Rights

fundamental human rights as ... set out in the Universal Declaration of Human Rights".[93] This decision was made "after much study and debate", and "it was concluded that this new form gave us the best approach to the work ahead".[94] The organisation bemoaned how support for the United Nations "amongst ordinary people, shows signs of waning", warning that governments risked "complete anarchy" in the world if they continued to "wreck a body by breaking its principles for selfish reasons, when it suits, and then to complain that it isn't any good".[95] ESHRAA responded to this by having the UDHR distributed to high school students, with the local United Nations Information Centre importing some 500 booklet copies for distribution and one large, framed version to each high school in the state "at great expense". One such wall-mountable copy made its way to a student-teacher's rented room, only to be smashed and disposed of by his landlady who did not want such "communist trash hung up in her house".[96] Additional to such attempted popularising of the document was a vernacularising of its principles to Australian circumstances. Theirs was a "non-party and non-sectarian" organisation that sought to "support the right of dissent", "support genuine conscientious objectors" and campaign in favour of "peaceful alternative forms of National Service". Waddington's abiding interest in Asia also shone through, with the organisation hoping for "a better informed public on all Australia, Asian and world affairs" – seeking in particular "peaceful co-operation [and] friendship with all Asian neighbours". The organisation diagnosed an "Australian sickness", where a population "whose ignorance and apathy is assiduously nurtured" is called to be "involved in a war ... to defend democracy [that] is made possible only by the virtual suspension of democracy at home".[97]

Waddington's organisation might have floundered and fallen into irrelevance if not for the RSL's reaction to their anti-war activities. As *Conscience* happily reported in June 1967, "there must be hardly anyone left in the country who has not now heard of our organisation and its aims, as a result of the tremendous news coverage given by all media" to Waddington's expulsion and the suspension of another member, Ashley Pascoe, for five years.[98] The same newsletter also welcomed the decision of the recently founded Victorian Ex-Servicemen's Protest Committee to

---

[93] Name change and objects as set out in *Conscience*, no. 6, 22 March 1967, 1.
[94] *Conscience*, no. 5, Undated, 1.   [95] Ibid., 1.   [96] *Conscience*, no. 11, August 1967, 5.
[97] *Conscience*, no. 10, July 1967, 1.
[98] *Conscience*, no. 9, 20 June 1967, 1. The group's foundation and the pair's expulsion were widely reported, *Canberra Times*, 12 October 1966, 10; *Sydney Morning Herald*, 14 October 1966, 5; *The Australian*, 2 June 1967, 3; *Sydney Morning Herald*, 8 June 1967, 1.

join ESHRAA, a "great increase in our membership".[99] ESHRAA was established just as the first of what were to be called "conscientious objectors", William "Bill" White, fell afoul of the law. White, a Sydney schoolteacher, announced his decision to defy a call-up notice to enter the National Service Scheme in July 1966 and was dragged from his home in front of waiting media in November of that year.[100] Australia's laws defined a conscientious objector as someone with a religious or otherwise moral belief against any armed conflict, and White's claim for such status was viewed as "insincere" by the presiding magistrate.[101] Rather than going "all the way with LBJ", in then Prime Minister Harold Holt's famous exhortation of national torpor, ESHRAA would "go all the way with William White", seeking to use their leverage as ex-service people to seek changes in the system.[102] It has been widely noted by scholars that a sort of "veteran privilege" came to exist in many Western nations after the world wars, as "[v]eterans were ... recognized as a status group with particular and special entitlements", including the right to have their own powerful voice in national affairs.[103] ESHRAA was very aware of their positioning, declaring that "[e]x-service men and women have a special responsibility to encourage public debate" on issues of individual and minority rights. When soldiers spoke, the public listened.[104]

White's case became a significant one for ESHRAA, with members joining those that camped outside his house for five days, congregating around an "eternal flame" before being dragged away by police during the non-complier's arrest. The review and subsequent acceptance of White's claim for conscientious objectors status, after nearly a month in custody, was greeted as "a success for human rights and for all those organisations and individuals who protested on his behalf".[105] The group became more focused and articulate in its particular meaning of the term as the decade progressed, and growing numbers of young men faced seeming persecution from government. In late 1967, *Conscience*'s Christmas issue carried a range of quotations from religious figures as well as from Thomas Jefferson, the Charter of the United Nations and Aldous Huxley, arguing

---

[99] Ibid., 1.   [100] *Canberra Times*, 24 November 1966, 1.

[101] On conscription in Australia, see Christina Twomey, "The National Service Scheme: Citizenship and the Tradition of Compulsory Military Service in Australia", *Australian Journal of Politics and History* 58, no. 1 (2012), 67–81; Michael E. Hamel-Green, "The Resisters: A History of the Anti-conscription Movement, 1964–72", in Peter King (ed.), *Australia's Vietnam: Australia in the Second Indo-China War* (Sydney: Unwin Hyman, 1983), 100–28; Greg Langley, *A Decade of Dissent: Vietnam and the Conflict on the Australian Home Front* (Sydney: Allen & Unwin, 1992).

[102] *Conscience*, no. 3, 25 November 1966, 1.

[103] Martin Crotty and Mark Edele, "Total War and Entitlement: Towards a Global History of Veterans Privilege", *Australian Journal of Politics and History* 59, no. 1 (2013), 18.

[104] *Conscience*, no. 6, 22 March 1967, 1.   [105] *Conscience*, no. 4, January 1967, 1.

106   Experimental Rights

that human rights had been in circulation "since Jesus spoke about them on the mount".[106] In 1968, the International Year of Human Rights, ESHRAA began an annual tradition of holding controversial discussions about Australian militarism on Anzac Day. Ashbolt spoke at this event alongside representatives of the Australian Council of Churches and the president of the newly founded Catholics for Peace. Rather than the memory of combatants past, the event focused on one Denis O'Donnell, who deserted his unit after being refused objector status. "Every Australian need[s] to be better acquainted with the dilemma of this gallant youth whose conscience should not be crushed by the pressure of the National Service Act", a flyer advertising the event read, noting his act as one of "the greatest bravery" owing to the "deep human principles involved." The timing of this event on Anzac Day was designed to elicit controversy: the "emotions of Anzac Day are the strongest Australia has produced", and International Human Rights Year placed the day "under the spotlight for all to see". Anzac was not a militaristic tradition, ESHRAA argued: instead, "it is the duty of all ex-service men and women, not only to prevent war on our own soil, but to do what we can to prevent it on other people's soil".[107]

Ashbolt, a public intellectual of some standing owing to his potted career with *Four Corners*, saw Australian attitudes of either violent support of or disinterested responses to Vietnam as pointing to "a society trapped in a repressive hysteria of fear and loathing".[108] Ashbolt contributed an essay to literary journal *Meanjin*'s collective thinking-through of the Australian condition after the departure of long-term Prime Minister Robert Menzies in January 1966. Ashbolt used his article to draw attention to the Cold War lifestyle Menzies' rule had fostered:

BEHOLD THE MAN – the Australian man of today – on Sunday mornings in the suburbs, when the high-decibel drone of the motor-mower is calling the faithful to worship. A block of land, a brick veneer, and the motor-mower beside him in the wilderness – what more does he want to sustain him, except a Holden to polish, a beer with the boys, marital sex on Saturday nights, a few furtive adulteries, an occasional gamble on the horses or the lottery, the tribal rituals of football, the flickering shadows [of TV] in his lounge-room.[109]

Ashbolt bemoaned how, for the average Australian, "the motor-mower has become ... an assertion of democratic rights", a measure of Menzies' success in making property the sole measure of human value, indeed

---

[106] *Conscience*, no. 14, November/December 1967, 1.   [107] *Conscience*, May 1968, 4.
[108] Rowan Cahill, "Vietnam Reading", *Overland* 150 (Autumn 1998), 12.
[109] Allan Asbbolt, "Godzone (3): Myth and Reality", *Meanjin Quarterly* 25, no. 4 (1966), 373.

a most valuable human right in his "forgotten people" speeches.[110] For Ashbolt, Anzac Day was the apotheosis of this – where "the Pioneer and the Common Man merged with the Warrior" to create the archetypal Australian and foster a national day marked by "both religiosity and bacchanalianism". Ashbolt quoted Sir William Yeo, head of the NSW RSL, as arguing "Anzac Day is bigger than the churches". Its "emphasis on heroism rather than murder" formed a national cult that could "embrace any and all of the spiritual idiosyncrasies promulgated by the competing sects of Christendom" while "endow[ing] with nobility the violation and destruction of the human person".[111]

While a non-believer, Ashbolt seems to have been deeply influenced by the liberalisation represented by the Second Vatican Council. His wife Jeanne was an active member of the newly established Catholics for Peace, who sought to illustrate the "growing divergence between Vatican ... pronouncements on ... Vietnam, and the attitudes of bishops and clergy here in Australia".[112] The group published a lengthy pamphlet by Denis Kenny, a Melbourne-based theologian, documenting the history of Catholicism and communism from the mid nineteenth century. Kenny and other radicals influenced by Pope John XXIII's liberalism argued that while the Church's attitude on "the primacy of the ... human person and human rights" arose from its opposition to communism, matters of war and poverty must "no longer [be] a corollary uneasily attached to ... more otherworldly concerns" but central to its role.[113] In a decade marked by questions of religion's gradual extinction, a Church for a modern world "must be and appear to be the champion of freedom in every sense of the world".[114] Ashbolt channelled Kenny in a lecture delivered to the prestigious Moore Theological College in Sydney in 1967. Therein, he directing his audience of priests-in-training to follow the example of Italian Catholic Father Ernesto Balducci, jailed in 1963 for supporting a young conscientious objector on the grounds "that total war is intrinsically unjust and that a truly Christian conscience is bound to disobey the State's command to bear arms".[115] If the Church wanted

---

[110] Ibid., 373.   [111] Ibid., 378–9.

[112] C. F. Bowers, "The Catholic Church in Sydney and the Vietnam Conflict", *Australian Left Review* 71 (1979), 32.

[113] Denis Kenny, *The Evolution of the Official Catholic Attitude towards Communism* (Longueville, NSW: Catholics for Peace, 1968), 49–50.

[114] Denis Kenny, *The Catholic Church and Freedom: The Vatican Council and Some Modern Issues* (Brisbane: University of Queensland Press, 1967), 104–5.

[115] For more on Balducci, see Jacopo Cellini, *Universalism and Liberation: Italian Catholic Culture and the idea of International Community* (Leaven, Belgium: Leuven University, 2017), 213–22.

108   Experimental Rights

a continuing role in society, with attendance rates dipping and its power waning, priests needed not to "encourage[e] the virtues of dissent and disobedience".[116] Referencing broader ructions as to "the relevance and authority of traditional institutions and formulations of beliefs" within Australian churches in the 1960s, Ashbolt encouraged the pious to break the bonds of "ecclesiastical authorities". It was time "to start thinking once more as individuals ... trying to reach some form of fellowship with other individuals, not merely as human units cut off from other human units except for certain institutional links".[117]

Such Christian sentiment often appeared in the pages of ESHRAA's publications, with *Conscience* voicing a hope in June 1968 that in light of objector Simon Townsend's position as a "prisoner of conscience ... every church will echo with songs of peace for the man who would not kill". ESHRAA shared many members with – and also held events, including its Anzac Day public meetings, alongside – Catholics for Peace.[118] The opening, albeit brief, of Catholicism's vistas in the 1960s, much like its vehement anti-communism in the early Cold War, led to new forms of political engagement by laity. Much as the power of conscience drove a new wave of anti-conscription protest, Catholics seized the term's power to push back against clerical authority in matters sexual and political. Equally, the decade's questioning of secular and religious authority saw a rupture within the seemingly monolithic force of the RSL, and human rights became a useful rallying cry for ex-servicemen tired of the organisation's lethargic conservatism. While the seeming moral unquestionability of "conscience" proved powerful for many, it was not so clear-cut for all, as another better-known group of campaigners was to discover.

Amnesty International and the Contested Politics of Conscience

Twenty-two people, a smattering of "lawyers, social workers, women at home, businessmen, industrial workers, minister of religion and students", attended a meeting at the Owen Dixon Chambers on Melbourne's William Street on the night of 2 March 1962 to establish the first Australian "section" of what is now the world's best-known human rights organisation. Peter Beneson, a British lawyer, former

---

[116] Allan Ashbolt, "The Needs of People in a Secular Situation", *The Australian Humanist* 1 (December 1967), 22.
[117] Ibid., 23–4; David Hilliard, "The Religious Crisis of the 1960s: The Experience of Australian Churches", *The Journal of Religious History* 21, no. 2 (June 1997), 209.
[118] *Conscience*, May–June 1968, 1.

Labour Party activist and recently converted Catholic, had published an article entitled "The Forgotten Prisoners" in *The Observer* newspaper some ten months earlier, sparking the formation of the first section of what is today Amnesty International (AI).[119] The organisation's remit was novel. Declaring itself above Cold War politics, local groups selected one unjustly incarcerated individual from a first-, second- and third-world nation – known as "groups of threes" – and sought to use the power of the pen to have them released. Hearing news of the organisation's founding over the radio "while standing at the sink one evening" hit Wendy Nott, a homemaker from the working-class suburb of Essendon, like "a bolt from the blue". She had been involved in the Student Christian Movement and Indigenous rights causes at university; she saw AI as representing "the idea of the brotherhood of man", an ambition not so distant from Benenson's own hope for "a sort of secularised religious community which would 'rekindle a fire in the minds of men'".[120] Sections were soon established nationwide and began earning media attention. The Canberra section secretary, Lesley Smith, spoke to AI's vital role: "A lot of organisations interested in the welfare of ... prisoners only take care of their own supporters while Amnesty will assist a man ... regardless of race, colour of creed."[121] Yet, the organisation's global growth was "a depressingly slow task", as historian Jan Eckel puts it, and AI was "by no means an instant success".[122]

Initial euphoria soon gave way to the difficulties of translating this new interpretation of human rights into Australian circumstances, as well as managing the London-based organisation's changing definitions of "prisoner of conscience" and significant divergences between members as to the limits of rights. Tensions between AI's transnational structure and the

---

[119] Works detailing the foundation of Amnesty are many, but for particularly incisive views on its early years see Tom Buchanan, "The Truth Will Set You Free: The Making of Amnesty International", *Journal of Contemporary History* 37 (2002), 575–597; Stephen Hopgood, *Keepers of the Flame: Understanding Amnesty International* (Ithaca, NC: Cornell University Press, 2006); Barbara Keys, "Anti-Torture Politics: Amnesty International, the Greek Junta, and the Origins of the Human Rights 'Boom' in the United States", in Akira Iriye, Petra Goedde and William I. Hitchcock (eds.), *The Human Rights Revolution: An International History* (New York: Oxford University Press. 2012), 201–21.

[120] Clare Wositzky, *Lighting the Candles: The First Thirty Years of Amnesty International in Australia* (Northcote, VIC: self-published, 1995), 18–19; Bastian Bouwman, "Outraged, yet Moderate and Impartial: The Rise of Amnesty International in the Netherlands in the 1960s and 1970s", *BMGN: Low Countries Historical Review* 132, no. 4 (2017), 55.

[121] *Canberra Times*, 21 August 1969, 19.

[122] Jan Eckel, "The International League for the Rights of Man, Amnesty International, and the Changing Fate of Human Rights Activism from the 1940s through the 1970s", *Humanity* 4, no. 2 (Summer 2013), 193.

110 Experimental Rights

necessity for action on domestic issues – particularly around Indigenous rights and non-compliance with the National Service Act – proved a powder keg for the new group's disciples in its first, troubled decade. While "little historical work has so far been done on national sections" of AI, looking closely at those who held its torch in the far corners of the world can uncover the local resonance of a global movement.[123] Rather than national sections, as was common around the world, Amnesty's haphazard formation in Australia saw separate state groupings emerge, speaking to "the tyranny of distance" that so often afflicts antipodean history.[124] A national organisation, albeit without the Queensland branch, would not be established until 1979. This meant that views on exactly which prisoners were covered by AI's seemingly broad yet, in reality, very precise and targeted area of work were wide and contested. By mid-1965, the Victorian section – by far the nation's largest – claimed some eighty-one financial members, an increase of fifteen on 1964, spread across ten suburb-based groups, who collectively had adopted some thirty-eight prisoners.[125] Globally AI struggled to maintain membership and interest during its first decade, yet the Victorian section grew steadily – with some 160 financial members in 1967 and 385 by 1973 – and while the New South Wales (NSW) section proved more sluggish, it claimed some 120 that same year.[126] The group had some initial successes – with the 1964–5 annual report recording the release of prisoners in Greece, Portugal and East Germany.[127] Aside from supporting prisoners abroad, Amnesty branches also took it upon themselves to recommend for adoption prisoners in their own countries, and the Victorian branch convened a study group in early 1965 to prepare a report on whether Indigenous Australians could become adoptees. The study group sought information from relevant organisations, principally the Federal Council for Advancement of Aborigines and Torres Strait

---

[123] Bouwman, "Outraged, yet Moderate and Impartial", 57. For other work looking at the "export" of Amnesty abroad, see Sarah B. Snyder, "Exporting Amnesty International to the United States: Transatlantic Human Rights Activism in the 1960s", *Human Rights Quarterly* 34, no. 3 (August 2012), 779–99; Lora Wildenthall, *The Language of Human Rights in West Germany* (Philadelphia: University of Pennsylvania Press, 2012), 76–88.

[124] A term most famously articulated in Geoffrey Blainey, *The Tyranny of Distance: How Distance Shaped Australia's History* (Sydney: Macmillan, 1966).

[125] "Third Annual Report of the Victorian Section – March 1964–March 1965", *Amnesty Bulletin* no. 10 (April 1965), 1.

[126] *Amnesty International Victoria Section – Annual Report, March 1966–March 1967* (Melbourne: self-published, 1967), 1; "Amnesty International Victoria Section: Eleventh Annual Report", *Amnesty Bulletin* 40 (April 1973), 2; Robert V. Horn to The Editor, Lateline, 10 May 1973, Robert V Horn Papers, MLMSS 8123, Box 33, State Library of New South Wales (henceforth SLNSW).

[127] "Third Annual Report of the Victorian Section – March 1964–March 1965", 1.

Islanders, and after seven months presented a final report, published as *The Situation of Australian Aborigines*.

In a way, it did not differ significantly from the work of a previous generation of rights translators around the Council for Aboriginal Rights in the early 1950s, except for its precise focus on "to what extent is curtailment of Aborigines' rights because of matters of policy which are outside the scope of Amnesty".[128] This was a vital question: what constituted imprisonment? Amnesty was devoted to the release of non-violent political prisoners, a stance strengthened by the organisation's rejection of African National Congress leader Nelson Mandela from such status in the aftermath of his 1962 incarceration in apartheid South Africa.[129] But what of oppressed minorities within states who, as the Victorian section's first constitution read, were "imprisoned because of race"?[130] Much as Charles Duguid and Yvonne Nichols had found the status of Indigenous peoples and the articles of the UDHR to be incongruent in nearly all instances, the final report laboriously mapped the inequalities of Indigenous Australians onto each relevant article yet came to mixed conclusions as to the role AI could play. While finding evidence of gross violations, particularly in terms of voting rights, lack of compensation for appropriated lands and freedom of movement, the group bemoaned that they could do little about these. While it "would seem that work for the removal of legal disabilities of Aborigines comes within the spirit ... of Amnesty if not the letter", the report concluded, that "Amnesty's objects refer to 'prisoners of conscience'" meant that "[i]n the absense of any militant pan-Aboriginalist movement, it is doubtful that there has ever been a true prisoner of conscience". The group's disappointment was almost palpable, with the report concluding that "Aboriginal people are certainly an enchained people", albeit one that AI's human rights agenda could do little to alleviate.[131] Key member and amateur historian Clare Wositzky described the report as "a milestone in the activities of the Victorian branch", albeit one which re-enforced the organisation's commitment to a very limited terrain of activity.[132] Amnesty was not to offer an indigenous Australian for adoption until a slackening of the group's definition of a "prisoner of conscience" in

---

[128] "The Situation of Australian Aborigines", *Amnesty Bulletin* no. 11 (August 1965), 3.

[129] This was a decision on which the NSW and Victorian sections both agreed; see Wositzky, *Lighting the Candles*, 57–8; letter from Robert V. Horn to Peter Beneson, "Your Recent Circular to Members", 31 June 1964, Robert V. Horn Papers, MLMSS 8123, Box 33, SLNSW.

[130] Wositzky, *Lighting the Candles*, 98.

[131] *The Situation of Australian Aborigines: A Factual Report Compiled by Amnesty International* (Sassafras, VIC: self-published, 1966), 36.

[132] Wositzky, *Lighting the Candles*, 100.

112   Experimental Rights

1988.[133] The group's other conclusion, that AI could forward this information to the United Nations for action, however, drew critical attention to the report, both from the media and from within AI.

The *Canberra Times* carried a brief story on the report in April 1966, remarking that it compared "the position of Aborigines in Australia ... to that of people living under a totalitarian state".[134] While the report never explicitly said this, Kim Beasley Snr, Member of Parliament for the ALP, who had raised his voice in 1940s deportation debates and was "a student of aboriginal affairs", penned a response "expressing some fears" that Amnesty's work could have unintended consequences. Beazley attempted to undermine the report's credibility, describing AI as an "international 'grievance' organisation" and condemning its authors for not inquiring with Indigenous people and their government-appointed protectors, instead only engaging with previously published reports. Beazley described AI's publication as a "warning of the twists of interpretation and the damage to Australia of 'investigations' of an abstract kind" – a less than subtle hint at the dangers of international eyes looking too closely in Australia's direction.[135] The Canberra AI section expressed similar concerns: the group's president, Michael McKerras, referred to the report as "regrettable" and viewed as dangerous the recommendation to "refer the matter of Aboriginal rights to the United Nations, where it might be used to discredit Australia, before ... all means of promoting their rights within Australia" were exhausted. McKerras concluded by remarking, "I personally do not feel that this comes within the scope of Amnesty", a debate which would continue to rage into the 1970s.[136] That another AI branch would take such a public step in shaming a sister section points to its haphazard and shifting forms of politics. The Victorian section made a "difficult decision" in 1968 not to publish an updated version of the report, owing to a "new ... statute" from London "which focused our work on ... political prisoners who are detained without trial", and limited its activities in the Indigenous rights area to collecting information.[137]

The issue of conscientious objection was to raise an even greater debate, this time between the organisation's Victorian and NSW branches. Bill White's imprisonment for refusing to abide his refusal of objector status sparked as much a flurry of activity in AI as it did in ESHRAA, with the cause of bringing those believed to be "prisoners of conscience" to light initially uniting both sections. The Victorian section

---

[133] Ibid., 101.   [134] *The Canberra Times*, 2 April 1966, 3.
[135] *The Canberra Times*, 27 April 1966, 20.   [136] *The Canberra Times*, 6 April 1966, 3.
[137] Wositzky, *Lighting the Candles*, 99–100.

released a statement in support of White's actions: "we feel it impossible ... to doubt the sincerity of his convictions and are gravely concerned at the prospect of his continued detention under the provisions of military law". Given "the grounds for an appeal to the Government on White's behalf based on the sanctity of the individual conscience are substantial", the section recommended White's case to AI's London office "for appropriate action".[138] The New South Wales section expressed near-identical sentiments, reporting in August 1966 that "[c]onscription had been the overriding issue in much of our new work". The section was collecting material on Australian cases while campaigning for the release of conscientious objectors in the USA and East Germany. "The fact that the predicament of Bill White is shared by young men all over the world" spoke, in the section president's view, to "the immediate domestic value of Amnesty International to safeguard our own civil liberties and our international reputation".[139] The NSW section's commitment to the anti-conscription cause should not be surprising, as the section president, Lincoln Oppenheimer, was also a member of ESHRAA and Les Waddington was the speaker at AI's "Human Rights Day" event on 10 December 1967.[140] White's public statement of conscientious objection, reproduced in the NSW section's newsletter, spoke of rights as "unalterable" and inhering in a person rather than being a "concession given by a government", and as such these were "not something which the government has the right to take".[141] White's statement reflected the development of a morally conscious form of politics percolating in both the CPA and ESHRAA at this time. "I respect people, I respect their feelings, I respect their property [and] I respect their equality ... on the basic conscientious assumption that they have, as I have, the unquestionable right to live", White concluded.[142]

White's release in December 1966 came before AI could adopt his cause internationally, but more objectors soon followed. What became problematic, however, was when the politics of conscientious objection moved to one of downright refusal – non-compliance with the laws of the land. This was part of a broader trend within the anti-conscription movement towards more militant opposition to the National Service Act. Unlike White, who was found to be a conscientious objector after a month in prison and

---

[138] "Statement from the Victorian Section of Amnesty International. Bill White Case", *Amnesty Bulletin* 16 (November 1966).
[139] Lincoln Oppenheimer, "President's Report", *Amnesty News* 10 (August 1966), 3.
[140] Waddington's speech is reproduced in *Amnesty News* 16 (February 1968), 5–6.
[141] "Copy of Statement by Mr W. White, Sydney Schoolteacher and Conscientious Objector", *Amnesty News* 10 (August 1966), 2–3.
[142] Ibid., 2–3.

114   Experimental Rights

a public backlash, part-time postman John Zarb applied not on the basis of his opposition to all war but only to that ongoing in Vietnam. He was jailed for two years in October 1968. "Free Zarb" became a rallying cry for the anti-war movement, with his imprisonment seen as representing the futility and double standards synonymous with the Vietnam War. As one activist leaflet put it: "In Australia – it is a crime not to kill".[143] The convenor of the Lane Cove AI section in Sydney's affluent north shore, Robert V. Horn, described in a long memorandum to London how "[c]onscription and Vietnam have become inter-mixed in public debate, and in contemporary style outbursts of demonstrations, protest marches, draft card burnings [and] sit-ins".[144]

Zarb's case was, however, nowhere near as clear-cut for Amnesty members as White's had been. Horn described how AI members held a "wide spectrum of political, religious and moral views", and, while "one might guess that many members are opposed to Australia's participation in the Vietnam war", these individuals held "many shades of views", particularly around the issues of the acceptability of law breaking.[145] Horn circulated a draft report on the situation in Australia that he had prepared for AI's London headquarters to other AI members within his section and the large Victorian one, reactions to which demonstrate just how divisive the issue of conscientious objectors and non-compliers was for an organisation deeply wedded to due legal process. David McKenna, in charge of the Victorian section's conscientious objection work, put this distinction quite clearly, arguing that those who "register for national service and apply for exemption" but whose "applications fail either through some apparent miscarriage of justice or because the law does not presently encompass their objections ... are prima facie eligible for adoption" as prisoners of conscience.[146]

However, those who "basically refuse to co-operate with the National Service Act" merely "maintain a right to disobey a law which they believe to be immoral" – and as such were not a concern for AI. McKenna here makes use of a similar typology as the Minister for National Service, casting refusal as a "purely political stand" as opposed to those who hold a "moral objection to conscription". By 1968 one of the Victorian

---

[143] "Australia's Political Prisoner", Undated leaflet, State Library of South Australia, available a: https://web.archive.org/web/20060501083814/, www.slsa.sa.gov.au/saatwar/collection/srg124_8_9.htm.

[144] Robert V. Horn, Untitled Report on conscientious objection and noncompliance in Australia, Robert V. Horn Papers, MLMSS 8123, Box 33, SLNSW.

[145] Ibid.

[146] David McKenna to Robert V. Horn, 2 March 1969, Robert V. Horn Papers, MLMSS 8123, Box 33, SLNSW.

section's primary objections to White's case – that the prisoner was held in a military jail – was amended by parliament in favour of civilian incarceration in state prisons.[147] The Victorian section's 1967 annual report also questioned a resolution of AI's most recent International Assembly, declaring that any person who refused to participate in a specific war was considered a prisoner of conscience, to which the section responded that "there is a need for clarification of Amnesty's modus operandi in democratic countries".[148] McKenna read the UDHR as in fact contradicting such a policy, noting that the limitations set forth in Article 29 meant "freedom of conscience is not an absolute, nor is freedom to disobey in a democratic society".[149] Concerns were raised about "to what extent we uphold disobedience to the law by adopting such persons", noting that AI had chosen not to adopt prisoners "who refuse obedience to laws [such as] in South Africa or Portugal". Adopting prisoners who refused to obey laws not only opened the road to what McKenna feared was a tidal wave of similar "freedom to disobey" claims – "are we to adopt people who refuse to have a T.B. X Ray on grounds of conscience[?]" – but also feared that in taking "such a radical step . . . our high repute would be seriously damaged".[150]

Horn and others in the NSW section "decr[ied] such legalistic interpretation" – insisting "the Non-Complier in gaol for conscientiously held and non-violently expressed views suffers no less than the [Conscientious Objector] who has tried in vain to act 'according to the law'".[151] While at first divisions on this issue were across and between sections, by late 1969 the Victorian section had solidly decided "that non-compliers should not be adopted", and sent a memorandum to London to this effect in preparation for the AI Executive Meeting, to be held in Stockholm in 1970.[152] The position of the NSW section was equally clear, expressed in a resolution adopted during "prisoner of conscience week" in November 1969 that requested Amnesty and the UN General Assembly adopt "firm restrains upon legal and political repression of conscience". "[P]rovided that the individual . . . has not used or advocated the use of violence", the resolution asserted, "the expression of honest opinions regarding matters of economics, politics, morality, religion or race is not a good and sufficient reason" to justify imprisonment,

---

[147] For more on these legal changes, see Murphy, *Harvest of Fear*, 214–16.
[148] *Amnesty International Victoria Section – Annual Report, March 1966–March 1967*, 4.
[149] David McKenna to Robert V. Horn, 2 March 1969. [150] Ibid.
[151] Horn, Untitled Report.
[152] David McKenna to Robert V. Horn, 19 February 1970, Robert V. Horn Papers, MLMSS 8123, Box 33, SLNSW

116   Experimental Rights

and "no person should be penalised for refusing to obey a law ... which infringes the[se] principles".[153]

Such disagreements both reflected and contributed to a much wider debate in AI globally. The organisation was convulsed with internal conflict over the period from 1966 to 1967, with evidence of Benenson's long collaborations with British intelligence and increasing signs of mental fatigue forcing the group's "founding father" to resign. This incident, while barely reported in the Australian sections, raised deep questions of whether it was "legitimate for Amnesty to draw when necessary on the resources of state" or to collaborate with the state in achieving domestic or foreign policy objectives.[154] Calls for a decentring of the London secretariat's authority also grew, with large sections in Sweden and Belgium making up a significant percentage of the organisation's global membership and demanding more of a say in the organisation's affairs. The 1970 Stockholm gathering's decision to back the NSW section's views was blamed by the Victorian section on the strength of their Swedish counterparts – "who have the same problem as Australia and have come to the opposite view".[155] This fundamental opposition in how both sections conceptualised human rights – as either inhering in the person, and as such not requiring compliance with the nation-state, or as the product and result of citizenship which imposed both rights and duties onto a subject – also tied into the most central debates on human rights during the decade. The idea of the state as guarantor and provider of rights was the central development of the highly contested First International Conference on Human Rights (Tehran 1968), where a collective notion of "development" based on self-determination of states within the global economy transformed the very meaning of human rights.[156] Notions of an indivisible humanity beyond borders were entirely alien to such proceedings, yet the concept of conscience and the universal approach to those objecting to military service adopted by AI gained more and more traction throughout the next decade, as the "human rights revolution" got under way.[157]

---

[153] "RESOLUTION – Prisoner of Conscience Week, November 1969", *Amnesty News* 24 (February 1970), 15–16.

[154] Tom Buchanan, "Amnesty International in Crisis, 1966–7", *Twentieth Century British History* 15, no. 3 (2004), 288.

[155] "International Council", *Amnesty Bulletin* 28 (October 1970), 4–5.

[156] Roland Burke, "From Individual Rights to National Development: The First UN International Conference on Human Rights, Tehran, 1968", *Journal of World History* 19, no. 3 (2008), 275–96.

[157] On the evolution of this concept amongst activists and in the UN, see Jeremy Kessler, "The Invention of a Human Right: Conscientious Objection at the United Nations, 1947–2011", *Columbia Human Rights Law Review* 44, no. 3 (Spring 2013), 753–91.

Conclusion

The year 1968 was far from a memorable one for Australian human rights activists. Legal historian and president of the United Nations Association of Australia Alex Castles reflected in Melbourne's *Age* that Australians had "become smug about our rights". "Unlike Canada, the United States and Great Britain ... we have, as yet, hardly begun the soul-searching process which has led already to new and improved standards ... of human rights", referencing in particular the US Civil Rights Act and Canada's 1960 Bill of Rights.[158] "Public apathy" and "complacency" was the order of the day, and a nation which once "set leads for other democratic countries" now "lagged markedly" in both legislation and public discussion.[159] This lack of a rights sensibility is clearly evident. AI found it "very difficult to arrange any worthwhile special activity which the organisation felt would be adequate to the occasion". An essay competition aimed at secondary students "on the subject of Freedom" was organised; however, "the response was very poor, and very few entries were received". "Prisoner of Conscience Week" was hoped to be "a focus part of Human Rights Year", but a planned talk by well-known journalist Arthur Koestler "proved disappointing to the audience" due to unexplained "circumstances we were unable to control".[160] Unlike many other nations, Australia did not print a commemorative stamp to mark the year, and attempts by the United Nations Association of Australia to distribute their own met with significant difficulty. Some 8,000 out of the original 20,000 remained undistributed by late November.[161] Governmental responses were equally tepid, with the External Affairs minister's brief statement acknowledging the year following closely that of 1963, when it was decided that only formulaic utterances should be made while the nation maintained, but publically denied, the existence of racial discrimination.[162] It is perhaps unsurprising, then, that some advocates found themselves dealing with "unrelieved depression and futility", as one AI member's resignation letter from 1970 put it: "I ... felt like the boy stemming the incoming tide with one finger against a hole."[163]

---

[158] *The Age*, 15 May 1969, 4   [159] *The Age*, 16 May 1969, 4.

[160] *Amnesty Bulletin* 24 (April 1969), 8.

[161] Circular from Lorraine Moseley on behalf of the Human Rights Year Sticker Committee, 21 November 1968, Records of the Australian Council for Civil Liberties, MS 5791, Box 10, National Library of Australia.

[162] J. Pomeroy, "Fifteenth Anniversary of the Universal Declaration of Human Rights", 24 September 1963, NAA: A1838, 929/1/1/1.

[163] Lily Heyde to Robert V. Horn, 2 December 1970, Robert V. Horn Papers, MLMSS 8123, Box 33, SLNSW.

118   Experimental Rights

While narratives of 1968 as a year of disappointment and depression for human rights activists can easily be made, these ignore other perhaps more interesting and vital perspectives from which to view the decades that followed. They were far from a dominant framework, but much as Jensen argues that some recently decolonised states used new readings of human rights to punch above their weight internationally, so too did old and emerging movements in Australia find that their needs to reorient or intervene in domestic political realities aligned with particular readings of the UDHR's universalism, if only briefly. The meanings of human rights were by no means stable in this period – they could mean democracy, the dismantling of national myths or the freedom of political prisoners. Nor were their sources clear: did the enjoyment of rights result from a citizen's compact with the state, granting rights and the compulsion to obey, or were they universal and inhering in the individual through a relationship with god or an inalienable secular conscience? Human rights served as a way of reconceptualising socialism in an advanced capitalist democracy like Australia, auguring socialist human rights movements such as Charter 77 in the 1970s and recasting the CPA as defenders and extenders of the rights it had long dismissed as bourgeois. The seemingly monolithic power of the RSL, claiming at once the mantle of freedom's defenders while pursuing fundamentally anti-democratic agendas, was shaken by a group claiming to be human rights' true advocates and supporting those whose consciences were being trampled by conscription. AI's uptake was quick in Australia, but the nascent group's novel reading of human rights posed as many challenges as it did opportunities, leading to often public internal disputes over the limits of human rights as domestic political tools. The Cold War's deep domestic impacts in Australia – creating subjectivities devoid of critical capacity that valued only the right to material goods, in Ashbolt's condescending description – lingered over each of these groups. In a way, though, each also contributed to finding new approaches that transcended its divisions and laid foundations for what was to come.

4 Whose Rights?

"The Aboriginal movement should be classified as a liberation movement rather than a civil rights movement or a land rights movement[;] in fact we have been colonised just as forcefully and arrogantly as anyone else."[1] Paul Coe, founder of the Aboriginal Medical Service, vice president of the Aboriginal Legal Service and one of the first Indigenous law students at the University of Sydney made this statement at a Canadian summit of indigenous political organisations in 1972. Sitting on a panel made up of representatives from the Mozambican guerrilla group FRELIMO and the American Indian Movement, Coe captured something of the 1970s "global" sensibilities and the contested nature of rights claiming in the decade of their so-called revolution. On average, the term "human rights" was mentioned only forty-eight times per year in the *Canberra Times* throughout the 1960s, but this increased to nearly 170 over the next decade.[2] The election of a Gough Whitlam–led ALP in 1972 marked not only an end to twenty-three uninterrupted years of conservative rule but also a sea change in governmental responses to human rights internationally and at home. After only six days in office, Australia adopted the "twin covenants" that gave effect to the Universal Declaration of Human Rights (UDHR). A human rights bill to ratify these documents and a Racial Discrimination Bill giving effect to the International Convention on the Elimination of all forms of Racial Discrimination (CERD) was introduced to parliament in 1973.[3] Australia finally seemed to be overcoming anxieties towards international treaties and concerns about their applicability within a federal system, although this last point was not to be resolved for some time. Internationally, bilateralism was quickly replaced with a new regard for

---

[1] Quoted in Kevin Gilbert, *Because a White Man'll Never Do It* (Sydney: Angus & Robertson, 1973), 111.

[2] Advanced search for keyword "Human Rights" in *Canberra Times*, 1970–9, available at https://trove.nla.gov.au/newspaper/result?q=%22human+rights%22&exactPhrase&any Words&notWords&requestHandler&dateFrom&dateTo&l-advtitle=11&sortby&l-decade=197.

[3] The most authoritative work on Whitlam's governmental record is Jenny Hocking, *Gough Whitlam: His Time* (Melbourne: Miegunyah Press, 2012).

120   Whose Rights?

the United Nations, and Whitlam expressed a desire for "a more independent Australian stance in international affairs ... an Australia which will enjoy a growing standard as a distinctive, tolerant, co-operative and well regarded nation ... in the world at large".[4]

But, as Coe's remarks imply, such an embrace of human rights was problematic at best. This chapter explores how Indigenous activists, second-wave feminists and their opponents in the emerging Right to Life movement imagined and engaged with the increasingly contested idea of human rights in the "long 1970s".[5] Moving away from the white-led advocacy groups of the 1950s, this chapter shifts focus to the increasingly vocal Indigenous activists of the 1960s and 1970s. Particular attention is paid to how civil and political human rights featured in events leading up to the 1967 "citizenship" referendum and how a reading that favoured economic and cultural rights came to the fore in its aftermath. This move was informed by the rise of "discrimination" as a specific concern, the signing of the CERD, and how ideas of self-determination and economic equality came to define the meaning of human rights at a UN dominated by proponents of what Vijay Prashad calls the "third world project".[6] Second-wave feminism had an equally problematic relationship with notions of rights, and the "human" that underpinned them, which is best viewed in debates and activities surrounding International Women's Year 1975. The Whitlam government hoped the year would recast Australia as "a pacesetter for the rest of the world in advancing basic human rights", while feminists – and in particular the Prime Minister's Advisor on Women Elizabeth Reid – looked askance at the term's dominant instrumentalist, development-centred meanings at home and abroad.[7] However, it was on the political right that human rights again received their strongest airing. The so-called Right to Life movement drew on a turn in Catholic social teaching marked by 1968's *Humanae Vitae* encyclical and a global "backlash" against the progressive movements of the 1960s – in particular the women's movement's demands for free and safe abortions – to once again employ ideas of universalism to stymie progressive change.

---

[4] Quoted in Dennis J. Murphy, "Problems in Australian Foreign Policy, January to June 1973, *Australian Journal of Politics and History* 19, no. 3 (December 1973), 340.

[5] The "long 1970s" is an increasingly meaningful term, particularly in human rights historiography, see Angela Romano, "Untying Cold War Knots: The EEC and Eastern Europe in the Long 1970s", *Cold War History* 14, no. 2 (2014), 153–73; Poul Villaume, Rasmus Mariager and Helle Porsdam, *The "Long 1970s": Human Rights, East-West Détente and Transnational Relations* (Abingdon: Routledge, 2016).

[6] Vijay Prashad, *The Darker Nations: A People's History of the Third World* (New York: The New Press, 2008).

[7] "FOR CABINET: International Women's Year 1975", Elizabeth Reid Papers (henceforth ERP), MS 9262, Box 32, Folder 13, National Library of Australia (henceforth NLA).

The 1970s appear in the emerging literature on human rights as something of a "breakthrough" moment.[8] Samuel Moyn has led this particular – and quite controversial – charge: identifying this decade as one in which human rights went from a set of ideas with little real life outside of inter-state disputation at the United Nations to a fully fledged political language to which activists and governments paid close attention. "Over the course of the 1970s", Moyn posits, "the moral world of Westerners shifted, opening a space for the sort of utopianism that coalesced in an international human rights movement that had never existed before".[9] That the (re)emergence of individual rights co-existed with the crescendo of a collective rights utopia – that of the developmentalist state seeking restitution for the wrongs of colonialism – is vital to understanding why this proved a slow, difficult process for Australians.[10] While Whitlam tied his political fortunes to the idea of human rights, responding to subtle shifts in the term's international meanings, few moves were made under his government to make such rhetorical gestures meaningful. As such, the term remained very much one open to debate and appropriation as the proliferation of treaties, conferences and concerns led to questions of exactly who the recipient of rights were.

Civil or Cultural, Law or Liberation? Indigenous Human Rights

In 1962 Oodgeroo Noonucall read a poem entitled "Aboriginal Charter of Rights" to the Adelaide national convention of the Federal Council for the Advancement of Aborigines (FCAA). The FCAA – which became the FCAATSI after the addition of "and Torres Strait Islanders" in 1964 to include Polynesian-descendant inhabitants of islands in Australia's northern-most territorial waters – had been founded in February 1958 to co-ordinate a renewed push for the federal government to end discriminatory policies in Australian states and territories. Though planned by Council for Aboriginal Rights secretary Shirley Andrews with the input of

---

[8] On the "breakthrough", see two key collections: Jan Eckel and Samuel Moyn (eds.), *The Breakthrough: Human Rights in the 1970s* (Philadelphia: University of Pennsylvania Press, 2013); Akira Iriye, Petra Goedde and William I. Hitchcock (eds.), *The Human Rights Revolution: An International History* (Oxford: Oxford University Press, 2010).

[9] Samuel Moyn, *The Last Utopia: Human Rights in History* (Cambridge, MA: The Belknap Press of Harvard University Press, 2010), 1. For examples of critiques of Moyn's approach, see Robin Blackburn, "Reclaiming Human Rights", *New Left Review* 69 (May–June 2011), 126–39; Jean H. Quatert, "The Last Utopia: Human Rights in History, by Samuel Moyn", *English Historical Review* 76, no. 521 (2011), 1028–9.

[10] See, for example, Antony Anghie, "Whose Utopia? Human Rights, Development, and the Third World", *Qui Parle: Critical Humanities and Social Sciences* 22, no. 1 (Fall/Winter 2013), 63–80.

122   Whose Rights?

Charles Duguid and Jessie Street – white humanitarians, Christians and communists – the organisation also brought together three Indigenous activists: Doug Nicholls, Jeff Barnes and Bert Groves.[11] In 1961, the organisation elected Queensland Indigenous leader Joe McGuiness to the position of president. This spirit, what was known as one of "black and white together", and a grand ambition of changing Australia's constitution to allow for federal intervention on Indigenous affairs is captured in Noonucall's poetry. "We want hope, not racialism" reads the first line of her "Charter", and "brotherhood not ostracism".

> Black Advance, not white ascendance:
> Make us Equals, not dependents . . .
> Give us welcome, not aversion,
> Give us choice, not cold coercion,
> Status, not discrimination,
> Human rights, not segregation.[12]

Noonucall, then known as Kath Walker and only at the beginning of a career that would make her one of Australia's best-known poets, articulated one of several charters and declarations developed by Indigenous Australians at this time, tying into both the ongoing civil rights movement in the United States and the seemingly exponential numbers of colonial nations declaring independence.

On 31 July 1960, in the far northern Queensland town of Cairns, a Declaration of Rights of Queensland Aborigines and Torres Strait Islanders was unanimously passed after several days of discussion. This was the foundation document of the Cairns Aborigines and Torres Strait Islander Advancement League, which declared that "the world-wide movement of subject peoples for full human rights, is a major feature of the times we live in", adding "The old colonial system is being swept aside." The year 1960 was the year of Africa, and the document welcomed the fact that "[m]any of the formerly colonial peoples have already established independent, self-governing republics", although in South Africa and the United States colonised peoples "are still pursuing the goal of full equality".[13] Such rhetorical flourishes – the grouping of

---

[11] The authoritative account of this organisation remains Sue Taffe, *Black and White Together: The Federal Council for the Advancement of Aborigines and Torres Strait Islanders, 1958–1973* (St Lucia, QLD: University of Queensland Press, 2005).

[12] "Aboriginal Charter of Rights", in Kath Walker, available at www.poetrylibrary.edu.au/poets/noonuccal-oodgeroo/aboriginal-charter-of-rights-0771030.

[13] "Declaration of Rights of Aborigines and Torres Strait Islanders, First Conference of the Aborigines and Torres Strait Islanders Advancement League, Cairns, North Queensland, 29–31 July 1960", Barry Christophers Papers (henceforth BCP), MS 7992, Box 28, NLA, 2.

Indigenous Australians as a colonial "subject peoples" and the conflation of "human rights" with national self-determination – owed much to the close involvement of many Communist Party–controlled trade unions, in particular the Waterside Workers Federation, to which key activists like Joe McGuiness belonged. This "community of the left", as Sue Taffe puts it, combined with "the large concentrations of aboriginal people ... and the close proximity of the Torres Strait" to bring over 100 people to this foundational gathering out of a total population of only 20,000.[14] The declaration was wide-ranging, covering the "sub-human" treatment of Indigenous people by "petty officials" to forced labour and the withholding of wages. It demanded the repeal of the Aborigines Preservation and Protection Act and the Torres Strait Islander Acts that controlled Aborigines' access to property, alcohol, marriage, social security benefits and housing. In a rare direct reference, the declaration concluded that these pieces of legislation "violate, completely or in part, every article of the Universal Declaration of Human Rights".[15]

Bain Attwood's *Rights for Aborigines* and John Chesterman's *Civil Rights: How Indigenous Australians Won Formal Equality* each focus on specific types of rights – "social" and "civil" – with "human" rights appearing largely indistinguishable amongst these other forms of claim making.[16] Ravi de Costa's *A Higher Authority* carefully examines the role of international instruments, including the International Labour Organisation's resolution 107 on the rights of "Indigenous and Tribal Populations" and the UDHR, in the work of campaigners. Yet, de Costa treats human rights as only a passing fancy, replaced with Black Nationalism in the late 1960s only to return in the late 1970s and early 1980s as work began towards what would become 2007's United Nations Declaration of the Rights of Indigenous Peoples.[17] The shift discussed here – from political and civil to economic and cultural conceptions of human rights, or what Dylan Lino described as one from "citizenship" to "peoplehood", in light of domestic realities and a changing international situation – is thus largely elided.[18] This section also discusses the development of the idea of racial discrimination, particularly tied in to the

---

[14] Sue Taffe, "The Cairns Aborigines and Torres Strait Islander Advancement League and the Community of the Left", *Labour History* 97 (November 2009), 149–67.

[15] "Declaration of Rights of Aborigines and Torres Strait Islanders", 3.

[16] Bain Attwood, *Rights for Aborigines* (St Leonards, NSW: Allen & Unwin, 2003); John Chesterman, *Civil Rights: How Indigenous Australians Won Formal Equality* (Brisbane: University of Queensland Press, 2005).

[17] Ravi de Costa, *A Higher Authority: Indigenous Transnationalism and Australia* (Sydney: UNSW Press, 2006).

[18] Dylan Lino, *Constitutional Recognition: First Peoples and the Australian Settler State* (Annandale, NSW: The Federation Press, 2018), 167–73.

124   Whose Rights?

formulation and enactment of an international mechanism to eliminate it: the CERD. Discussions of this document and its applicability to Australia – and whether law was the best way to address Indigenous disadvantage at all – are here closely analysed.

"Racial Discrimination", rarely discussed in Australia during the 1950s, became a hot-button topic in the 1960s.[19] The Cairns Declaration of Rights noted that such prejudice could be "open or concealed" and found Queensland Indigenous people to be discriminated against in "employment, in the use of many public facilities, in some theatres, and other places of entertainment". It called for a campaign to ensure that such "bars" become seen as "morally wrong and impermissible, punishable by the law where necessary".[20] Such colour consciousness was also apparent in moves by a small number of students and academics to challenge the discriminatory nature of Australia's immigration policy, which was dubbed a "colour bar" and contested on similarly moral grounds.[21] Accusations of its practice in Australia and Papua New Guinea – a trustee territory until 1975 – have also been found to be a primary motor behind Commonwealth changes to voting laws and other federal restrictions on Indigenous peoples in the early 1960s.[22] Christerman tells how one 1962 case – involving three non-Indigenous children being kept home from school "following the admission of five Aboriginal children to regular classes" at a school 500 kilometres outside of Darwin, made domestic and international headlines. This was "testimony to the international disapproval now greeting evidence of racial discrimination".[23] Similarly newsworthy was the famous "Freedom Ride" of 1965, though those involved were rankled by such "flamboyant"

[19] The term appears only sixty-two times in the *Canberra Times* across the entire decade but turns up seven times as often in the 1960s. Advanced Search "Racial Discrimination", available at https://trove.nla.gov.au/newspaper/result?q=%22racial+discrimination%22 &exactPhrase=&anyWords=&notWords=&requestHandler=&dateFrom=&dateTo=& l-advtitle=11&sortby.

[20] Declaration of Rights of Aborigines and Torres Strait Islanders, BCP, MS 7992, Box 28, NLA, 5–6.

[21] See Kate Darian-Smith and James Waghorne, "Australian-Asian Sociability, Student Activism and the University Challenge to White Australia in the 1950s", *Australian Journal of Politics and History* 62, no. 2 (June 2016), 203–18.

[22] On this, see John Chesterman, "Defending Australia's Reputation: How Indigenous Australians Won Civil Rights, Part One", *Australian Historical Studies* 32, no. 116 (2001), 20–39; John Chesterman, "Defending Australia's Reputation: How Indigenous Australians Won Civil Rights, Part Two", *Australian Historical Studies* 32, no. 117 (2001), 201–21; Jennifer Clark, "Something to Hide": Aborigines and the Department of External Affairs, January 1961–January 1962", *Journal of the Royal Australian Historical Society* 83 (1997), 71–84; Jennifer Clark, "'The Wind of Change' in Australia: Aborigines and the International Politics of Race, 1960–1972", *The International History Review* 20, no. 1 (1998), 89–117.

[23] Chesterman, *Civil Rights*, 55.

American terminology.[24] After having been charged with "overlooking racial discrimination in Australia" in their zeal to highlight injustice abroad, students at Sydney University under the leadership of that institution's first Indigenous graduate Charles Perkins adopted a successful tactic from the American South, launching a fact-finding bus tour that uncovered and contested social practices of segregation in rural towns.[25] In that same year, the UN's General Assembly adopted and opened to signature the CERD, and in 1966 South Australia became the first Australian jurisdiction to implement anti-discrimination legislation. Don Dunstan, Australian Labor Party premier, proudly noted that his state "was the first ... to comply with the conditions of the 1957 ILO Convention", having removed the last remaining legal discrimination – prohibiting the consumption of alcohol – early in 1965.[26]

Australia adopted the CERD in November 1966, using a "narrow understandings of ... disputed clauses" to ensure the final Convention was at least perceived to allow for the continuation of "protective" regimes in various states.[27] In July 1965, a letter from the secretary of the Department of External Affairs was sent to each state requesting their particular interpretations of the then-draft CERD's provisions in regards to their own separate legal arrangements for Indigenous Australians under their jurisdiction. "The question of racial discrimination, in present world circumstances, is a particularly important one and it is essential that the Australian government should be able to speak authoritatively on the matter," the letter cautioned.[28] The Queensland government's submission argued that the almost unrestricted powers of the Director of Aboriginal and Island Affairs over lives of "assisted aborigines", including the ability to move individuals under his control between reserves at will, were allowable under the "special measures" provisions of Article II.[29] Western Australia reiterated concerns about the watchful eyes of international opinion, that "from time to time discriminations ... which are – allegedly at least – made on the basis of colour" occur, and "the convention affords marvellous facilities to those who have an

---

[24] Ann Curthoys, *Freedom Ride: A Freedom Rider Remembers* (St Leonards, NSW: Allen & Unwin, 2002).

[25] *The Canberra Times*, 13 February 1965, 4.

[26] *The Canberra Times*, 10 August 1965, 4.

[27] Annemarie Deveraux, *Australia and the Birth of the International Bill of Human Rights, 1946–1966* (Annandale, NSW: The Federation Press, 2005), 236–7.

[28] Secretary, Department of External Affairs, Canberra to Secretary, Prime Minister's Department, Canberra, 12 July 1965, National Archives of Australia (henceforth NAA), A463, 1964/1826.

[29] Under Secretary, Premier's Department, Brisbane to Secretary, Prime Minister's Department, Canberra, 3 September 1965, NAA: A463, 1964/1826.

126 Whose Rights?

interest in magnifying and distorting" them.[30] While Australia abstained from the final UN vote on the Convention's wording in 1965, Minister for External Affairs Paul Hasluck signed the Convention in October 1966, owing as much to the United States, the United Kingdom and Canada having already done so as to the hope that "difficulties" at a state level could be ironed out at a later date.[31]

Removing discrimination from the Australian Constitution and empowering the federal government to take control of Indigenous affairs was the central driving force behind a famous referendum on 27 May 1967. Over 90 per cent of Australians voted to alter two clauses that precluded the counting of Indigenous people in the estimation of each state's total population and restricted the ability of the federal government to make laws governing them.[32] The enthusiasm that this process engendered "is baffling when one considers the terms of the constitutional changes" campaigners sought, Bain Attwood remarks, and indeed these small technical changes were presented by some campaigners as the final step towards full citizenship.[33] This was a bipartisan campaign, with Menzies' replacement as prime minister, Harold Holt, making the referendum a point of differentiation between himself and his long-serving predecessor. The idea of human rights had some traction: the Australian Council of Salaried and Professional Associations released a poster titled "The Rights of the Australian Aborigines ... and you", which quoted Article I of the UDHR and claimed that all white Australians had to do to "make this a reality for their fellow-Australians of Aboriginal Descent" was to "Vote YES".[34] Perhaps the campaign's most famous leaflet, featuring an Indigenous child framed by the words "Right Wrongs, Write Yes for Aborigines", captured the sense in which this minor constitutional amendment became a fundamental step in the nation's history.[35] The vote had few practical outcomes, bar the establishment of a new Office of Aboriginal Affairs within the Prime Minister's Department, which was not to gain any real momentum until well into the 1970s.

---

[30] Premier, Western Australia to Prime Minister, Commonwealth of Australia, 19 September 1966, NAA: A463, 1964/1826.

[31] Assistant Secretary, UN Branch, Department of External Affairs to Secretary, Prime Minister's Department, 14 October 1966, NAA: A463, 1964/1826.

[32] Key texts on the referendum include Bain Attwood and Andrew Markus, *The 1967 Referendum: Race, Power and the Australian Constitution* (Canberra, ACT: Aboriginal Studies Press, 1997); Larissa Behrendt, "The 1967 Referendum: 40 Years On", *Precedent* 82 (September–October 2008), 4–8; Lino, *Constitutional Recognition*, chapter 5.

[33] Attwood, *Rights for Aborigines*, 162.

[34] The Australian Council of Salaried and Professional Employees, "The Rights of the Australian Aborigines and You", undated, Gordon Bryant Papers (Henceforth GBP), MS 8256, Box 175, NLA.

[35] Federal Council for the Advancement of Aborigines and Torres Strait Islanders, "Right Wrongs, Write Yes for Aborigines on May 27", GBP, MS 8256, Box 175, NLA.

Joe McGinness detected a sense of "self-congratulatory complacency" after the vote, calling a report arising from the post-referendum meeting of Commonwealth and state ministers "a reaffirmation of the policy of assimilation formulated by government in the 1950s" which "can only result in the absorption of Aborigines and Islanders into the white community".[36] McGinness' formulation, that Indigenous people represented "a people" with "history, customs, culture of our own", marked a turn in rights readings: less the universalism and "brotherhood of man" that framed the 1960 Declaration than the assertion of a new Indigenous sovereignty and cultural rights. Equally, McGinness pointed to how the acquisition of political rights – now largely complete in many states – would not be sufficient for Indigenous Australians: "most have not been able to acquire the knowledge, skills and experience necessary to make enjoyment of formal equal rights a reality". This would require not just negative rights but also new legislation that would "guarantee our rights to communal lands and local self-government, prohibit discrimination in any form against us [and] provide long term technical and other aid to help us advance ... something like a Colombo Plan for Aboriginal and Islander communities".[37] McGinness provided a long analysis of newly passed Queensland state laws, known colloquially as "The Act", which replaced those the 1960 Declaration had attacked. Yet, these were little but window dressing in McGinness' opinion, as Queensland "continues to violate the United Nations declaration of Human Rights [sic]". International Human Rights Year provided an opportunity for Australians to ensure that "Aborigines and Islanders ... gain and enjoy full human rights in the land of their birth", lest activists "feel compelled to go over to violent forms of action" as African Americans had.[38] Noonucall made a similar rhetorical move after a trip to the United Kingdom in 1968 to attend a World Council of Churches conference, returning with warnings that based on her encounters with black power radicals Australia had "10 years to bring about instant evolution or face the consequences of a bloody revolution".[39] Faith in gradual processes of domestic reform was quickly fading.

On 15 October 1970, five Indigenous travellers – Bruce McGuinness, Patsy Kruger and Bob Maza from Victoria, Sol Belear of New South

---

[36] Joe McGinness, "The Aboriginal and Torres Strait Islanders Affairs Act of 1965 – and Regulations of 1966 – Address given to Inter-Racial Seminar, Townsville, 1967". BCP, MS 7992, Box 7, NLA, 1.

[37] Ibid., 2.   [38] Ibid., 6.

[39] Kath Walker, "Report to the Australian Council of Churches on the World Council of Churches 'Consultation on Racism' held in London 19th May 1969", Oodgeroo Noonuccal Papers, UQFL84, Box 30, Fryer Library, The University of Queensland.

128   Whose Rights?

Wales and Jack Davis of Western Australia – visited the United Nations in New York to meet with post-colonial leaders and deliver a petition to the United Nations Commission on Human Rights.[40] While several appeals had been directed to UN Secretary General U Thant in 1965–6, reflecting the General Assembly's discussion of and adoption of the CERD, this was the first time such a petition had been lodged directly with the Commission.[41] Its contents demonstrated how well the economic and cultural human rights claims McGinness and others were articulating chimed with the dominant readings of rights at the United Nations: that of self-determination. The Right to Self Determination was the first article in both the Human Rights Covenants of 1966 and was front and centre at the First International Conference on Human Rights (Tehran 1968) as the foremost right, the realisation of which was a precondition for the extension of others.[42] A pivotal paragraph in the gathering's official Proclamation claimed that as:

human rights and fundamental freedoms are indivisible, the full realization of civil and political rights without the enjoyment of economic, social and cultural rights is impossible. The achievement of lasting progress in the implementation of human rights is dependent upon sound and effective national and international policies of economic and social development.[43]

The Indigenous petitioners delivered their paperwork to the deputy director of the Human Rights Division wearing red headbands to symbolise the blood of their ancestors, and indeed the claim of genocide – another central term in UN nomenclature – was central. "This genocide started when the Europeans first invaded us almost two hundred years ago ... [T]hey poisoned us, they methodically and brutally murdered us", and while today "the techniques of the invaders are more subtle", the petitioners said, the aim remained the same. They spoke particularly of life in the Northern Territory, where "gastroenteritis, dysentery and pneumonia" were rife and dwellings were marked by "squalor": more than one-third, 37 per cent, of housing was classed as "shacks", and more

---

[40] Full text of petitions can be found in *Aborigines visit the U.S.: Report on Trip by Five Aborigines to Congress of African People and United Nations* (Melbourne, Abschol, 1971).

[41] Such claim making by "sub-national" or other non-state entities to "legitimate" status under international law were increasingly common from the 1960s onwards. See in particular Lydia Walker, "Decolonisation and the 1960s: On Legitimate and Illegitimate Nationalist Claim-Making", *Past and Present* 242 (February 2019), 227–64.

[42] Roland Burke, "From Individual Rights to National Development: The First UN International Conference on Human Rights, Tehran, 1968", *Journal of World History* 19, no. 3 (2008), 275–96.

[43] "Proclamation of Teheran, Final Act of the International Conference on Human Rights, Teheran, 22 April to 13 May 1968", A/CONF 32/41, available at http://hrlibrary.umn .edu/instree/l2ptichr.htm.

than half of people slept in houses without sufficient beds. "We speak of the literal, physical destruction of our people," the petition continued, and readers were instructed to see "the policy of the Australian government in light of what it does ... rather than what it says". Improvements or extensions to Indigenous citizenship rights would not solve these problems; instead the petition concluded with three demands:

1. Cease the ... systematic obliteration of our people.
2. Provide us with the housing ... and medical services which will enable us to survive.
3. Pay us the sum of 6 billion dollars so that we can achieve economic parity with those who have sought to wipe us out.[44]

Such assertiveness contrasted with the assimilationist claims of only a few years prior. An unnamed "full-blood Aboriginal" wrote to the secretary general in 1965 stating a desire "to live like white people": "The government says we should assimilate [and] we are willing", the letter concluded, "[b]ut help us to get our land back first so we can do it in our own ways".[45] The tonality of the 1970 claimants could not have been more different. These new demands – in keeping with a rising chorus of third world states demanding that colonisers grant not only formal independence but also significant compensation to eliminate underdevelopment – came as a significant shock to the Australian government.

External Affairs Department bureaucrats quickly began assembling material and wording statements to discredit and undermine the petitioners. While responses to the petitioners of 1965–6 relied on the language of assimilation that had been in place since 1951 – of "achieving for Aborigines and part-Aborigines the same rights, privileges, responsibilities ... and loyalties characteristic of Australian Society" – it was clear this would not do for claims of genocide and compensation.[46] If criticism were not stymied and "the issue is brought up under the general discussion of human rights, it would be certain to get the support of certain Asian, Arab and Communist Bloc delegations if for no other reason than to embarrass the Australian government".[47] The petitioners, who "know something about the Human Rights Commission's procedures for handling petitions", hoped that "an African delegation [would] speak about their petition during the

---

[44] *Aborigines Visit the US*, 35–7.
[45] "COPY of a communication dated 11 August 1965 from an individual in Australia", NAA: A452, NT1966/167. A further petition was sent from the Northern Territory Council for Aboriginal Rights in July 1966, reproduced in *Tribune*, 21 September 1966, 11.
[46] "Human Rights Communication Referring to Australia", 6 January 1966, NAA: A452, NT1966/167.
[47] Telegram, 16 October 1970, NAA: A1838, 929/5/3 PART 3.

130   Whose Rights?

Third Committee's discussion of Racial Discrimination", and the report warned that either Tanzania or Guinea would possibly do so.[48] The government prepared an official response and a series of talking points, beginning by discrediting the petitioners themselves, who, according to the Department of the Interior (that administered the Northern Territory), "do not represent the Aboriginal people of Australia [or] the Northern Territory" and were "part Aborigines" who "think as Europeans not as Aboriginals".[49] In responding to the petition's substantive points, the word "assimilation" was noticeable in its absence, but many of the racialized assumptions that underlay it re-emerged. What the petitioners called "invasion" was merely a "culture clash" leading to "intolerance and misunderstanding that expressed itself in occasional violence".[50] Rather than dying out, the government estimated that the population was growing at a rate of 4 per cent and that infant mortality was improving; it also claimed that "increased interest by Aboriginal citizens in maintaining and re-asserting their social and cultural identity" was actually the result of government policy of assisting "these citizens [to] realise fully their potential".[51] In response to demands for compensation, the government noted that "specific educational, work training, economic development [and] welfare programmes" were in place so that "the people may confidently elect to participate fully in the wider community", and "paying lump sums to individual Aborigines ... will not contribute to this goal".[52] In the end, the petition fell victim to the Commission's own institutional failings: it was not spoken to in the Third Committee, and in any case the Australian government was not even obligated to respond.

Such international disappointments sat alongside a more successful attempt to connect the return of traditional land to a narrative of long-standing occupation of the Australian continent. Miranda Johnson speaks to the significance of Indigenous rearticulation of rights in the early 1970s, particularly in the Gove Land Rights case of 1971. While the case was lost, Johnson sees it as significant for two reasons. Firstly, the Northern Territory Supreme Court judge, Richard Blackburn, allowed the admission of Indigenous oral traditions and claims to land ownership – previously considered hearsay – to be heard for the first time. This in turn allowed for Indigenous traditional owners to make a claim to being the "First

---

[48] Australian Mission to the United Nations, New York to Department of External Affairs, 14 October 1975, NAA: A1838, 929/5/3 PART 3.

[49] Department of the Interior, "Aborigines: Petition to the United Nations. Pont Brief in Relation to Northern Territory", 22 October 1970, NAA: A1838, 929/5/3 PART 3.

[50] Ibid.

[51] "Petition from Australia Aborigines", undated, NAA: A1838, 929/5/3 PART 3.

[52] Department of the Interior, "Aborigines: Petition to the United Nations", NAA: A1838, 929/5/3 PART 3.

Civil or Cultural, Law or Liberation? Indigenous Human Rights   131

Australians", a significant political and legal claim that laid the foundation for both the famous granting of land rights to the Gurindji people in 1975 and the passage of the Northern Territory Land Rights Act in 1976.[53] Whitlam's government, elected in 1972 amidst a groundswell of progressive opinion, was also able to ratify the CERD through the passage of the Racial Discrimination Act 1975 (RDA). While stalled by significant debate in parliament over the existence of racism in Australia and the creation of a "race relations industry", it is remembered as a watershed in Australian politics.[54] Yet, not all were pleased with the final shape the RDA took.

As early as 1966, Indigenous Australians had been calling for bans on the use of racist terminology in public, with the Northern Territory Council for Aboriginal Rights making the outlawing of "derisive terms" part of its programme in July of that year. Don Dunstan, then South Australia's minister for Aborigines, dismissed such laws as "not practicable" for inclusion in the state's racial discrimination legislation, noting that "if these words were outlawed the Government would have to list every derisive word against other national groups" as well.[55] The Bill's final passage in October 1975, outlawing discrimination in employment and access to public spaces on the basis of race, occurred without the inclusion of measures "relating to incitement and the promotion of racial hatred that are required by the International Convention", struck out by a Liberal-dominated Senate. The government begrudgingly accepted these amendments with "a total lack of enthusiasm", while the newly elected Liberal MP for the Sydney seat of Bennelong, John Winston Howard, applauded his party's achievements, saying that "one does nothing towards reducing the incidence of racial tension by legislative coercion".[56] While Indigenous leaders had campaigned for the RDA's passage, Pat O'Shane remarked that the Bill had been "thoroughly emasculated", noting that its focus only on "attitudinal" rather than "behavioural" racism meant that its value "as a weapon against the perpetuation of racial attitudes and ideology is minimal". The argument put by conservatives like Howard – that education, facilitating the free flow and debate of racist ideas rather than their curtailment, was the RDA's true purpose – ignored that "racism is thoroughly entrenched in . . . our educational, social, cultural and economic institutions, and it is through these institutions that individual attitudinal

---

[53] Miranda Johnson, *The Land Is Our History: Indigeneity, Law and the Settler State* (Oxford: Oxford University Press, 2016), chapter 2.

[54] Tim Soutphommasane, *I'm Not Racist But: 40 Years of the Racial Discrimination Act* (Sydney: NewSouth Publishing, 2015), chapter 2.

[55] *Canberra Times*, 27 July 1966, 3.

[56] Commonwealth Parliamentary Debates, House of Representatives, 3 June 1975, 3249.

132   Whose Rights?

racism is preserved and maintained".[57] As such, the expression of racism by individuals in a society structured by racism "denies [indigenous] people their dignity as human beings", and it was unsurprising that O'Shane had "not yet talked to anyone who greeted the existence of the Act with overwhelming, or any, enthusiasm".[58]

Similar sentiments emerged at a conference on "Aborigines, human rights and the law", held in July 1973 by the Australian Branch of the International Commission of Jurists (ICJ) and the newly established University of New South Wales Law School. Charles Perkins, who had led to the 1965 Freedom Ride and was now working in the Office of Aboriginal Affairs in Canberra, called for "virtually unlimited funds" to be made available to Aboriginal-run organisations.[59] Land rights were clearly spelt out as the granting of "ownership and control of existing reserves" as a step towards "the restoration of traditional land" and "[c]ompensation for all land excised from reserves since the[ir] establishment ... to be paid into a trust fund ... to be administered by Aboriginals".[60] Such clarity of purpose was also met with a strident rejection of law as the place to make these changes. The legal system was incomprehensible to many Indigenous people, and while the emergence in 1971 of the Aboriginal Legal Service in Sydney provided some respite, law spoke in a language alien to many. As Perkins put it: "I distrust the law, I distrust the police, in fact I hate them at many times".[61] Such distrust was well earned: one speaker reflected on how the ICJ had only a decade previously refused to use its wide international apparatus to publicise Indigenous legal issues for fear it would "likely cause embarrassment to Australia".[62] Paul Coe again attested to the power of Indigenous people's emerging global consciousness – "we are now starting to realise the struggle that we are faced with is not contained simply within the legal confines of Australia" – and the need for "black groups and Indian groups ... to link up and try and build an international front".[63] Roberta "Bobbi" Sykes, journalist and Indigenous rights advocate, argued that the "[Tent] Embassy was more productive than twenty years of legal attack", referring to the erection in January 1972 of a makeshift Indigenous Embassy outside Parliament House in Canberra that had made international headlines.[64] Human rights were

---

[57] Pat O'Shane, "Law and Justice as Experienced by Aborigines", in *Seminar on the Implications of the Racial Discrimination Act 1975* (Sydney: Department of Services, 1976), 55–6. On Indigenous campaigning for the RDA, see Lino, *Constitutional Recognition*, 177–85.

[58] O'Shane, "Law and Justice", 56.

[59] Garth Nettheim (ed.), *Aborigines, Human Rights and the Law* (Sydney: Australia and New Zealand Book Company, 1974), 13.

[60] Ibid., 104.   [61] Ibid., 10.   [62] Ibid., 128.   [63] Ibid., 139–40.   [64] Ibid., 155.

not to be won by reform or within the courtroom, a sentiment shared by that other great social movement of the 1970s, women's liberation.

"Women Are a Colonised Sex": Human Rights and International Women's Year

The centrality of self-determination and economic empowerment in 1970s rights discourse was equally apparent in Australian Elizabeth Reid's speech at the first United Nations Conference for International Women's Year (IWY), held from 19 June to 2 July 1975, in Mexico City. Declaring that "women are a colonised sex", Reid pressed the 2,000 official delegates for the term "sexism" to be classified alongside racism as equally injurious to global politics. "We must cease being afraid of these words," she remarked, before declaring that the conference's stated theme of equality was a "limited and possible harmful goal".[65] While gaining significant publicity, Reid's impassioned speech made little difference to the conference's preordained outcomes. Sexism was not to appear in the conference's declaration, written months in advance, and was to be only a footnote in that presented to the second conference, held in Copenhagen, Denmark, in 1980.[66] However, it was one of the opening salvos in a long struggle to fundamentally transform the UN human rights program, cemented in 1995 when American First Lady Hillary Clinton declared "human rights are women's rights and women's rights are human rights" at the Fourth World Congress on Women in Beijing, China.[67] It also offers a valuable insight into what uses the idea of human rights were put to by the Women's Liberation Movement (WLM) in a decade during which the term was almost invisible in its publications or domestic activism.

The decision to designate 1975 as International Women's Year was the product of a decades-long struggle to have women's rights taken seriously in global power politics. The UN's Commission on the Status of Women (CSW) was established in 1946, under the umbrella of the Economic and Social Council. It wasn't until 1967, however, that the Declaration on the Elimination of Discrimination against Women (CEDAW) was passed by the General Assembly, which then took twelve years to gain sufficient

---

[65] "Statement by the Leader of the Australian Delegation – Ms Elizabeth Reid", 21 June 1975, ERP, MS 9262, Box 42, Folder 84, NLA.

[66] Kristen Ghodsee, "Revisiting the United Nations Decade for Women: Brief Reflections on Feminism, Capitalism and Cold War Politics in the Early Years of the International Women's Movement", *Women's Studies International Forum* 33, no. 1 (2010), 7.

[67] Hillary Rodham Clinton, "Remarks to the U.N. 4th World Conference on Women Plenary Session", 5 September 1995, available at www.americanrhetoric.com/spee ches/hillaryclintonbeijingspeech.htm.

134   Whose Rights?

signatures to come into force as a Covenant.[68] With aims to "promote equality, ensure the full integration of women in the total development effort", and achieve the "strengthening of world peace", member nations were requested to "ensure the full realisation of the rights of women".[69] What this meant in different nations varied widely, but in Australia it was welcomed as part of the newly elected Whitlam government's commitment to human rights at a domestic and international level. Such hopes however clashed with the dominant rights claims of the period, those of the third-world developmentalist state.[70] The now largely forgotten Charter of Economic Rights and Duties of States (1974) and calls for a New International Economic Order (NIEO), reflecting at least in part the needs of third-world populations like Indigenous Australians, leant International Women's Year a somewhat obscure phraseology.[71] Rhetoric of "integrating" women into the development project is indicative of how much those crafting the UN's rights program and activities viewed the individual as a potential resource or roadblock in the way of the national, masculinised right to development.[72]

While remarkably distinct in content, Reid's contribution must be seen within a longer traditional of Australian women abroad. The internationalism and experimentation of the first-wave feminists, who distrusted national formations as opposed to international or local ones, gave way from the 1920s onwards to a peculiar reverence for the importance and growth of the individual nation.[73] The Women's Charter Movement, first convened in 1943, drew up a list of demands reflecting its national focus: women "as citizen, mother, home maker, wage earner [and] member of the services". The 1946 Conference established official links between the

---

[68] On CEDAW's long germination and contested implementation, see Susanne Zwingel, *Translating International Women's Rights: The CEDAW Convention in Context* (Basingstoke: Palgrave Macmillan, 2016).

[69] General Assembly Resolution 3010, *International Women's Year*, A/RES/3010(XXVII), 18 December 1972, available at www.un.org/en/ga/search/view_doc.asp?symbol=A/RES/3010(XXVII).

[70] Burke, "From Individual Rights to National Development".

[71] General Assembly Resolution 1514, *Declaration on the Granting of Independence to Colonial Countries and Peoples*, A/RES/1514(XV), 14 December 1960, available at www.un.org/en/decolonization/declaration.shtml; General Assembly Resolution 29/3281, Charter of the Economic Rights and Duties of States, A/RES/29/3281, 12 December 1974, available at www.un-documents.net/a29r3281.htm. On the NIEO, see Nils Gilman, "The New International Economic Order: A Reintroduction", *Humanity* 6, no. 1 (2015), 1–16.

[72] This argument is made in Roland Burke, "Competing for the Last Utopia?: The NIEO, Human Rights, and the World Conference for the International Women's Year, Mexico City, June 1975", *Humanity* 6, no. 1 (2015), 47–61.

[73] James Keating, "'An Utter Absence of National Feeling': Australian Women and the International Suffrage Movement, 1900–14', *Australian Historical Studies* 47, no. 3 (2016), 462–81.

Australian movement and the newly established CSW, the foundation of which Australian Jessie Street had played a not-insignificant part in, but this was less about international solidarity as it was about using the organisation's commitment to the "principle of equality as between men and women" to effect national change. Women wished to share in the spoils that the nationally delimited postwar order promised to bring.[74] Reid's experience places her firmly within this legacy of a feminism that embraced internationalism while remaining closely tethered to the growth of the state as a rights-giving organisation. Her intimate involvement in Australian government during the 1970s, however, also contested the limitations of such a practice. Reid's appointment as adviser to Labor Prime Minister Gough Whitlam on women's affairs in 1973, a position she held until late 1975, was the first such appointment in the world.

Described in one profile as "tall, lithe, with light brown hair and facts at her fingertips", Reid had travelled widely, separated from her husband and occupied the position of senior tutor at the Australian National University.[75] The first of those sometimes condescendingly dubbed "femocrats", Reid's work was guided by a focus on changing archaic legislation on issues like equal pay and ensuring access to child care that she shared with earlier generations of feminists. What differentiated her practice were more culturally attuned positions such as "end[ing] the invisibility of women" and changing "basic attitudes towards women in our society".[76] It was through this last demand, the changing of attitudes, that Reid's and the broader movement's ideas broke with those articulated in the Women's Charter movement. The WLM began emerging in Australia in 1969, drawing inspiration from overseas, in particular the USA. While varying in their form of politics, one view the movement shared was that not just political or economic but also cultural change was necessary.[77] Reid explained in a 1975 interview: "Much can be done by enlightened legislation. But you can't legislate away entrenched attitudes. You may get equal pay, but it won't mean equal opportunities, until those attitudes are changed."[78]

---

[74] Marilyn Lake, *Getting Equal: The History of Australian Feminism* (Sydney: Allen & Unwin, 1999), 193–4.

[75] *Canberra Times*, 9 April 1973, 1.

[76] Elizabeth Reid, "Creating a Policy for Women", in *The Whitlam Phenomenon: Fabian Papers*, Australian Fabian Society (Melbourne: McPhee Gribble/Penguin Books, 1986), 145–9. On femocrats, see in particular Hester Eisenstein, *Inside Agitators: Australian Femocrats and the State* (Sydney: Allen & Unwin, 1996).

[77] Lake, 254–6.

[78] Kay Keavney, "There Ought to Be a Lot of Joy in a Special Year for Women", *The Australian Women's Weekly*, 12 March 1975, 5.

136   Whose Rights?

While the WLM saw it as a continuation of a long struggle, IWY appeared to Whitlam as an opportunity to present Australia's newly rediscovered human rights credentials. Whitlam, whose father had worked closely with H. V. Evatt during marathon drafting sessions for the UDHR in 1947–8, argued for the need to invest significantly in IWY, to the tune of some $2 million in the first six months alone. The year "presents us with the opportunity to focus on women in our society, [to] consolidate improvements already achieved and to enable Australia to become once again a pacesetter for the rest of the world in advancing basic human rights". This is consistent with what scholars locate as the ALP's understanding of Australia as an independent middle power, capable of acting as a facilitator in discussions between the developed and the developing worlds – something the increasing assertiveness of third-world states problematized.[79] The state development ethos Whitlam brought to this project was made clear when he noted: "If we are to properly utilise our human resources, ensure basic human rights and improve the quality of our lives we must release the energy and develop the talents of all of our population."[80] Whitlam quickly moved to establish a National Advisory Committee (NAC) to facilitate Australia's implementation of IWY, headed by Reid. The NAC's task was to "ensur[e] that women enjoy the dignity of basic human rights, that they are integrated into society, and that there is a recognition of the importance of their contribution to society".[81] How different members of the NAC imagined their wide scope taking concrete form, however, proved controversial.

The NAC was made up of ten women assisted by two male bureaucrats. The assembled women expressed diverse views regarding their understanding of the year's scope and proposed activities. Maria Pozos, a migrant women's leader from Victoria, thought a main activity should be the education of women from non–English-speaking backgrounds, while Jeanette Hungarford from Queensland believed women's experience of health care was vital. Ruth Ross, president of the Australian Association of Business and Professional Women's Clubs, saw IWY as an opportunity to "clear away those obstacles that obstruct women from doing what they really want to do".[82] What exactly women wanted to do

---

[79] See, in particular, Carl Ungerer, "The 'Middle Power' Concept in Australian Foreign Policy", *Australian Journal of Politics and History* 53, no. 4 (December 2007), 538–51; David Lee and Christopher Waters (eds.), *Evatt to Evans: The Labor tradition in Australian Foreign Policy* (St Leonards, NSW: Allen & Unwin, 1997).

[80] "FOR CABINET: International Women's Year 1975", ERP, MS 9262, Box 32, Folder 13, NLA.

[81] Ibid., 2.

[82] "Notes on comments made by Jeanette Hungarford, Queensland, Occupational Therapist", 20 August 1974, NAA: A4223, W/NAC 1; "Notes on comments made by

"Women Are a Colonised Sex"

was of no concern to Ross: if women wished to be housewives "they should be able to do so without incurring pity or criticism", while if an appropriately credentialed woman wished to be a CEO "she should be able to be appointed to that position".[83] These ideas very much represented one particular strand of Australian feminism: a wish for instrumental, piecemeal reform culminating in formal equality with men. Owing to the "geographic dispersal of the members", Reid and the small IWY Secretariat she headed were given discretion to set the tone of the year via press releases and other announcements, and they used this position to argue that equalitarian feminism did not go far enough. Instead, it was necessary to challenge the patterns of behaviour and ideological structures that enforced women's disempowerment, a complex web the activists came to call "sexism". First coined in the United States in the late 1960s, the term "sexism" was soon widely used across North America to describe, as one populariser put it, someone "who proclaims or justifies or assumes the supremacy of one sex over the other".[84] Shirley Castley – feminist, bureaucrat and leading participant alongside Reid in Australia's IWY activities, defined the term similarly in one of the NAC's major publications: "Sexism ... describes a set of assumptions about the world, which are then imposed on the world."[85] Inculcated from birth, when a person is defined as a male or female based on their physical attributes alone, sexism "divides up all the qualities a human being has, or potentially has, and says that women should have and be valued for half of these qualities".[86] Breaking with the ideas of earlier generations, Castley wrote firmly in a NAC newsletter that "equality is not the answer so long as our society remains sexist. Equality would mean women becoming more like men. What is needed is for people to become more like human beings."[87]

The many groups that participated in IWY far from universally supported the line Reid and her WLM colleagues articulated. On the one hand, Sydney Women's Liberation received funding for work on its Rape Crisis Centre, and numerous conferences and seminars were held alongside various art, film and documentary projects, including the film *Caddie*,

---

Ms Maria Pozos, who is active amongst migrant women in Melbourne", 20 August 1974, NAA: A4223, W/NAC 1.

[83] Ruth W. Ross, "Australian Federation of Business and Professional Women's Clubs Proposed Programme for International Women's Year", NAA: A4223, W/NAC 1.

[84] Fred R. Shapiro, "Historical Notes on the Vocabulary of the Women's Movement", *American Speech* 60, no. 1 (1985), 7.

[85] Shirley Castley, "Sexism: Introductory Remarks", in *Women in Australian Society: Analyses and Situations* (Canberra: Australian National Advisory Committee for International Women's Year, 1975), 5; emphasis in original.

[86] Ibid., 7.   [87] Ibid., 8.

138   Whose Rights?

the first of Australia's "new wave" late-1970s cinema.[88] On the other hand, the women of Bland Shire, New South Wales, received IWY funding to hold a forum discussing "Women on the Land", venerating the family unit and arguing that rural women "in nearly every instance accept their responsibilities as a wife and a mother, and are equal partners in the business of living".[89] The Tasmanian IWY committee, under the auspices of the UNAA, made more overt criticisms of the NAC's line, arguing that "women do not want to 'take over', but wish to preserve their feminine attributes and qualities, but with equal opportunities to choose their own life-style – to be part of the total world".[90] The Tasmanian committee's closing report labelled IWY a "controversial" year, the "constructive side" of which was lost in the "radical, aggressive and sensational aspects". "Two sets of aims for the year" – the Australian government's and the UN's – were at odds, the Tasmanian Committee claimed. The year in particular was "fail[ing] in putting across the UN aim of promoting equality between men and women", what they defined as "equality of opportunity in responsible partnership". Echoing negative, often virulent and condescending media coverage, the Tasmanian committee charged Reid as championing "women wanting to reverse the discrimination and make it a woman's world".[91] It is clear that, for some, reinforcing rather than questioning complimentary gender roles was the order of the day. Lawyer Naida Haxton put this differently in a speech at a United Nations Association of Australia forum in Sydney: "so-called women's liberationists" should remember that "no one was ever endowed with a right without being saddled with a responsibility".[92]

Such cleavages between radicals and reformers were equally on display in Mexico City. Work towards the IWY conference was somewhat ad hoc. As Reid, attending a preparatory meeting for the conference in New York, wrote to Whitlam in November 1974, "planning for the conference ... was a chaotic last minute mess". Still, she was able to convince Whitlam to have her appointed to the year's Executive Committee, which met in

---

[88] Eisenstein, *Inside Agitators*, 25–7.

[89] Beryl Ingold, "The Status of Women on the Land in New South Wales", Report of Bland Shire International Women's Year Seminar, Saturday, 5 July 1975 (West Wyalong, NSW: Advocate Publishing, 1975), 12.

[90] Joyce Dulfer-Hyams, "Tasmanian State Committee International Women's Year – IWY Assessment and Consolidation Report", August 1975, ERP, MS 9262, Box 31, Folder 7a, NLA.

[91] *Report of the National Committee for International Women's Year* (Sydney: United Nations Association of Australia, 1975), 28–9. On negative media coverage of the year, see Eisenstein, 25–7.

[92] Naida Haxton, "Recognition of the responsibilities of equality", Unpublished Paper, 22 March 1975, Ruby Rich Papers, MS 7493, Box 31, NLA. Thanks to Emma Sarian for drawing this source to my attention.

"Women Are a Colonised Sex"

February 1975. The focus of this committee, aside from behind-closed-doors discussions on the World Plan of Action that would be voted on in Mexico City, was a public, eighteen-member panel discussion on the topic of "Women and Men – the next 25 years", on which Reid spoke. The Australian highlighted how the UN's governing rhetoric of decolonisation and development excluded women. In a sign of how much ideas of colonialism and development had gained global currency, Reid protested that "[w]omen are the oldest colonial and under developed group in the world", insisting that dominant discourses of development would do little for women "unless, simultaneously, a genuine effect is made to change ... attitudes".[93] As well as economic development or legal equality, Reid argued that the Mexico conference should focus on the "social attitudes ... society's prejudices, myths and beliefs" – sexism, although at least at this preparatory gathering, the word was not used. "Notions such as the breadwinner and the homemaker ... the dichotomy between the public and the private, work and the home, between the personal and the political" needed to be the central focus of the World Plan of Action.[94] While McGinness and others saw Indigenous economic empowerment as a prerequisite for the enjoyment of rights, the WLM found talk of development and economic improvement to be an impediment to and distraction from real discussion of women's place in society.

Development, Reid argued based on her experience of its outcomes in Australia, "went hand in hand with the Westernisation of peoples of other cultures ... a further form of colonialism from which women in particular are forced to suffer – cultural colonialism".[95] Australian media reported Reid's contribution as a success, with *The Australian Women's Weekly* declaring that her "articulate contribution" to the Committee made the world aware that "Australia is doing more ... than any other industrialised nation" to secure IWY's aims.[96] Reid was much more circumspect in her assessment, returning to Australia to bemoan the year's World Plan of Action, which remained "very disappointing in its insensitivities to the problems of women in the developing world".[97] The Department of Foreign Affairs concurred, describing the draft as "lengthy, verbose and poor in style", noting that despite Reid's "helpful but inadequate attempts to come to grips with the document", it still ran to an unwieldly 150 paragraphs.[98] Foreign Affairs

[93] "Inward Cablegram", 11 March 1975, ERP, MS 9262, Box 1, Folder 7, NLA, 2–3.
[94] Ibid., 8.   [95] Ibid., 3–4.
[96] Phillipa Day Benson, "Australia Wins", *The Australian Women's Weekly*, 16 April 1975, 4.
[97] Minutes of meeting, 11 April 1975, ERP, MS 9262, Box 32, Folder 15.
[98] "Overall Approach of the Australian Delegation", ERP, MS 9262, Box 41, Folder 72, NLA. The Department of External Affairs was renamed the Department of Foreign Affairs in November 1970.

140   Whose Rights?

bureaucrats prepared a lengthy booklet for Australia's Mexico City delegation to ensure they had maximum chance of success in their dual task of representing Australia's women and its economic interests. Despite hopes of working as a "bridge" between the developed and developing worlds, Australia's position as a white settler colonial state placed it at a distance from other resource export–based economies. This is made particularly clear in the DFA's guidance of the representatives to "head off moves ... to inject extraneous political and economic issues" such as those of the global south seeking economic equality via the NIEO. Instead, the Australians were instructed to "promote fundamental human rights in terms of womens' [sic] dignity and their right to have the major say in determining their part in the ... community".[99]

Australia sent ten representatives – a mixture of feminist activists such as Castley, Susan Ryan and Sara Dowse, women's activist (and Gough Whitlam's wife) Margaret Whitlam and foreign affairs bureaucrats – to the IWY main sessions and another ten to the unofficial "Tribune". Extending on a new initiative at the 1974 Bucharest conference on World Population, the IWY's Tribune made it the first UN gathering truly opened to non-government organisations (NGOs) and independent activists. The Australians made a point of speaking not of their own national achievements but to (what they imaged as) the needs of the world's poorest women. As Reid summarised in a later report: "The delegates did not emphasise the problems and achievements of Australasian women in isolation, but related them to those needs that all women have in common ... in short, for freedom from sexism."[100] Yet such communion was problematised by organisation and geography, not to mention food poisoning effecting "some of every delegation all of the time", conspiring to make proceedings cumbersome and hinder any positive dialogue.[101] Reid was still able to play a larger-than-life role in the gathering, described in one American report as "one of the most outspoken feminists at the official UN conference".[102] Her major speech at the Conference's third plenary sparked significant interest. Reid told

---

[99] Ibid.

[100] Australian National Advisory Committee, International Women's Year, *International Women's Year Conference, Mexico City 1975* (Canberra: Government Printer, 1975).

[101] Quoted in Burke, "Competing for the Last Utopia", 51. For more on the conference, see Jocelyn Olcott, "Cold War Conflicts and Cheap Cabaret: Sexual Politics at the 1975 United Nations International Women's Year Conference", *Gender and History* 22, no. 3 (2010): 733–54; Jocelyn Olcott, *International Women's Year: The Greatest Consciousness-Raising Event in History* (Oxford: Oxford University Press, 2017); Ghodsee, "Revisiting the United Nations Decade for Women".

[102] Helena Papanek, "The Work of Women: Postscript from Mexico City", *Signs: The Journal of Women in Culture and Society* 1, no. 1 (1975), 217.

"Women Are a Colonised Sex" 141

the assembled delegations that "[t]he basis of racism, racial discrimination, alien domination and the taking of territories by force is similar to the basis of the violence against women which we call sexism".[103] The strong if unsuccessful push from the Australians to have sexism included in the final conference documents reflects both the deep impact that understandings of racism, particularly as experienced by African Americans, had on the second-wave feminist movement's ideas and the delegation's desire to blunt the edges of the dominant statist reading of development and rights.[104]

While acknowledging that "economic rights are as important if not more so than political ones" for women and that, consequently, "the demand for a new international economic order is far from a peripheral issue", Reid critiqued the conference's developmentalist agenda and sought to keep proceedings focused on the needs of women. Yet, Reid tempered her rhetoric, no longer rejecting development outright but instead championing a more women-attuned version. "Women must not only not be forgotten" in striving for a just global economic order or risk becoming a matter of "vague exhortations, insincere rhetoric and token gestures", Reid insisted, but "their present oppression and subjugation must be recognised and steps taken to correct them".[105] The Australians tried to use their experiences to argue for a universal position, that the discourse of development demanded by Western and now developing powers – "productivity and efficiency at any cost" – must not "make the personal a female trait and then deprive women of ... economic and political power" as had been Reid's experience in Australia. This was not the only way, Reid said; instead, "new and culturally appropriate concepts of development" that acknowledge "the specific problems and experiences of women ... including the poorest and least articulate" must be employed.[106]

After the conference, it was remarked that Reid's contribution in particular had put Australia on the map. *The Australian Women's Weekly* happily reported that while representatives of other nations "trumpeted national achievements – real or imagined", Reid had "time and again ... brought the issues back to women", proving a vital and near solo voice against the perceived developmentalist tide. The world was now "looking

---

[103] "Statement by the Leader of the Australian Delegation – Ms Elizabeth Reid", 21 June 1975.
[104] On the interrelationship between women's liberation and racism, the key text is Sarah Evans, *Personal Politics: The Roots of Women's Liberation in the Civil Rights Movement and the New Left* (New York: Vintage Books, 1980).
[105] "Statement by the Leader of the Australian Delegation – Ms Elizabeth Reid", 21 June 1975.
[106] Ibid.

142   Whose Rights?

to Australia for a lead in women's politics", the *Women's Weekly* claimed.[107] The delegation itself was far from effusive on the conference's success, and that of the year itself, in their closing report. While changes in "deep-seated attitudes in a community will inevitably be gradual and cannot be assessed in the short term", the year was judged a success owing to the funding of some 700 different feminist projects. Despite often derogatory and dismissive media commentary, "the scope and variety of activities which took place in virtually all community and governmental organisations as a direct result of the declaration of International Women's Year requires no elaboration".[108] Of their attempts to globalise Australia's campaign, Reid and the NAC were more circumspect, looking askance at their position as Australians abroad. A *New York Times* report on the conference quoted Reid as adopting a "pessimistic" tone, fearing the World Plan of Action she had fought desperately to change would "wind up in the bottom draw of government", leading only to "token gestures [and] hollow promises".[109]

The NAC noted that while "recent advances made in Australia on the status of women are widely recognised and Australia is looked to as a global leader", the delegates "had a great deal to learn from women of other countries". In particular, Reid's report on the conference outcomes noted a strong divide between "women from the Third World [who] tended to discuss the physical conditions of their lives, whereas those from 'developed' countries were pre-occupied by social attitudes and relationships".[110] While Reid's carefully worded sentiments of the centrality of a human-focused development had sought to bridge these opposing perspectives, her discomfort at being a first-world feminist abroad is palpable. A sign of Reid's disillusionment was her decision to leave Whitlam's services in October of 1975, as the ALP government careened from crisis to crisis in its last months, taking on a role in Iran as head of the UN-affiliated Asia and Pacific Centre for Women and Development.[111] Reid's experiences of women from the third- and non-

---

[107] Phillipa Day Benson, "Looking to Australia for a Lead on Women's Policies", *The Australian Women's Weekly*, 30 July 1975, 4–5.

[108] *International Women's Year: Report of the Australian National Advisory Committee*, Parliamentary Paper no. 201/1976 (Canberra: Government Printer, 1976).

[109] Judy Klemesrud, "A Plan to Improve Status of Women Approved at Parley", *New York Times*, 3 July 1975, 59.

[110] Australian National Advisory Committee International Women's Year, *International Women's Year Conference, Mexico City 1975* (Canberra: Government Printer, 1975).

[111] Christine Osborne, "Fighting for Basic Women's Rights in Iran's Male-Dominated Society", *The Australian Women's Weekly*, 31 August 1977, 51–2. On Reid's time in Iran, see Roland Burke, "'My Work Does Not Wait for Revolutions': Elizabeth Reid and the Possibilities of State Feminism in Iran", in Joy Damousi and Judith Smart (eds.), *Contesting Australian History: Essays in Honour of Marilyn Lake* (Clayton, VIC: Monash University Press, 2019), 80–93.

The Backlash: Right to Life

aligned world seemed to have fostered an acknowledgement that the process of decolonisation made the white metropole just one of the world's political and intellectual centres.[112] Other members of the delegation were to go on to have significant roles in constructing the human rights state, to be discussed further in the next chapter. Susan Ryan, in particular, played a significant role in bringing Australia into line with the CEDAW via the *Sex Discrimination Act 1983*, administered by the recently established Human Rights Commission.[113] As both the Indigenous and women's movements adopted different, conflicting perspectives on human rights that both transcended ideas of equality and aligned with their emerging worldviews, conservatives sought to introduce a new rights-bearing entity to public discussion: the unborn child.

The Backlash: Right to Life

Pope Paul VI received a welcome reception to Australia in November 1970. In the first papal visit to the Eastern Asian region, the pontiff conducted mass at the Royal Randwick Racecourse in Sydney before a crowd of some 150,000 people, instructing the assembled to "denounce un-Christian attitudes in today's 'permissive society'".[114] Having replaced Pope John XXIII in 1963, Paul VI closed the Second Vatican Council and oversaw a conservative turn in the Church, culminating in the significant 1968 encyclical *Humanae Vitae*. This statement reaffirmed the pro-natalist foundations of Church dogma, which had been challenged by the rise of the Pill and the global questioning of papal authority. The trip was welcomed as evidence of a "new style" – communicative and consultative rather than authoritarian – while *The Australian Women's Weekly* reported on the pontiff's sumptuous accommodations and lavish gifts.[115] Such reportage belied significant ructions within the Church. *Humanae Vitae* proved deeply divisive amongst Australian Catholics, as it did globally. While the hierarchy affirmed the encyclical as an "authentic and authoritative document" and conservatives were "pleased that the Pope had made a stand against modern materialism and the demand for

---

[112] See Tracey Banivanua Mar, *Decolonisaiton and the Pacific: Indigenous Globalisation and the Ends of Empire* (Cambridge: Cambridge University Press, 2016), chapter 6, for an exploration of how decolonisation cemented new networks of non-metropolitan communication and activism.

[113] *The Canberra Times*, 30 November 1983, 2.

[114] *The Canberra Times*, 3 December 1970, 1. A total of 400,000 people, or roughly one in seven residents of Sydney, attended one of the pope's masses on his three-day visit.

[115] *The Canberra Times*, 25 June 1970, 13; "Where the Pope Will Stay", *The Australian Women's Weekly*, 30 September 1970, 34–5.

144   Whose Rights?

self-fulfillment", many lay Catholics rebelled. Catholic university groups called meetings to protest it, several priests were ousted for decrying it while many Catholic families simply ignored it: at the time of the Pope's visit, 58 per cent of Catholics were found to disagree with the pontiff's proclamation.[116] Anglican Archbishop of Sydney Marcus L. Loane warned that the pope's visit would "strengthen conservatism" in the Church and threaten the ecumenical movement that had flourished throughout the 1960s.[117] One man was ejected from a town hall meeting for wearing a protest sign challenging the pope's authority, while the communist paper *Tribune* – where progressive religious activism and Christian-Marxist dialogue was regularly reported – labelled him the "world's biggest shareholder" and condemned the need to set aside public hospital beds for "casualties expected during [his] appearance".[118] Warnings of a growing conservatism seem to have been prescient. Over the next eighteen months, groups of Australians drawing on both the pope's encyclical and the array of ideas associated globally with the "backlash" movement began forming chapters of a new political organi-sation – Right to Life.

The idea of a particular "right to life" has a long history. The American Declaration of Independence proclaimed the "unalienable rights" of "life, liberty and the pursuit of happiness", and Article 3 of the UDHR declared, "Everyone has the right to life, liberty and security of the person". The exact meaning of that term "life" was subject to significant debate in the drafting process and remained unsettled. The Catholic hierarchy made life one of the fundamental human rights spelt out in the 1940 Social Justice Statement, drawing on centuries of the term's usage in Catholic scripture, though with various focuses. Equally, pacif-ists and conscientious objectors such as Bill White made use of a "right to live" to justify their non-compliance with national service for the Vietnam war, many of whom were influenced by liberalised Catholic social teach-ings of the early 1960s.[119] For the campaigners that occupy this section, the right to life was overlaid with that of the child, particularly as articu-lated in the Declaration of the Rights of the Child (1959), which did not gain the status of Covenant until 1989. Originally produced by the League of Nations in 1924, often considered the first international

[116] David Hilliard, "The Religious Crisis of the 1960s: The Experience of the Australian Churches", *The Journal of Religious History* 21, no. 2 (1997), 218–19. For more on the global response to *Humanae Vitae*, see Alana Harris (ed.), *The Schism of '68: Catholicism, Contraception and Humanae Vitae in Europe, 1945–1975* (Basingstoke: Palgrave Macmillan, 2018).

[117] *The Canberra Times*, 1 October 1970, 13.

[118] *Tribune*, 18 November 1970, 1; *Tribune*, 2 December 1970, 9.

[119] See Chapter 1 and Chapter 3 of this volume, respectively.

The Backlash: Right to Life   145

human rights instrument ever adopted, the Declaration's rearticulation and adoption by the United Nations in the 1950s demonstrated not unified commitment but "a careful fabric of compromises and unresolved moral issues", in the words of one observer.[120] Its wording, that "every child without any exception whatsoever shall be entitled to these rights" and that such "special protection" should "enable him to develop physically, mentally, morally, spiritual and socially in a healthy and normal manner and in conditions of freedom and dignity", left the question of who a child was unexamined amidst the verbiage.[121] Such lack of clarity was only furthered by the Declaration's preambular reference to the need to protect the child both before and after birth, though this wording was dropped from the draft Covenant. This vagueness, coupled with the lack of consultation beyond a few hand-picked NGOs, produced a consensual document but also created a "gap between legislation and social reality" that ensured popularising the Declaration around the world "achieved limited success".[122] While early drafting processes received some coverage in the Australian press, the Declaration's adoption was almost entirely ignored.

The emergence of abortion as a significant political issue in Australia saw the "rights of the child" enter public discourse in a new, pronounced way. While neither the Women's Charters of 1943 or 1946 included a demand for access to birth control or abortion, plans by the New South Wales government to ban the advertisement of birth control in 1946 "forced feminists into articulating a new right, not to contraception as it happened, but the 'right to free enquiry into and free discussion of a vitally important social question'".[123] Abortion was an undeniable fact in Australia – it is estimated that between one in three to four pregnancies were terminated by illegally operating doctors or "backyard abortionists" in the 1930s – yet cases were rarely prosecuted and convictions even less common.[124] Only eleven women were convicted in 1960 out of an estimated total of some 90,000 abortions across New South Wales, and such low figures seem to have made activists largely silent on decriminalisation.[125] Indeed, as Barbara Baird argues, the figure of the unsafe, dangerous backyard

---

[120] Zoe Moody, "Transnational Treaties on Children's Rights: Norm Building and Circulation in the Twentieth Century", *Paedagogica Historica* 50, no. 1–2 (2014), 163.

[121] General Assembly Resolution 1386, *Declaration of the Rights of the Child*, A/RES/14/1386 (XIV), 20 November 1959, available at www.ohchr.org/EN/Issues/Education/Training/Compilation/Pages/1DeclarationoftheRightsoftheChild(1959).aspx.

[122] Moody, "Transnational Treaties on Children's Rights", 164.

[123] Lake, *Getting Equal*, 200–1.

[124] Lisa Featherstone, *Let's Talk about Sex: Histories of Sexuality in Australia* (Newcastle upon Tyne: Cambridge Scholars Publishing, 2011), 150.

[125] *Tharunka* (NSW), 6 July 1964, 2.

146   Whose Rights?

abortionist was a tool for women campaigners in seeking the medicalisation and strengthened professional compliance of the industry.[126] Women's liberation groups, which began emerging in Australia from 1969 onwards, broke with this tradition and made a new demand: for abortion law reform. As "Jenny" put it in a 1972 letter to Melbourne WLM journal *Vashti's Voice*:

> What right has any church or government, or anyone else ... to decide whether or not a woman should have a child. Women have the right to control their own bodies. If we can't decide if and when to have children then we can't decide anything.[127]

Yet, as Emma Sarian highlights, the foundation of the UDHR – based on the premise of the family as the building block of social order – offered little to this new generation of radicals who often rejected that very institution. Instead of seeing society as a kind of organism in the more classical sense of the "social", Sarian writes, there emerged a more cynical view of social relations that saw the reproduction of inequality not as an accident but as an active recreation that resisted being dismantled. While feminists of the 1940s and 1950s venerated the family unit as a funda-mental institution of human society, a member of the WLM described how "the ways in which ... entrenched power is maintained are complex, but certainly the nuclear family is at its base".[128] Thus, the maternal rhetorical tools that women's rights campaigners had effectively employed since the nineteenth century and which had been codified in the UDHR were rejected.

   Britain's 1967 legalisation of abortion up to twenty-eight weeks' gesta-tion – moves towards which were widely reported in Australian from 1965 onwards – soon saw jurisdictions in Australia considering similar moves. Already, there was evidence of a backlash on the question of "rights". Julie Cunliffe wrote to the *Canberra Times* to protest the sentiments of another letter writer, Elizabeth Richardson, that it was an individual's right to "control the size and timing of their families", asking, "[W]ho, in this conflict ... between parents and 'accidental' babies, is the individual?" "The 'rights' of the parents are obvious" to Mrs Richardson, and they "enable them to do away with the life of their unborn child without loss of dignity and responsibility".[129] Such rarely expressed sentiments were only an opening shot, however. In 1969 South Australia became the

---

[126] Barbara Baird, "'The Incompetent, Barbarous Old Lady Round the Corner': The Image of the Backyard Abortionist in Pro-Abortion Politics", *Hecate* 22, no. 1 (1996), 7–26

[127] Quoted in Lake, *Getting Equal*, 223.

[128] Emma Sarian, "Identity Has a History: Rethinking Identity Politics through Historical Discourses of the Self" (PhD Thesis, Macquarie University, 2018), 45–6, 138.

[129] *The Canberra Times*, 10 December 1965, 2; *The Canberra Times*, 4 December 1965, 2.

first jurisdiction to liberalise abortion laws, passing amendments to the Criminal Law Consolidation Act 1935, while in that same year the "Menhennitt ruling" in Victoria established precedent allowing for abortion to occur if such action was considered both "necessary" and "proportionate".[130] The year 1969 was also a federal election year, and the Catholic hierarchy began swinging into action against this new turn towards abortion reform. In March, Catholic Archbishop of Melbourne J. R. Knox warned that abortion would "have a strong influence on the way Catholics voted in the forthcoming election". "[M]orality, human rights and social justice" would be at the core of such decisions, and Knox named the two most pressing issues to be termination of pregnancies and the perennial concern of state aid for Catholic schools.[131] In May, priests gathered in Canberra to discuss a national organisation of anti-abortion societies to pressure government, as "[t]he State existed only to guarantee the individual rights of its members, and therefore it could not legislate away the right to life of unborn children".[132] Such sentiment reflected threads in Catholic social thought present since the 1930s, when human rights became a way of accepting the existence and limiting the authority of the nation-state through acting as a guarantor of the rights that man enjoyed as a product of god. Indeed, when in 1967 the American National Conference of Catholic Bishops took steps to establish a Right to Life movement in America, founding member Fr. James McHugh "encouraged them to cite the UN declaration as evidence that their campaign was a human rights cause that had the imprimatur of the United Nations behind it".[133]

Opposition leader Gough Whitlam made his first public utterance on the issue of abortion in September 1970, in a statement regarding provision for the freedom of conscience in Australia. As he put it, "[t]he Australian community and legislature were becoming increasingly concerned with matters of private morality and conscience" such as "abortion, prostitution and homosexuality", and the "mental suffering of women who wish to terminate pregnancy of an unwanted child warranted reform of the existing law".[134] While Whitlam's modernised ALP had lost the 1969 election, it had won a significant number of seats, and it seemed only a matter of time until a new progressive government was formed.

---

[130] For more on the still-ongoing process of abortion legalisation in Australia, see Gideon Haigh, *The Racket: How Abortion Became Legal in Australia* (Carlton, VIC: Melbourne University Press, 2008).

[131] *The Canberra Times*, 10 March 1969, 3. [132] *The Canberra Times*, 14 May 1967, 9.

[133] Daniel K. Williams, "The Partisan Trajectory of the American Pro-Life Movement: How a Liberal Catholic Campaign Became a Conservative Evangelical Cause", *Religions* 6 (2015), 455.

[134] *The Canberra Times*, 1 September 1970, 3.

148 Whose Rights?

Thomas J. Connelly, professor of moral theology and Vicar of the Religious for NSW, condemned Whitlam's approach in an address to the recently founded Randwick-Coogee Right to Life movement, describing it as an "extra-ordinary statement by a national party leader aspiring to the highest public office".[135] It is clear that Right to Life organisations began emerging in the early 1970s, but the National Right to Life Association did not come into existence until 1973, bringing groups in all states and territories under its umbrella. This action was taken in response to the new government's attempts to pass a Commonwealth bill to legalise abortion, but it also reflected the emergence of a backlash against "rights" politics overseas.

By 1973, the American movement had become an independent, technically non-sectarian national organisation operating as the National Right to Life Convention.[136] That same year saw growing momentum for an Equal Rights Amendment to the US Constitution, as well as the path-breaking decision in Roe v Wade that declared laws criminalising abortion to be constitutionally invalid on privacy grounds, effectively allowing abortion in all first- and some second-trimester cases. Similar legislative conditions and the air of social movement ascendency made conditions in Australia ripe for the emergence of a sister organisation – indeed reflections of Right to Life activists themselves attest to the centrality of American developments.[137] One edition of the South Australian branch newsletter declared that the tactics of the American movement "are a good example to follow", while American guests were regular fixtures at conferences and meetings.[138] This was not the limit of their global connections, however. Daniel Overduin, well-known Lutheran pastor, bioethicist, orator and editor of the Right to Life South Australia branch's newsletter, travelled to the UN Population Congress in Bulgaria in 1974, which he claimed to be well attended by anti-abortion activists. In a lengthy report to members, Overduin lamented that "[i]t was frightening to realise that in the heart of a communist country representatives of the so-called 'free' world were advocating dehumanising policies under

---

[135] *The Canberra Times*, 20 October 1970, 3.

[136] On the American right-to-life movement, see Williams, "The Partisan Trajectory of the American Pro-Life Movement"; Prudence Flowers, "Fighting the 'Hurricane Winds' of Abortion Liberalization: Americans United for Life and the Struggle for Self-Definition before *Roe v. Wade*", *The Sixties: A Journal of History, Politics and Culture* 11, no. 2 (2018), 131–55; Gillian Frank, "The Colour of the Unborn: Anti-Abortion and Anti-Busing Politics in Michigan, United States, 1967–1973" *Gender and History* 26, no. 2 (2014), 351–78.

[137] Joclyn Hedley, "'On the Side of the Saints': A History of the Sydney Catholic Pro-life Organisation Family Life International with Reference to Identity Formation" (PhD Thesis, University of Notre Dame, Sydney, 2017), chapter 2.

[138] *Right to Life* [South Australia] 2, no. 2 (November/December 1974), 5.

The Backlash: Right to Life   149

a Joseph's cloak dipped in the blood of the innocent". That socialist and "free" societies supported abortion and other forms of contraception "as legitimate measures of population control" unsettled Overduin: "with a mind influenced by Alexander Solzhenitsyn's *The Gulag Archipelago*, I could only reflect on the hidden realities of suffering . . . caused by regimes which do not tolerate the individual's freedom to act in accordance with his or her own conscience".[139] References to the newly famous Soviet writer, whose work proved popular in Australia and is now read as a significant signpost in the making of 1970s human rights politics, shows anti-abortion activists seeking to ride the emerging movement's coattails.[140]

The power of the individual's conscientious objection, similar to the anti-conscription campaign that had wound up with Whitlam's 1972 election, proved a powerful tool. The Australian Capital Territory (ACT) Right to Life Group's submission to the 1974–7 Royal Commission into Human Relationships (RCHR), for example, quoted a statement of the Royal Australian Nursing Federation which noted such practitioners "have a right to refuse to participate in medical or surgical procedures to which they have a conscientious objection".[141] They also shared a similar form of politics: the raising of individual rights issues – of an unborn child, in this instance – through the medium of letters from concerned individuals, a tactic of course pioneered by Amnesty International.[142] Indeed, as Daniel K. Williams points out, the American movement on which the Australians modelled themselves began as a corollary of the anti-war and civil rights movement and emerged from the same liberal Catholic influences as Amnesty International had. The newsletters of the Australian movement also carried articles opposing euthanasia, nuclear testing and uranium mining in their early years. When the ALP sought passage of a bill legalising abortion in the Australian Capital Territory and the Northern Territory, the only two jurisdictions subject to Commonwealth law on the matter, in 1973 "all members of the parliament were deluged with material for and against the bill, with the bulk of it emanating from the opponents and, notably, from the National Right to

---

[139] Pastor Daniel Ch. Overduin, "Population Tribune – Bucharest – August, 1974", *Right to Life* [South Australia] 3, no. 1 (October 1974), 1–3.

[140] For more on the global impacts of Solzhenitsyn's writings, see Sarah B. Snyder, *Human Rights Activism and the End of the Cold War: A Transnational History of the Helsinki Network* (Cambridge: Cambridge University Press, 2011).

[141] ACT Right to Life Association, *Submission to the Royal Commission on Human Relationships, February 1976* (ACT: self-published, 1976), 8.

[142] On the politics of Amnesty's letter-writing campaigns, see, for example, Vannessa Hearman, "Letter-Writing and Transnational Activism on Behalf of Indonesian Political Prisoners: Gatot Lestario and his Legacy", *Critical Asian Studies* 48, no. 2 (2016), 145–67.

150   Whose Rights?

Life Association".[143] As the Victorian Branch newsletter put it in 1973, "almost every member wrote to their Federal representative" to oppose what was known as the McKenzie-Lamb Bill – something which was "a task for every right to life member".[144] The NRLA also made significant use of petitions, some 407 all up, in opposition to the Bill, with over 200 nearly carbon-copy petitions submitted on a single day.

The Bill was defeated in parliament after a conscience vote; however, in the end a nebulously defined Royal Commission was proposed – initially into "Abortion" specifically, then broadened to "Male-Female" and finally – in line with the emerging critique of the WLM and organisations like Gay Liberation, simply "Human Relationships". Michelle Arrow has written widely on how the commission became a forum for articulating new forms of sexual citizenship, of breaking the gender and sexual compact that constructed white, straight men as the normalised Australian. "[G]round-breaking in its scale and scope and its acceptance of women's reproductive autonomy", Arrow writes, the RCHR also acknowledged "the ways that this troubled the boundary between public and private".[145] Right to Life members sought to utilise horrific images of what were claimed to be aborted foetuses to secure this very distinction; the rights of the unborn needed protection from the secular state through legal frameworks. One leaflet carried an image of a pregnancy ultrasound scan, emblazoned with the words "It's asking how to write 'Human Rights'".[146] This merging of humanitarian imagery with the legalistic political language of human rights seem to augur as well the increasing merging of these two phenomena during the decade and into the 1990s.[147]

The RCHR received over 1,300 written submissions, and transcripts of its oral testimony ran to some 4,000 pages. The family was at the centre of the conservative intervention, with the ACT Right to Life submission quoting well-known social-conservative Clair Isbister to the effect that "the rights of men, women and children" were best respected in the "stable family unit". Isbister shared with the UDHR an understanding that the hetero-normative family was the building block of society, and there existed "responsibilities of individuals, groups . . . and governments

---

[143] Ian Hancock, *John Gorton: He Did It His Way* (Sydney, NSW: Hatchett Press, 2002), 368.

[144] *Right to Life* [Victoria] 1, no. 3 (October–November 1973), 1.

[145] Michell Arrow, "'Everyone Needs a Holiday from Work, Why Not Mothers?' Motherhood, Feminism and Citizenship at the Australian Royal Commission on Human Relationships, 1974–1977", *Women's History Review* 25, no. 2 (2016), 320–36.

[146] "It's Asking How to Write 'Human Rights'", undated, University of Queensland Pro-Life Club, FVF449, Fryer Library, The University of Queensland.

[147] On this, see, in particular, Michael Barnett, *Empire of Humanity: A History of Humanitarianism* (Ithaca, NY: Cornell University Press, 2011), chapter 10.

Conclusion 151

to create and preserve this type of family".[148] The New South Wales Right to Life Association drew on the 1959 Declaration: "the unborn child has a fundamental right to life", "an absolute right on which all other rights depend".[149] The RCHR's final report, released in April 1977 after having its period of inquiry shortened by the incoming Liberal government of Malcolm Fraser, ran to some six volumes. The commissioners upheld many more of the concerns of the decade's "liberation" movements than those of their conservative enemies and did so by critiquing conceptions of universal rights. Contrasting the "right to life" with a "right to be wanted", the commissioners concluded that "in our view the abortion issue cannot be resolved by reference to a category of legal rights such as the right to be born", for "[t]he assertion of any right has to be considered in the light of other competing or conflict rights", after all, "legal rights attach to legal persons and an unborn child has no legal personality".[150] While seemingly definitive, rearticulations of rights language to reflect and protect the human-ness of the unborn were to grow and become even more politically challenging in the 1980s.

Conclusion

When participants arrived at the Canberra venue of August 1975's Women and Politics conference – a signal event of IWY organised in conjunction with the United Nations and attended by women from all over the globe – they were confronted by small but vocal group of Indigenous women demonstrators. Condemning ideas of gender equality as "at best an abstraction", the leaflet that these women distributed offered a trenchant critique of the "elitist and bureaucratic" machinations that had excluded Indigenous voices from the gathering. "We will not be divided", the protesters declared, "because we know that the real enemy is racism", to which the demands of "liberation" from white middle-class women ran a distant second. Their leaflet concluded with two key demands:

We want CONSULTATION – not LIBERATION
We want RECOGNITION – not DISCRIMINATION.[151]

---

[148] ACT Right to Life Association, *Submission to the Royal Commission on Human Relationships*, 3.

[149] Elizabeth Evatt, Felix Arnott and Anne Deveson, *Royal Commission on Human Relationships, Final Report, vol. 3* (Canberra: Australian Government Publishing Service, 1977), 149–50.

[150] Ibid., 150.

[151] "Why Are We Demonstrating Here Today", undated, ERP, MS 9262, Box 38, Folder 51, NLA.

152   Whose Rights?

In the 1970s, more Australians were talking about a wider array of rights than ever before. While activists of previous decades had upheld a fairly restrictive reading of rights – the legacy of British birthright had furnished them a gradualist, equalitarian visions of political change – a new generation of militant Indigenous activists and young women saw the need for new or reimagined conceptions. An absence of racial discrimination within law proved dramatically insufficient for Indigenous radicals who, buoyed and subsequently disappointed by the remarkable referendum victory of May 1967, were soon petitioning the UN over structural and endemic economic and cultural rights infringements. Reflecting dominant international readings, activists placed the right to restitution for the wrongs of colonialism at the centre of their human rights agenda.

Women's liberationists on the other hand rejected calls for a new international order that merely replicated the division of private and public, breadwinner and homemaker, which defined women's experience of welfare states in the global north. Not only would such a plan potentially weaken gains by Western feminists, but merely replicating the demands of a UN dominated by voices of underdeveloped states – who sought to extend the welfare state model globally – might dramatically limit the rights of women in developing nations.[152] In focusing on equality with men, the conference placed male traits and masculinised economic imperatives – "increasingly larger institutions, distant workplaces [and] a dehumanising environment that suppresses the social, spiritual and cultural lives of its workers" – above those universal "human" traits the activists articulated.[153] The so-called Right to Life movement sought to appropriate the concept of "human" at the same time, pushing its definition beyond birth to the time of conception. Drawing on a long history of Catholic teachings and the ecumenical movements of the 1960s, the Right to Life movement applied the tactics of its opponents – dramatic leaflets, petitioning and street protests – to contest the so-called permissive society and its liberationist proponents. As rights became more a focus of public discussion, battle lines were also being drawn as to what rights were and who could claim them. Such divisions laid foundations for the contentious construction of Australia's "human rights state" in the 1980s, the legacies of which continue to reverberate today.

---

[152] On such plans for a global welfare state, see Samuel Moyn, *Not Enough: Human Rights in an Unequal World* (Harvard: Harvard University Press, 2018), chapter 6.

[153] "Statement by the Leader of the Australian Delegation – Ms Elizabeth Reid", 21 June 1975.

5   Implementing Rights

Prime Minister Malcolm Fraser opened Australia's first Human Rights Commission on 10 December 1981, "33 years since the United Nations Declaration of Human Rights [sic] was proclaimed". Drawing on "traditions of rights . . . [which] are obviously centuries old", those original fifty-six nations had established "a common standard of achievement for all peoples and all nations". Speaking to assembled dignitaries and media outside the organisation's Canberra offices, Fraser remarked that the day "symbolises the commitment of Australia and many other nations to giving greater reality to human rights", a fact that was "carved in the honour rolls of every city and country town".[1] Fraser's claims of human rights' deep roots in the Australian psyche, even to the extent of connecting their protection to the nation's much-exulted cult of the soldier, speaks to the newfound place such ideas had in political and public discussion. This was experienced as a remarkable and disconcerting shift, for some. Keith Suter, New South Wales branch secretary for the United Nations Association of Australia, wrote in that same year of a "thorough . . . transfer of attention" towards human rights amongst Australian and world leaders, and while this meant the movement had "certainly come a long way in a comparatively short time" their new place at the centre of politics was "unfortunate". Significant questions over which rights – political and civil or economic and social – and indeed whether "human rights are equal in significance" were left unanswered. What Suter dubbed the "human rights explosion" risked "human rights considerations [being] elevated from . . . one factor in international and national politics . . . to being the overall target to which all actions on all factors should be aimed", turning what he saw as an ongoing process of compromise and reinterpretation into an unchallengeable national and global order.[2]

[1] Malcolm Fraser, "Inauguration of the Human Rights Commission", 10 December 1981, available at: https://pmtranscripts.pmc.gov.au/release/transcript-5712.

[2] Dr Keith Suter, *Human Rights: Today and Tomorrow* (Sydney: United Nations Association of Australia, 1981), 4–6.

154   Implementing Rights

The 1980s saw human rights enter the Australian mainstream in an unprecedented way, surpassing even the era of immediate postwar enthusiasm for declarations and new world orders. While human rights did not feature in judgements of the High Court of Australia from 1949 until 1975, in 1978 the International Covenant on Civil and Political Rights (ICCPR) – one half of the so-called international bill of rights that gave enforceability to 1948's Universal Declaration of Human Rights (UDHR) – was found to have relevance in several domestic cases. In two judgements, regarding a prisoner's rights to take civil action and the rights of non-parent primary caregivers to seek custody of children in family law matters, presiding justices found not only that such rights were protected by international instruments but also that these instruments could have bearing on Australian common law.[3] Such judgements preceded the two most significant decisions of the era, *Koowarta* v *Bjelke-Petersen* (1982) and the *Tasmanian Dams Case* (1983) which tested and upheld the use of the External Affairs power in Australia's constitution (s. 51 xxxix) to enforce international treaties – and as such potentially overriding state laws on a wider range of concerns than ever before.[4] This was not just a judicial story, however. Fraser's personal commitment to human rights reflected his social liberalism, the quickly changing international environment marked by Jimmy Carter's presidency and the need to foster a more cohesive, multicultural Australian polity – an agenda continued under his Australian Labor Party (ALP) successors. Groups also emerged, or were rebadged, to meet the new rights discourse. The Gay Rights Lobby was founded in Sydney in 1981, an Australian Human Rights Council emerged in Canberra in 1978 and a new focus coalesced from both government and movements: an Australian Bill of Rights.

This chapter critically understands the seemingly spontaneous emergence of this rights consciousness, exploring first the politics of the so-called human rights explosion, focusing firstly on government and activist responses to 1978's thirtieth anniversary of the passage of the UDHR. Stalled bids for an Australian Bill of Rights under the Hawke government (1983–91) and the creation of a national Human Rights Commission (1981–6) occupy the remainder of this chapter. These developments are explored alongside synchronous campaigns for a treaty or Makarrata with Indigenous Australians and recognition of gay and lesbian rights, as well

---

[3] *Dugan* v *Mirror Newspapers Ltd* [1978] HCA 54 (19 December 1978); Dowal v Murray [1978] HCA 53 (19 December 1978).

[4] For strong overviews of the significance of these cases, see the special issues of *Griffith Law Review*, both edited by Ann Genovese: "Critical Decisions: *Koowarta* v *Bjelke-Petersen*, 1982" 23, no. 1 (2014); "Critical Decision 1983: *Commonwealth* v *Tasmania*" 24, no. 1 (2015).

"Human Rights Begin at Home"   155

as the continued intransigence of conservatives – in particular
Queensland Premier Joh Bjelke-Petersen and the decade's "New
Right".[5] Invented in the 1940s, ignored, experimented with or contested
in later decades, superficially at least the 1980s saw government, the legal
system and many social movements adopt human rights' precepts at
a startling pace. There was also a dramatic rise in the number of non-
government organisations (NGOs), in and of itself a term popularised in
the decade, associated internationally with groups like the Helsinki Watch
(now known as Human Rights Watch).[6] By 1983, the Human Rights
Commission's National Consultation conference was attracting some
fifty self-described Australian NGOs, from religious to child rights, par-
ent support and ethnic community organisations.[7] The number of articles
addressing the topic of human rights nearly quadrupled over the decade
from 1975 in one of the nation's key broadsheet newspapers, and issues
covered were no longer purely international.[8] An explosion, even
a revolution, was clearly underway: but there was seemingly as little
clarity as ever on what human rights actually meant. Was this, in the
end, a popular groundswell or a revolution from above?

"Human Rights Begin at Home": 1978 and the Human Rights Breakthrough

The dismissal of Gough Whitlam as prime minister on 11 November 1975,
replaced by opposition Liberal party leader Malcolm Fraser at the orders of
Governor General Sir John Kerr after months of scandals and crisis at the
hands of an obstructive Senate, is one of contemporary Australia's defining
moments. Fraser and Whitlam seemed to represent polar opposite strands
of the nation's self-imagination: the latter's multilateralism and social
democratic vision versus the American-focused and austerity-driven

---

[5] On the Australian new right, see Verity Archer, "Dole Bludgers, Tax Payers and the New
Right: Constructing Discourses of Welfare in 1970s Australia", *Labour History* 96 (May
2009), 177–90; Damien Cahill, "The Radical Neo-liberal Movement as a Hegemonic
Force in Australia, 1976–1996" (PhD Thesis, University of Wollongong, 2004).
[6] See Akira Iriye, *Global Community: The Role of International Organizations in the Making of
the Contemporary World* (Berkeley: University of California Press, 2002); Sarah B. Snyder,
Human Rights Activism and the End of the Cold War: A Transnational History (Cambridge:
Cambridge University Press, 2011); Thomas Richard Davies, *NGOs: A New History of
Transnational Civil Society* (Oxford: Oxford University Press, 2014).
[7] *Human Rights Commission Annual Report 1983–84* (Canberra: Australian Government
Publishing Service, 1985), 34.
[8] Advanced search for "Human Rights" in *The Canberra Times*, 1975–85, reveals that over
the decade the term appeared 4,126 times, with 142 times in 1975 and 542 in 1985;
available at https://trove.nla.gov.au/newspaper/result?q=%22human+rights%22&exact
Phrase&anyWords&notWords&requestHandler&dateFrom=1975-01-01&dateT
o=1985-12-31&l-advtitle=11&sortby&openFacets=true.

attitude of the former. Yet while Fraser's "razer gangs" slashed government spending and attacked trade unions – the beginnings of Australia's adoption of neoliberalism that was properly rolled out under the Australian Labor Party (ALP) government of 1983–96 – the new prime minister seemed just as animated as his predecessor in the field of human rights. Unlike his conservative forebears, Fraser was socially progressive, a staunch opponent of apartheid and a believer in the importance of international human rights law. In an electorate speech delivered on 6 March 1977, Fraser was clear that "reforms to improve the position of individual men and women" – including the creation of a Human Rights Commission, the passage of a Freedom of Information bill and the introduction of a legal aid system with the states – were "of equal importance to this Government" as his ongoing economic restructuring.[9] What differed between Whitlam and Fraser was not so much tonality as content, for the very meaning of human rights was undergoing one of its many – and potentially its most significant – re-imaginations. The Fraser government's continuation and extension of Whitlam's rights legacy was the product of the swiftly changing international landscape. In March 1976, ten years after first opening for signature and twenty-eight years after the UDHR's signing, the ICCPR came into force, having finally gained the necessary thirty-five ratifications. In 1977, Jimmy Carter made "human rights" a central plank of his successful campaign for president of the United States, and Amnesty International won a Nobel Peace Prize, having gained significant international attention from its anti-torture work.[10] As Eckel puts it: "Human rights ceased to be a topic confined to states' policies toward international organizations ... Now they entered the mainstream of bilateral relations ... moving human rights issues to the center [sic] of international relations."[11]

This turn towards enforceable standards of individual liberties saw Australia play an abnormally significant role in pushing for a convention prohibiting torture from the mid-1970s onwards and seek a seat on the United Nations Commission on Human Rights for the first time in two decades. The origins of Australia's sponsorship of anti-torture measures in the General Assembly, a break from previous attitudes of abstention in matters of rights, can be found in Amnesty International's (AI) campaign

---

[9] Malcolm Fraser, "Electorate Talk", 6 March 1977, available at https://pmtranscripts.pmc.gov.au/sites/default/files/original/00004338.pdf.

[10] On Carter's foreign policy and the American turn to human rights, see Barbara Keys, *Reclaiming American Virtue: The Human Rights Revolution of the 1970s* (Cambridge, MA: Harvard University Press, 2014).

[11] Eckel, "The Rebirth of Politics from the Spirit of Morality", 231.

"Human Rights Begin at Home" 157

against torture, which has been noted by scholars like Barbara Keys as a central formative moment in the rights ascendency.[12] AI President Sean MacBride wrote fawningly to the new prime minister in May 1973 of being "lost in admiration at the rapidity at which you and your government had moved" in its first few months, calling Whitlam's quick uptake of international law a "breath of fresh air in our otherwise rather dismal world situation". MacBride saw such enthusiasm as an opportunity for Australian to co-sponsor two resolutions the organisation had prepared, one requesting the establishment of a permanent commission to examine compliance with international humanitarian law and another to appoint a working group to prepare a draft convention "outlawing torture and other inhuman and degrading treatment" of prisoners.[13] In that same year, the first moves were made to found a Parliamentary Group associated with Amnesty, initiated by ALP representative Richard Klugman with the aim of "obtaining government support ... for prisoners of conscience". The first meeting of this group convened on 23 November 1973 over dinner in Parliament House, chaired by the recently elected Liberal Member for Parramatta Phillip Ruddock and attended by some sixteen members of both the House of Representatives and the Senate, with attendance from all major and minor parties. Addressed by long-time Victorian Amnesty stalwart Clare Wozitsky, this first meeting was dominated by discussion of torture and unjust imprisonment in Indonesia – a close regional ally – and in Chile.[14]

After significant consultation and discussion, MacBride's push for an enforceable convention was deemed premature amidst long standing fears that such debates would be unduly "politicised" by the non-Western majority. Links were maintained, however, with an Australian representative attending AI's Conference on the Abolition of Torture in December 1973.[15] The unlikely passage in November 1974 with only one abstention of a more limited General Assembly resolution recommending, amongst other things, that torture be a key focus of the upcoming UN Congress on the Prevention of Crime and the Treatment of Offenders to

---

[12] See Barbara Keys, "Anti-Torture Politics: Amnesty International, the Greek Junta, and the Origins of the U.S. Human Rights Boom", in Akira Iriye, Petra Goedde and William I. Hitchcock (eds.), *The Human Rights Revolution: An International History* (New York: Oxford University Press, 2012), 201–21.

[13] Sean MacBride to Gough Whitlam, 11 May 1973, in National Archives of Australia (henceforth NAA): A1838, 929/6/3 PART 3.

[14] "Minutes of the Meeting Held on Tuesday November 23, 1973 (Preliminary Meeting to Establish Parliamentary Amnesty Group)", National Archives of Australia (henceforth NAA): M5048, 18.

[15] "Draft UN Resolutions Proposed by Amnesty International on Abolition of Torture and Humanitarian Law", 25 September 1973, NAA: A1838, 929/6/3 PART 3.

158   Implementing Rights

be held in Geneva in September 1975 augured well for the push for an enforceable Convention.[16] Whitlam's government could more easily support calls for the bodily autonomy of the individual, which would overwhelmingly target offending states in the second and third worlds, than the calls for global economic redistribution it had combated during International Women's Year. Australian foreign affairs bureaucrats met with Amnesty's Martin Ennals in August 1975, who expressed that he was "entirely in agreement with our thinking in favour of a Convention", drafts of which had already been prepared in Canberra. However, a more developed, if poorly publicised, plan by the Netherlands and Sweden to instead push for a Declaration caught both parties off-guard.[17] Instead of seeking a Convention, the Australians worked with Amnesty to prepare amendments to this draft Declaration to include intimidation and other forms of coercion, and the amended document was adopted by the General Assembly in December 1975, a month after Whitlam's dismissal.[18] Ennals reached out to Fraser in April 1976 hoping that "the new government would show the same interest and support as its predecessor", and, while such verbal support remained forthcoming, privately Australian diplomats and government figures dramatically cooled on the prospect of an enforceable Convention.[19] C. L. Lamb, Australia's first secretary at the United Nations in New York, observed "some doubt in the minds of Western countries" as to the manner of proceeding on this issue, concerned that hasty moves might "only serve to narrow general prohibitions" on torture in the UDHR and the ICCPR "which now serve us relatively well".[20]

Despite his unwillingness to take the leadership role Whitlam had sought to craft, Fraser's government could not adopt the attitude of previous conservative governments of largely ignoring or derailing UN human rights discussions. The old bilateral relationship with the United States, central to Liberal foreign policy from Menzies on, would now necessitate not only engagement with, but also leadership in, multilateral human rights discussions. It was in this context that Australian diplomatic

---

[16] General Assembly Resolution 3218, *Torture and Other Cruel, Inhuman or Degrading Treatment or Punishment in Relation to Detention and Imprisonment*, A/RES/3218(XXIX) (6 November 1974), available at www.un.org/en/ga/search/view_doc.asp?symbol=A/RES/3218(XXIX).

[17] "Fifth UN Congress on Crime", 21 August 1975, NAA: A432, 1977/5938.

[18] General Assembly Resolution 3452, *Declaration on the Protection of All Persons from Being Subjected to Torture and Other Cruel, Inhuman or Degrading Treatment or Punishment*, A/RES/3452 (XXX) (9 December 1975), available at www.ohchr.org/EN/ProfessionalInterest/Pages/DeclarationTorture.aspx.

[19] G. J. L. Coles to Secretary, Department of Foreign Affairs, "Amnesty International", 7 April 1976, NAA: A1838, 929/6/3 PART 3.

[20] C. L. Lamb to Secretary, Department of Foreign Affairs, "UNGA 32: Torture", 19 May 1977, NAA: A1838, 929/34/2 PART 1A.

"Human Rights Begin at Home" 159

officers, newly acquainted with UN processes around the issue of torture, entered contestation in 1977 for a seat on the United Nations Commission on Human Rights (UNCHR). Australia had not sat on the UNCHR for two decades, the longest absence of any Western nation, seen by many as a protest against the Commission's agenda. Australia's UN representative in New York warned, "[W]e are ... vulnerable to the suggestion that Australia makes beautiful speeches but does little to follow them up with detailed work on international bodies."[21] Replaced in 2005 by the current United Nations Human Rights Council, the UNCHR had two key functions: the standard setting – that is, drafting the Declaration itself and then numerous covenants and instruments; as well as implementation, on which it had a significantly less stellar record.[22] Seats on the commission were distributed between the African, Asian, Eastern European, Latin American and Caribbean and the so-called Western European and Others – to which Australia belonged – groupings, and elections were for three-year terms. Fraser hoped his government's removal of discriminatory pieces of legislation and ratification of the International Covenant on Economic, Social and Cultural Rights (ICESCR) – which required only progressive implementation – in 1975 as well as hosting a UN world forum in 1976 and organising another for 1980 would work to his favour.

With a close eye on the incoming American president, Australia's representative in New York again cautioned the Department of Foreign Affairs that it was "likely to find itself grappling more and more frequently with human rights questions in the context of foreign policy formulation in the future".[23] In particular, attention was drawn to the coming into force of the ICCPR in March 1976, which meant that the UNCHR would "now be looking to find ways of bridging the gulf that exists between the setting of standards in international treaties and their implementation".[24] While Roland Burke has described the pace at which the human rights breakthrough reached the halls of the UN as "glacial", Australia wanted to be on the front foot.[25] Hosting a United Nations symposium on

---

[21] Ralph Harry, Australian Permanent Representative to the United Nations, New York, to Secretary, Department of Foreign Affairs, "Human Rights Activities", 6 December 1976, NAA: A1838, 929/1 PART 6.

[22] Andrew S. Thompson, "Tehran 1968 and Reform of the UN Human Rights System", *Journal of Human Rights* 14, no. 1 (2015), 85.

[23] Harry, "Human Rights Activities", 6 December 1976.

[24] "UN Commission on Human Rights: Australia a Candidate", *DFA Backgrounder*, 11 February 1977, 8.

[25] Roland Burke, "Human Rights Day after the 'Breakthrough': Celebrating the Universal Declaration of Human Rights at the United Nations in 1978 and 1988", *Journal of Global History* 10, no. 1 (2015), 148.

160   Implementing Rights

Human Rights and the Administration of Justice in December 1976 in Canberra allowed Department of Foreign Affairs (DFA) officials to put forward Australia's proposed candidacy to Marc Schreiber, director of the UN's Division of Human Rights in Geneva.[26] Acknowledging that "Australia was not as involved in the United Nations institutions concerned with human rights as it could be", Mark Bourchier of the DFA's Legal and Treaties division asked why the UN's enforcement mechanisms for human rights were so "selective" – and particularly why socialist states seemed beyond rebuke. Schreiber responded that many nations "operated deftly within the United Nations system", as "regional solidarity helped to blanket criticism". However, the new enforceability of the ICCPR and pronounced focus by emerging NGOs was already leading to successes in breaking such solidarities. Schreiber particularly noted the release of 300 Chilean political prisoners only five days after a condemnatory resolution was tabled in the General Assembly, something which he presented as a "breakthrough".[27]

Schreiber intoned the new moral sense that was seeping into the UN's previously abstracted, state-based Human Rights agenda. The released prisoners, socialists and communists arrested by the dictator Augusto Pinochet after his bloody seizure of power in 1973, whom Schreiber had made it a priority to meet in person reported their torture was "not as intolerable as 'feeling alone'", a sense that "had been genuinely ameliorated by the knowledge that 'important people' outside of Chile were actively trying to help them".[28] This success was owed to Chile's status as a palatable target for both first world advocates against torture and false imprisonment as well as second and third world propagandists against its hard-right government: both shared what Patrick William Kelly calls a "politics of emergency".[29] "Many things not possible just a few years ago had now become plausible", Schleiber related, as "[d]iscussions about human rights had become more open".[30] Such openness was also present domestically, with Foreign Minister Andrew Peacock noting in the 1978 Foreign Policy Statement the inseparability of the domestic and the international in human rights issues, as well as the interconnection of political, economic and cultural concerns with rights issues. "It is no longer possible to identify separately issues as having only a political,

---

[26] On the symposium, see *The Canberra Times*, 15 December 1976, 26.
[27] "Summary Record of Meeting with Mr Marc Schreiber, Director, Division of Human Rights, Geneva", 16 December 1976, NAA: A1838, 929/1 PART 6.
[28] Ibid.
[29] Patrick William Kelly, *Sovereign Emergencies: Latin America and the Making of Global Human Rights Politics* (Cambridge: Cambridge University Press, 2018), 96.
[30] "Summary Record of Meeting with Mr Marc Schreiber", NAA: A1838, 929/1 PART 6.

"Human Rights Begin at Home" 161

strategic, economic or social nature", Peacock mused, adding that "like most things, human rights begin at home".[31] Fraser's government also took steps to popularise the UDHR and educate Australians on the emerging human rights machinery that he hoped to construct. 1978 marked the thirtieth anniversary of the Declaration's adoption, and it was the first time an Australian government took such an occurrence seriously.

A Cabinet Submission on behalf of Minister for Foreign Affairs Andrew Peacock remarked of the government's "strong public commitment to human rights which the commemorative program would enhance".[32] The "program of observance" was announced in a prime ministerial press release that mentioned the "growing international recognition of the importance of fundamental human rights", particularly after "the world-wide outcry in recent days against the trials of Soviet dissidents".[33] Australians should be "justly proud" of their nation's commitment to human rights and the UDHR, the release said, adding that "government had a role to play in promoting public awareness of its universal significance". While Paul Hasluck had dismissed it as "controversial" only a decade earlier, Fraser described the UDHR as "a most highly regarded document" both internationally and at home.[34] The practicalities of this initiative involved the distribution of educational kits – including a simplified version of the Racial Discrimination Act as well as posters and films – which were to be sent to every Australian secondary school and some 3,000 "ethnic (including Aboriginal) groups and relevant organisations". An additional 20,000 copies of the UDHR were to be prepared, as well as 8,500 copies of the RDA, which was also to be recorded in selected Indigenous languages and distributed on cassette.[35] The postmaster general was also instructed to produce its first-ever Human Rights Day commemorative stamp, and after a public competition a winning design was chosen, featuring an illustration of four children – one clearly Anglo-Celtic next to one each of Mediterranean, Asian and Indigenous backgrounds.[36] The choice of these ethnically diverse children

---

[31] *CPD* (House), 9 May 1978, 2029, 2041.

[32] Andrew Peacock, "Confidential for Cabinet – Commemoration of the 30th Anniversary of the Universal Declaration of Human Rights", NAA: A12909, 1948.

[33] Malcolm Fraser, "For Press: Programme for the Observance of the 30th Anniversary of the Universal Declaration of Human Rights", available at https://pmtranscripts.pmc.gov.au/sites/default/files/original/00004759.pdf.

[34] Andrew Peacock, "Confidential for Cabinet – Commemoration of the 30th Anniversary of the Universal Declaration of Human Rights", NAA: A12909, 1948.

[35] Ibid.

[36] "Human-Rights Stamp Issue", *The Canberra Times*, 29 November 1978, 33. For a discussion of the peculiar politics of human rights stamp making, see Roland Burke, "Premature Memorials to the United Nations Human Rights Program: International

162   Implementing Rights

demonstrates how the government's push for human rights awareness was entwined with another concept in the process of vernacularisation: multiculturalism.[37] Indeed, discussions of the two terms were nearly inseparable. The Office of Community Relations, established by the RDA and headed by former Labor immigration minister Al Grassby was incorporated into the Human Rights Commission, to be discussed more fully later in this chapter.

Overall, it was thought that while "some criticism may occur of any perceived shortfall between government policy and rights set out in the Declaration", not to mention continued inability to ratify the ICCPR, this was outweighed by the benefits of the program, which it was thought would be "long lasting", particularly amongst "future opinion formers (students)".[38] Beyond government, 1978 also showed that a new sense of human rights' potential was evident amongst the old hands and new faces in what for the first time could meaningfully be called a human rights movement. The United Nations Association of Australia (UNAA), established in 1946 out of what had been the League of Nations Association, welcomed delegates and attendees to a public symposium on Australia and Human Rights – "a cause [that] gains respectability day by day" in the opinion of chairperson and UNAA President Richard Alston. Meeting in May 1978, the gathering heard of how the "international spotlight ... on gross human rights violations" was shining all the brighter, with "President Carter's [having] conferred a new legitimacy on the cause".[39] Discussion centred on Australia's failure to ratify the ICCPR, with the USA's decision to do so seemingly illegitimating the traditional defence of the complexities of a federal system. Keith Suter pointed out that "[i]f a 50-state federation can ratify the covenant, a 6-state federation can certainly do so", particularly as "there are a number of 'Queenslands' in his country", highlighting the intransigent position of the northern state to the idea of human rights that was to be a hallmark of the 1980s.[40] The senior vice chair of the Ethnic Communities Council of NSW, Vladimir Menart, brought the perspective

Postage Stamps and the Commemoration of the 1948 Universal Declaration of Human Rights", *History and Memory* 28, no. 2 (Fall/Winter 2016), 152–81.

[37] On the emergence of multiculturalism in Australia, see Jatinder Mann, "The Introduction of Multiculturalism in Canada and Australia, 1960s–1970s", *Nations and Nationalism* 18, no. 3 (July 2012), 483–503.

[38] Andrew Peacock, "Confidential for Cabinet – Commemoration of the 30th Anniversary of the Universal Declaration of Human Rights", NAA: A12909, 1948.

[39] Richard Alston, "A Chairman's Opening Remarks", *Australians and Human Rights: Proceedings of a Public Seminar held in Sydney on Saturday, 13th May, 1978* (Sydney: UNAA, 1978), 3.

[40] Keith Suter, "The International Protection of Human Rights", *Australians and Human Rights: Proceedings of a Public Seminar Held in Sydney on Saturday, 13th May, 1978* (Sydney: UNAA, 1978), 18.

of "ethnic minorities" to the gathering, seeking to articulate the new relationship between multiculturalism and human rights. Since the Universal Declaration had been signed, Australia's population had nearly doubled, growth which was roughly half owed to migrants. Less than 10 per cent of Australia's population had been born overseas in the late 1940s, a figure that more than doubled by 1978, owing to both postwar migration programs and the gradual slackening and abolition of the White Australia Policy.[41] The arrival of Vietnamese refugees - dubbed "boat people" – fleeing political upheaval in their homeland marked the first significant numbers of Asian migrants as well, and the complexion of the nation began to change.[42]

If Australia was to become "a multicultural society in fact and not only in composition", Menart told the gathering, this could only be achieved "through the full and genuine adoption of the principles of human rights as enunciated 30 years ago", particularly through diversifying the education system and encouraging the growth of ethnic organisations. "Laws may look beautiful in the statute books ... but without people supported by free and independent associations acting as watchdogs, the beautiful laws often remain a dead letter".[43] One such association was launched that very year. The Human Rights Council of Australia (HRCA) first met on 13 May 1978, ten years since the First International Conference on Human Rights had convened in Tehran, creating the first national organisation specifically devoted to the universal application of human rights in Australia. Thomas Millar, professor of International Relations at the Australian National University and member of the HRCA's Organising Committee found that while "some Australians do care"– including civil liberties groups, Amnesty International and the International Commission of Jurists, the federal government was "edging into human rights legislation" and "concerns over human rights questions [were] seeping into society" – this was "only a tiny fraction of the Australian population". The HRCA was "trying to remedy some of the many gaps in the fabric of our concern with human rights at home and abroad" by taking as its modus operandi the ICCPR rather than the collective rights

---

[41] Phillip Lowe, "Demographics, Productivity and Innovation", Speech to the Sydney Institute, 12 March 2014, available at www.rba.gov.au/speeches/2014/sp-dg-120314 .html. For more on the end of White Australia, see Gwenda Tavan, *The Long, Slow Death of White Australia* (Melbourne: Scribe, 2005).

[42] See Rachel Stevens, *Immigration Policy from 1970 to the Present* (New York: Routledge, 2016); Claire Higgins, *Asylum by Boat: Origins of Australia Refugee Policy* (Sydney: NewSouth Publishing, 2017)

[43] Vladimir Menart, "Ethnic Minorities and Human Rights", *Australians and Human Rights: Proceedings of a Public Seminar Held in Sydney on Saturday, 13th May, 1978* (Sydney: UNAA, 1978), 54–5.

164   Implementing Rights

articulated at Tehran. While "civil and political rights … do not compensate a person dying of starvation", it was noted, "we do not need to accept the corollary that [their] denial is a prerequisite to a full stomach".[44] The economic, social and cultural rights that Evatt and other Australians had worked to secure in the 1940s, and which Indigenous Australians and others continually demanded, received no hearing at the UNAA's May gathering.

Human rights were also increasingly entering public discussions, becoming what Lora Wildenthal calls a "strategic political language".[45] The Indonesian invasion of East Timor in 1975 was one eye-opening example of human rights violations for Australians, not because of the Indonesian's denial of the right of self-determination but due to reports of torture and massacres appearing with regularity alongside rumours of Western government involvement.[46] The HRCA's president, Canberra public servant Bill Dunn, wrote to the *Canberra Times* in December 1978 castigating the Australian government for embracing a more human rights–focused foreign policy while "condon[ing] a particularly flagrant abuse of those rights in a neighbouring territory". "Those of us who really care about human rights", Dunn protested, "might well now take stock of Australia's role in this terrible episode in our diplomatic history. Those unheeded anguished cries for help from the Timorese should really haunt us forever."[47] Such sentiment marked a shift in the way leftists understood third world struggles, a movement from solidarity with necessarily violent national liberation struggles to the transformation of unknown others into distant victims in need of moral sympathy.[48] Communist activist Denis Freney retrospectively bemoaned Australian Party support for Indonesia during its occupation and integration of West Papua. Though cloaked in the language of anti-imperialism, their support for the "Indonesian revolution" under Sukarno meant that "the rights of West Papuans to self-determination" were not considered, something the author described as "paternalism".[49] As well as a language in which to analyse Australian foreign policy, human rights were becoming a way

---

[44] *Canberra Times*, 25 July 1978, 2.
[45] Lora Wildenthal, *The Language of Human Rights in West Germany* (Philadelphia: University of Pennsylvania Press, 2013), 168.
[46] For more background, see Clinton Fernandes, *Reluctant Saviour: Australia, Indonesia and the Independence of East Timor* (Melbourne: Scribe, 2004).
[47] *The Canberra* Times, 21 December 1978, 2.
[48] For more on the left's general turn against solidarity to human rights, see Eleanor Davey, *Idealism beyond Borders: The French Revolutionary Left and the Rise of Humanitarians, 1954–1988* (Cambridge: Cambridge University Press, 2015).
[49] Denis Freney, *The Politics of Solidarity: Supporting Liberation Struggles in the Australian Context* (Sydney: Communist Party of Australia, 1986), 5.

to link the domestic and the international. N. V. Barry of Walgett NSW wondered whether "Australian human-rights campaigners should ... observe the old motto of shovel the dirt from your own door before you start throwing it at others", noting injustices against Indigenous peoples and the ever-developing surveillance powers of police agencies.[50] After 1,500 people protested in Melbourne against the mistreatment of dissidents and minorities in the Soviet Union, abortion rights campaigner Dr Bertram Wainer asked whether "these people are equally as concerned about the total lack of human rights in Uganda, East Timor and Irian Jaya" or, for that matter, "the draconian penalties in Queensland against the right to assemble".[51]

Queensland, increasing referred to as the "Deep North" in an unflattering parallel with the Deep South of the United States, was governed by the Country Party under Premier Johannes Bjelke-Petersen. A peanut farmer from the rural town of Kingaroy, two hours from the State's capital of Brisbane, it was in Bjelke-Petersen's Queensland that "most of the issues which cast a shadow over human rights in Australia arise", as Alston put it in a four-page statement to mark Human Rights Day in his capacity as UNAA president. "The sight of hundreds of police massed in the streets of an Australian city to prevent a march" – referring to the Queensland Government's 1977 ban on all unpermitted public gatherings of over four people – made "it seem that in Queensland human rights were the privilege only of those who chose not to exercise them".[52] The HRCA targeted Queensland's ongoing efforts to displace Indigenous communities to make way for mining operations, particularly in Aurukun and on Mornington Island, including attempts to "strike 'dropouts, hanger-ons and agitators' from the electoral roles [sic]".[53] Action for World Development, the HRCA's predecessor, accused the state and federal governments of "ignoring the human rights of aborigines" by having "put Queensland State rights first".[54] The premier did not take kindly to critics either. In 1981 he labelled AI "simply an arm of communist propaganda" after the rights group condemned his rule "repressive" and "anti-human rights".[55] For his critics, though, the Queensland premier's approach was "not distinguishable from that of hard-line Soviet leaders towards dissidents and revisionists" – indicating that perhaps the premier's long term use of Cold War fear-mongering was waning in believability.[56] Such conflicts were but an opening salvo for what was to come in the 1980s.

---

[50] *The Canberra Times*, 10 October 1978, 2.   [51] *The Canberra Times*, 6 August 1978, 2.
[52] *The Age*, 11 December 1978, 5.   [53] *The Canberra Times*, 31 August 1978, 3.
[54] *The Canberra Times*, 24 April 1978, 3.   [55] *The Canberra Times*, 8 June 1981, 3.
[56] *The Canberra Times*, 22 July 1981, 17.

166   Implementing Rights

Coming Together? Makarrata and a Bill of Rights

"In the next few years we will have some new words to understand", Stewart Harris, journalist, Senior Fellow at the Australian National University's Centre for Pacific Studies and secretary of the newly formed Aboriginal Treaty Committee (ATC), wrote in the *Canberra Times* in July 1980. The word "Makarrata", drawn from the Yolngu region of Northern Australia and meaning "a coming together after a struggle", first appeared in a report of the National Aboriginal Conference (NAC) in 1979 to describe that organisation's desire for a treaty with settler Australians.[57] Treaties had been signed between British colonising forces and indigenous peoples in the United States, Canada and New Zealand but almost never in what became Australia.[58] A National Aboriginal Consultative Council (NACC) had been established in 1973 by the Whitlam government to give greater effect to the mandate Commonwealth authorities received from the 1967 referendum. Australia's first-ever Indigenous representative body, it was reconstituted as the NAC in 1978.[59] Indigenous transnationalism was gaining more results and institutionalising during this period, with Bruce McGuinness as chair of the-then NACC attending the foundation of the World Council of Indigenous Peoples in Canada in 1975.[60] Commenting on the impending bicentenary of the first settlement of Australia, Bruce Miles of the Aboriginal Legal Service remarked in 1979 that "there can't be a proper celebration until we get a treaty" governing ongoing land use and reparations –now described as compensation – for the loss of Indigenous land.[61] The appearance of a short book by Harris in that same year, entitled *It's Coming Yet: An Aboriginal Treaty within Australia between Australians*, marked the first sustained argument for such a venture. It quickly sold out of a print run of 5,000 and soon received "influential interest – even support" from within the legal fraternity.[62]

---

[57] *The Canberra Times*, 5 July 1980, 2.
[58] On the politics of European treaties and expansionism, see Saliha Belmessous (ed.), *Empire by Treaty: Negotiating European Expansion, 1600–1900* (Oxford: Oxford University Press, 2014); Saliha Belmessous (ed.), *Native Claims: Indigenous Law against Empire* (Oxford: Oxford University Press, 2012); Marcia Langton et al. (eds.), *Honour among Nations? Treaties and Agreements with Indigenous People* (Melbourne: Melbourne University Press, 2004).
[59] Ravi de Costa, *A Higher Authority: Indigenous Transnationalism and Australia* (Sydney: UNSW Press, 2005), chapter 5.
[60] "Submission No 3405: Assistance to the National Aboriginal Conference (NAC) to Host the Third General Assembly of the World Council of Indigenous Peoples (WCIP)", 20 August 1979, NAA: A12909, 3405.
[61] *Canberra Times*, 15 May 1979, 12.
[62] Stewart Harris, *It's Coming Yet: An Aboriginal Treaty within Australia between Australians* (Canberra: Aboriginal Treaty Committee, 1979). On sales, see Tim Rowse, "From

Coming Together? Makarrata and a Bill of Rights

J. G. Stark QC, editor of the *Australian Law Journal*, described the book as "informative to an extent out of proportion with its brevity", highlighting that it "serves to challenge some of the central assumptions on which the case-law, unfavourable to Aboriginal claims of nationhood and sovereignty, is founded".[63] Starke invoked the spectre of international law, arguing that

it is not at all clear that the whole of Australia was acquired by settlement, that is to say by a form of international law occupation, rather than by – at least in certain areas of Australia – a form of dispossession tantamount to conquest according to the traditional nineteenth century rules of international law preceding the foundation of the League of Nations, and the establishments of its successor, the United Nations.[64]

"When lawyers become involved in an issue we can be sure of its gravity", Harris wrote, "so Makarrata and Yolnu [sic] will be words we might as well get used to".[65]

The turn to treaty occurred in the same temporality as the re-emergence of calls for an Australian Bill of Rights. While arguments for constitutionally enshrined rights were made during the debates surrounding Australian federation, these were only in a minor key, and the Australian Labor Party's plans to codify some basic rights in its "powers referendum" of 1944 were defeated.[66] Interest in such a notion was piqued again somewhat in 1968, with an Australian Civil Liberties Council created to campaign for a Bill of Rights modelled on the ICCPR. The Australian Council for Civil Liberties, discussed in Chapter 2, had fallen victim to the Cold War and largely ceased to operate after 1955.[67] To fill this gap, a National Convention of Councils of Civil Liberties was held in Sydney in early 1968, hoping to constitute an Australia-wide organisation from a new wave of state-based councils in New South Wales (1963), Victoria (1966) and Queensland (1966). Robert Hope QC, president of the New South Wales Council, warned the gathering that "with the vast extension of bureaucracy and the increasing withdrawal of the regulation of our day-to-day activities from the realm of judicial rights to the sphere of administrative decision, the tendency to slowly erode into these rights must surely grow".[68] Hope's words demonstrated not only renewed interest in rights but a wider reading of their scope,

---

Enforceability To Feel-Good: Notes on the Pre-history of the Recent Treaty Debate", in Peter Read, Gary Meyers and Bob Reece (eds.), *What Good Condition: Reflections on an Australian Aboriginal Treaty, 1986–2006* (Canberra, ANU E-Press, 2006), 73.

[63] J. G. Stark, "Current Topics", *The Australian Law Journal* 54, no. 5 (May 1980), 248.

[64] Ibid. [65] *The Canberra Times*, 5 July 1980, 2. [66] See Chapter 1 of this volume.

[67] Stuart Macintyre and James Waghorne, *Liberty: A History of Civil Liberties in Australia* (Melbourne: Melbourne University Press, 2011), 105–9.

[68] *The Australian*, 8 October 1968, 7.

168   Implementing Rights

with topics discussed at the gathering ranging from "censorship and police powers" to "abortion, vagrancy and prostitution". Special consideration was also given to emerging concerns around privacy, particularly as "recording devices, ever smaller and more powerful" were becoming available.[69] Lionel Murphy, lawyer and then leader of the Labor opposition in the Senate, agreed with Hope's sentiment, warning the assembled delegates that "[w]e live in an age where we see the enlargement of government and private bureaucracies [and] there is a real danger that human personality might be submerged".[70] Speaking in August of that year to a Young Labor conference, Murphy reiterated his desire to tackle "one of the greatly increasing problems" of the era, the "tremendous concentration of power in the hands of government and an increase in the power ... of private groups and individuals unprecedented since the breakdown of the feudal system". A Bill of Rights would do much to ensure that "the upsurge in rioting and discontent around the world" that marked 1968 would not reach Australian shores. While the new national organisation floundered, and the Victorian council struggled to grow its membership or influence, Murphy's ALP made the incorporation of a Bill of Rights into Australia's constitution a key plank of its successful 1972 election campaign.[71]

In November 1973, Murphy in his position of attorney general introduced two pieces of legislation – a Human Rights Bill and the Racial Discrimination Bill (discussed in Chapter 4) – which he hoped "would form the basis for a constitutional bill of rights ... in two or three years".[72] Based on the ICCPR, indeed the document was annexed to the Human Rights Bill when presented to the House of Representatives, Murphy declared that while "we believe these rights to be basic to our democratic society, they now received remarkably little protection in Australia".[73] Australia's constitution, he said, "does not touch the most significant of these rights", and "Common Law is powerless to protect them against the written laws and regulations made by parliament". Former prime minister Robert Menzies quickly and publicly weighed in – "like a ghost from the Victorian era", as one Communist scribe put it[74] – in defence of that "unwritten law of England administered by the Queen's courts [and] based on ancient and universal usage". Menzies' three-part commentary, widely reported and reproduced in the press, impressed on readers that "one of the functions of the Common Law, devised over a course of centuries in England and adopted by us by inheritance, has been to protect the individual against infringement on his personal rights". "Why Senator Murphy should

---

[69] Macintyre and Waghorne, *Liberty*, 119–20.   [70] *The Australian*, 8 October 1968, 7.
[71] *The Canberra Times*, 29 November 1972, 19.
[72] *The Canberra Times*, 22 November 1973, 1.   [73] Ibid.   [74] *Tribune*, 9 April 1974, 7.

Coming Together? Makarrata and a Bill of Rights 169

wish to substitute for the Common Law a long category of various rights as if they had no existence apart from his legislation", Menzies added, "I will never understand", and in any case he doubted whether the Commonwealth had adequate powers to implement such a bill.[75] Murphy's retort, delivered in the press, parliament and in talks to the International Council of Jurists and the NSW Council for Civil Liberties, challenged the efficacy of handed-down legal traditions. "We only have to look at the way in which the common law upheld the rights of owners of mines and factories in the nineteenth century to engage children of tender age to work for sixteen hours or more a day to see how the common law in fact has operated in a particular situation," he protested.[76] That Murphy's bill did not cover any aspect of these employment rights, a central concern of Australian negotiators in the 1940s, went unmentioned.

While the wind rather quickly fell out of Murphy's sails – the Human Rights Bill was widely criticised, lapsed with the double dissolution election of May 1974 and was not reintroduced – the idea of constitutionally enshrined protections continued to appeal to Indigenous Australians. While 1967 had led to disappointing outcomes for many, advocates recognised that "a limiting factor like the Constitution" remained necessary to ensure that Indigenous rights – increasingly reimagined in terms of sovereignty – were "binding on the government and all subsequent governments" and as such take the issue outside of partisan politics.[77] In April 1973, the vice chair of the Victorian Aboriginal Affairs Advisory Council, David Anderson, proposed that, as well as a Human Rights Bill, additional protections were required "to ensure the satisfaction of human needs", covering in particular "the right to employment and training in decentralised regions of Australia, adequate medical care, social security and dual culture and minority relations education".[78] Charles Perkins struck a similar note, arguing that a Bill of Rights was a necessity to "protect Aboriginal people right throughout the nation" as well as "any other person in Australia from discrimination on the grounds of race, nationality or whatever it may be".[79] The transition from demands for a Bill of Rights to a treaty with Australia's First Peoples occurred largely as

---

[75] *Sydney Morning Herald*, 14 March 1974, 7; *Sydney Morning Herald*, 15 March 1974.

[76] Lionel Murphy, "Address to the United Nations Associations [sic] of Australia Human Rights Seminar", 20 April 1974, 111, available at http://parlinfo.aph.gov.au/parlInfo/search/display/display.w3p;query=Id%3A%22media%2Fpressrel%2FHPR04005492%22.

[77] *The Canberra Times*, 5 July 1980, 2

[78] *The Canberra Times*, 14 April 1973, 9. For more on the rise of "basic needs" as a discourse in this period, see Samuel Moyn, *Not Enough: Human Rights in an Unequal World* (Cambridge, MA: Harvard University Press, 2018), chapter 5.

[79] Garth Nettheim (ed.), *Aborigines, Human Rights and the Law* (Sydney: Australia and New Zealand Book Company, 1974), 12.

170   Implementing Rights

a result of the growing international awareness and connections of the 1970s. A historical treaty signed by John Batman, an early white settler in the region of what became Melbourne, and the Kulin people of that region in 1835 had been embraced by Indigenous campaigners for generations as evidence of their continued ownership and occupation of the continent. However, its unenforceable status, having been declared "null and of no effect as against the rights of the crown" in an 1835 proclamation, and deeply problematic articles forced a turn from old to new.[80] Anderson, in his capacity as a member of Whitlam's NACC, remarked in March 1974 that the organisation's very existence rested on an "unstated recognition that the Aboriginal people of Australia have unique, not special, rights rooted in international law relating to treaty rights", a recognition extending far beyond the narrow geographical and conceptual parameters of the Batman Treaty.[81]

A year later Anderson deployed recent developments in Canada – particularly renewed interest in historic treaties signed with "Indian" groups and new mechanisms to develop further agreements "where Indian title was never extinguished by treaty or superseded by law" – to argue for a similar process in Australia "of funding ... research into rights, treaties and negotiating settlements of claims".[82] "Australian Aborigines are not alone any more", one commentator wrote, "because their leaders are widely travelled, to London, Moscow, Peking, New York, Israel and the Arab World".[83] Anderson put it bluntly that if "the world is moving into a planetary culture, it is vital that justice be done, not through Aboriginal or white man's law, but international law".[84] In 1976, the first sustained calls for what was then termed a "treaty of commitment" were made. The election of the Fraser government had "direct ... personal and, already, disastrous" implications for Indigenous people, with the breaking up of the NACC into three different bodies "illustrat[ing] the present Government's determination to divide and conquer our race" in Anderson's words.[85] The susceptibility of Indigenous issues to such political whims spawned the need for a "treaty of commitment" between all political parties and Indigenous people, promising "an unchanging proportion of the total [Commonwealth] budget every year", as Harris

---

[80] See Bain Attwood, *Possession: Batman's Treaty and the Matter of History* (Melbourne: Miegunyah Press, 2009), 269–74.

[81] *The Canberra Times*, 11 March 1974, 2.

[82] *The Canberra Times*, 26 September 1972, 2. For more on the transnational power of such "treaty talk", see Miranda Johnson, "The Case of the Million-Dollar Duck: A Hunter, His Treaty, and the Bending of the Settler Contract", *American Historical Review* 124, no. 1 (2019), 56–86.

[83] *The Canberra Times*, 3 August 1976, 2.   [84] *The Canberra Times*, 21 April 1977, 21.

[85] *The Canberra Times*, 3 August 1976, 2; *The Canberra Times*, 13 July 1977, 12.

Coming Together? Makarrata and a Bill of Rights 171

put it.[86] Such a plan would "replace charity ... with real responsibility", taking the "recovery" of Indigenous society "out of the area of our domestic politics" into the area of international obligation.[87] Anderson commended Harris' views, arguing for "special aboriginal electorates, seats in Federal parliament, inside the constitutional parliamentary process" alongside a treaty of commitment to ensure Indigenous people had "a hope or a home under this continent's sky".[88]

Building on this momentum, the ATC was founded in Canberra in April 1979,[89] with Harris as secretary and H.C. "Nugget" Coombs, the well-known former public servant, Reserve Bank governor and rights advocate, as president.[90] Coombs had been the architect of Australia's postwar reconstruction and played a central role in developing the additional Commonwealth powers defeated in 1944, which – as well as freedom of expression and religion – proposed for the first time Commonwealth responsibility over Indigenous affairs.[91] Coombs then provided a particularly strong connection between the postwar idea of human rights and new demands for an internationally recognised treaty between Indigenous and settler Australians. Coombs' reputation saw him represent the ATC at numerous forums, including a widely reported address as the guest of honour at Amnesty International's celebration of Human Rights Day 1979, where he connected the need for a treaty with the UDHR's Article 17 regarding the right to own property "alone as well as in association with others".[92] "We stand in open breach of this principle," Coombs warned, and asked for Amnesty International to help push "the Commonwealth Government ... into negotiations with the Aboriginal people to conclude a treaty".[93] This would function as a constitutionally enshrined rights-giving document, Coombs hoped, "recording Aboriginal acknowledgment of the right of other Australians to share this land, of the validity of property rights, legally and justly

---

[86] *The Canberra Times*, 3 August 1976, 2   [87] *The Canberra Times*, 8 September 1976, 2.

[88] *The Canberra Times*, 13 July 1977, 12.

[89] For more on this period of treaty negotiations and their links to ongoing politics of constitutional recognition, see Dylan Lino, *Constitutional Recognition: First Peoples and the Australian Settler State* (Annandale, NSW: The Federation Press, 2018), 16–22. On how these discussions deployed different ideas of sovereignty, see Julie Fenley, "The National Aboriginal Conference and the Makarrata: Sovereignty and Treaty Discussions, 1979–1981", *Australian Historical Studies* 42, no. 3 (2011), 372–89.

[90] On the ATC, see Rowse, "From Enforceability to Feel-Good".

[91] On Coombs, see Tim Rowse, *Nugget Coombs: A Reforming Life* (New York: Cambridge University Press, 2002).

[92] H. C. Coombs, "A Treaty with Aboriginal Australians: Talk Given to Amnesty International on Human Rights Day, 10 December 1979", H. C. Coombs Papers, MS803, Box 53, National Library of Australia (henceforth NLA).

[93] Ibid.

172   Implementing Rights

granted to, or acquired by, white Australians and the acceptance of the sovereignty of the Australian parliament". In exchange, settler Australians would acknowledge the "rights of Aborigines to ... maintain their distinctive identity ... laws, languages and culture", to "acknowledge their title to land to which they can show valid claim in Aboriginal law and custom" and to "acquire other lands necessary for their social and economic purposes".[94] Coombs' framing of demands for a treaty as a human rights issue saw AI adopt the treaty principle publically, along with the HRCA to whom he presented similar ideas in October of 1979.[95]

The Third General Assembly of the World Council of Indigenous Peoples in Canberra in 1981 also provided a confluence of Indigenous transnationalism, human rights and treaty demands. Held from 27 April to 1 May, this gathering followed two earlier meetings in Canada and received a $90,000 grant from the Fraser government, which saw hosting as "significant in promoting multi-culturalism" as well as "demonstrate[ing] that other countries have problems similar to those in Australia resulting from past treatment of indigenous people".[96] Some 500 delegates attended from twenty-seven countries, making it the largest global gathering of indigenous peoples to date, and the NAC delivered a position paper to the General Assembly on its ongoing work towards a Makarrata.[97] They placed this campaign within postwar "development of the law of self-determination to a point where the concept is now established in international law", having been "asserted as a fact" by third world nations, amongst whom the NAC – as the representative body of Indigenous Australians – counted itself. The "convenient falsehoods" of *terra nullius* provided "no impediment to the Australian government recognising the Aboriginal Nation as an international entity with whom it may treat". Such a recognition would allow the Commonwealth government to sidestep issues of federalism and negotiate directly via constitutional amendment, not only legitimating the sovereignty of the Australian settler state but also ensuring "that land handed over in any settlement is not the subject of 'just compensation' to the States".[98] The WCIP adopted calls for self-determination and land rights for Indigenous Australians as part of the Canberra gathering's final

---

[94] Ibid.   [95] *Canberra Times*, 25 October 1979, 2; *Canberra Times*, 11 December 1979, 3.

[96] "Submission No 3405: Assistance to the National Aboriginal Conference (NAC) to Host the Third General Assembly of the World Council of Indigenous Peoples (WCIP)", 20 August 1979, NAA: A12909, 3405.

[97] De Costa, *A Higher Authority*, 126. On the processes leading to the formation of the WCIP, see Hanne Hagtvedt Vik, "Indigenous Internationalism", in Glenda Sluga and Patricia Meria Clavin (eds.), *Internationalisms: A Twentieth-Century History* (Cambridge: Cambridge University Press, 2016), 315–39.

[98] National Aboriginal Conference, *The Makarrata: Some Ways Forward* (Canberra: National Aboriginal Conference, 1981), 1–4.

declaration, recognised the status of the NAC as an international representative body and for the first time issued its own Declaration of Human Rights.[99] This document included rights to self-determination, culture and language, to national resources and to economic assistance, the foundations of what would in 2007 become the United Nations Declaration of the Rights of Indigenous Peoples.[100] Several months later, the Senate Standing Committee on Constitutional and Legal Affairs convened an inquiry into "the feasibility of a compact or 'Makarrata'" between Indigenous and settler Australians, which handed down a report two years later recommending that such a proposal be put to a referendum.[101]

In December 1980, Stewart Harris reported a "developing consensus" around calls for Makarrata, with not only prominent legal endorsement but "qualified support" from both sides of mainstream politics, and it was at this moment that proposals for a Bill of Rights emerged with renewed vigour.[102] Michael Kirby, president of the Australian Law Reform Commission and long-time Bill of Rights advocate, optimistically declared to a conference on "Legislating for Human Rights" in February 1980 that while "there are acute differences between our political leaders on many things, it is reassuring that on the fundamental question [of an enforceable system for rights protections] there is harmony".[103] The only issue was "precisely what the rights are and whether they should be enforceable by a general charter or in some other way" and, indeed, the limitations of the ICCPR as the litmus test of rights. The Australian Council of Social Services (ACOSS), the peak body of Australia's community services sector, drafted a Bill of Rights for the Unemployed in 1977, calling for higher payments and less stringent eligibility criteria as "stagflation" saw Australia experience a significant rise in the number of job seekers for first time since World War II.[104] Criminologist Jocelynne Scutt, then at the beginning of a career that would make her one of Australia's best-known human rights lawyers, told a September 1980 conference on Women and Human Rights that a Bill of Rights would specifically aid women. She envisaged provisions for guaranteed income despite employment status, for the right to

---

[99] "Resolutions", *Identity* 4, no. 3 (1981), 22–3.
[100] "WCIP Declaration of Human Rights", *Identity* 4, no. 3 (1981), 20–1.
[101] Senate Standing Committee on Constitutional and Legal Affairs, *Two Hundred Years Later: Report by the Senate Standing Committee on Constitutional and Legal Affairs on the Feasibility of a Compact or "Makarrata" between the Commonwealth and Aboriginal People* (Canberra, ACT: Australian Government Publishing Service, 1983).
[102] *Canberra Times*, 17 December 1980, 22.
[103] Michael Kirby, *A Bill of Rights for Australia? Paper Presented at UNSW and ICJ's 1980 Seminar: Legislating for Human Rights – Saturday, 16 February 1980* (Canberra: Australian Law Reform Commission, 1980), 24.
[104] "Workless or Worthless? An Extract from the ACOSS Bill of Rights", *Legal Service Bulletin* 10 (December 1977), 368–71.

174   Implementing Rights

economic self-determination and to "enter into affectional relationships without regard to race, colour, sex, national or social origin".[105] Such claims lay well outside the remit of the ICCPR, as did those for Indigenous rights. As Kirby put it, "the endeavour to recognise and provide for the enforcement of Aboriginal customary laws runs into problems with the [ICCPR]", for, despite the covenants allowance for "self-determination", its promise of the extension of rights "without distinction of ... race or colour" entirely flew in the face of demands for sovereign treaty rights, demonstrating "the difficulty of applying ... internationally agreed upon standards of human rights which originated in Western Europe".[106]

Implementing a Bill of Rights was a campaign promise of Bob Hawke's ALP, elected in 1983. Gareth Evans – long-time vice president of the Victorian Council for Civil Liberties, lawyer and academic before becoming an ALP senator in 1978 – was a key proponent, citing Canada's Charter of Rights and Freedoms in 1982 and the British House of Lords 1980 Bill of Rights, based on implementation of the European Convention on Human Rights, as precedent.[107] Australia's was to be a document similarly based on an existing declaration, the ICCPR. "[T]o map the areas of deficiency" in Australia's adherence to the ICESCR would not only be lengthy, Evans cautioned, but "beyond the scope of the topic 'human rights' as that term has currency in this country".[108] Human rights' return in the 1970s, as many scholars have highlighted, occurred without the social and economic rights that sat at the core of the UDHR. Evans' minimalist Bill still came in for criticism, however. Its tepid language about any potential Commonwealth overriding of state laws and significant leeway period for reform was questioned in a submission by Queensland civil libertarians, who drew attention to the High Court's upholding of such actions via the external affairs power in the Tasmanian Dams case (1983). They claimed that such equivocation "bear[s] stark witness to the political obstacles to implementing the ICCPR in an incremental and selective fashion".[109]

---

[105] Jocelynne Scutt, "An Australian Bill of Rights?", in *Women's Rights: Human Rights? Conference* (Canberra: Law Foundation of New South Wales/Office of Women's Affairs, 1981), 56–9.

[106] Kirby, *A Bill of Rights for Australia*, 24.

[107] Gareth Evans, "An Australian Bill of Rights", *Human Rights* 1, no. 5 (July/August 1983), 6–9.

[108] Gareth Evans, "Human Rights in Australia", paper presented at Australian Council for Overseas Aid Summer School, Hobart, 22 January 1978, Allan Missen Papers (henceforth AMP), MS 7258, Box 336, NLA.

[109] Peter Applegarth, "The Australian Bill of Rights: A Submission by the Queensland Council for Civil Liberties", AMP, MS 7258, Box 336, NLA.

Coming Together? Makarrata and a Bill of Rights 175

For others, the Bill went too far. The Institute of Public Affairs, a conservative think tank founded in 1943 that by the 1980s had become a standard-bearer of the New Right's mixture of economic liberalism and social conservatism, argued that the Bill was "social engineering". "Similar 'Human Rights' Bills have been adopted by Warsaw Pact countries," the author warned, and the real agenda of "code words" like rights and freedom was to "promote and entrench values, ideologies and lifestyles that are unacceptable to the vast majority of Australians".[110] Unsurprisingly, perhaps, the Bill soon became something of a dead letter. After two rewrites and a lengthy period in the Senate Standing Committee on Constitutional and Legal Affairs, a disgruntled Evans withdrew the bill in November 1986. While the basic intent had been "to provide a legal avenue ... for people to remedy government acts and practices", the legislation "had been widely misunderstood, with some opponents claiming it was a communist document which would have all sorts of adverse effects".[111]

Tellingly, the Bill was pulled only days after the introduction of controversial "Australia Card" legislation to federal parliament that "exposed a raw nerve of suspicion of the state".[112] Loosely modelled on the American Social Security Number and introduced under the pretext of controlling tax evasion, critics quickly labelled it a "big brother" initiative to trace citizens using new computer technologies.[113] In a sign of popular angst, the *Australian* newspaper received over 800 letters concerning the proposal, at a rate of seventeen to one against.[114] Liberal member John Watson remarked on the auspicious timing of the Bill's debate in the Senate – 10 December 1986 – expressing hopes that "on this day, the 38th anniversary of the ... Declaration of Human Rights in 1948, this human rights infringing Australia Card will be defeated in the Senate".[115] Poet Les Murray opined, just prior to the proposal's inglorious scrapping in 1987:

> Well you have or claim more rights than a dingo pup has bites
> More rights than any brumby in the yard
> But bluey that's all wrong, for your "rights" will soon belong
> Not to you but to that little plastic card.[116]

---

[110] J. K. Bowen, *The Proposal for a Bill of Rights – Some Implications for our Society* (Sydney: Institute of Public Affairs, 1985),

[111] *Canberra Times*, 27 November 1986, 10.

[112] Frank Bongiorno, *The Eighties: The Decade That Transformed Australia* (Melbourne: Black Inc., 2015), 209.

[113] On "big brother" responses to the Australia Card, see the *Canberra Times*, 27 October 1986, 23.

[114] Bongiorno, *The Eighties*, 208.   [115] *CPD* (Senate), 10 December 1986, 3747.

[116] Les Murray, "The Australia Card", *The Daylight Moon* (North Ryde, Sydney: Angus & Robertson, 1987), 52.

176   Implementing Rights

That government could propose a sweeping rights charter while also seeking what seemed a dramatic extension of its powers invoked the spectre of 1944: of an intention to curb rather than cultivate rights. Though much more ink was spilt on the topic in later years, a Bill of Rights has not been seriously considered by the Commonwealth parliament since. Plans for a Makarrata met a similar fate. Harris' greeting of emerging bipartisanship on the issue in fact proved a high point of conviviality, for while the incoming ALP government promised to "fully investigate" the idea of a treaty in 1983, Malcolm Fraser's Liberals proposed only to work "in consultation and cooperation" with the states rather than foster "conflict and confrontation".[117] By 1987, Hawke was no longer using treaty terminology, declaring himself "bored with the discussion about whether it's a treaty, compact or another word" and warning that "I don't think we should be creating unreal expectations by using a word now which may have connotations that are inappropriate or unbelievable".[118] A particularly harsh blow, however, came in 1988: the much-vaunted bicentenary year where wrongs might be righted. Moves towards an enforceable treaty were "torpedoed", as the opposition Liberal party under John Howard "outright reject[ed]" any future treaty, finally severing the pretence of agreement expressed by his predecessors. Labelling the idea a "sick and sorry joke", Howard called for the "real needs" of Indigenous people to be met rather of focusing on "stupid symbolism" – words that were to define his years in public life.[119]

The Human Rights Commission and Its Discontents

Craig Johnston was perhaps an unlikely human rights activist. He joined the Communist Party of Australia (CPA) in 1973 as a 22-year-old university student, the same year he became involved in the emerging Gay Liberation Movement in Sydney, a radical offshoot of the Campaign Against Moral Persecution (CAMP).[120] These campaigns exploded in prominence in the early years of the 1970s, thanks in no small measure to the international success of Australian Dennis Altman's 1971 book *Homosexual: Oppression and Liberation*, which drew on emerging critiques of psychoanalysis as exemplified by Frantz Fanon to critique the social

---

[117] *Canberra Times*, 26 February 1983, 12.   [118] *Canberra Times*, 4 September 1987, 1.
[119] *Canberra Times*, 18 June 1988, 2; *Canberra Times*, 16 November 1988, 16.
[120] For histories of Australia's gay liberation and queer rights movements, see Robert Reynolds, *From Camp to Queer: Remaking the Australian Homosexual* (Carlton, VIC: Melbourne University Press, 2002); Graham Willett, *Living Out Loud: A History of Gay and Lesbian Activism in Australia* (St Leonards, NSW: Allen & Unwin, 2002); Liz Ross, *Revolution Is for Us: The Left and Gay Liberation in Australia* (Brunswick, VIC: Interventions, 2013).

status of the homosexual.[121] Despite only being one group within a broader movement, Johnston explains how "Gay Liberation gave its name to the whole homosexual movement, as well as a certain militancy, structure, analysis and 'image'" that drew heavily on its forbears in black and women's liberation as well as Western Marxism.[122] Johnston soon became a leading figure in the movement and lent it socialist political insights, but by the end of the 1970s he was concerned as to its direction. Writing in the CPA's theoretical journal, Johnston identified two splintering currents – "the maximum program of liberation and the minimal program of democratic rights", with the full social, cultural and political emancipation of the former increasingly being replaced with the latter's strictly legislative, incremental agenda.[123] Johnston did not see this as an either/or question; instead he drew on the CPA's critical embrace of rights talk to argue that the "homosexual movement must fight for democratic rights, but must be alert to the opportunity for exposing the social function of sexual repression". This idea that a successful movement "cannot just demand 'gay rights', but sexual liberation for all" underlay Johnston's spearheading the establishment of the Gay Rights Lobby (GRL) in Sydney in 1980.[124]

At the same moment, a years-long debate was coming to an end in the Australian parliament, with the latest Human Rights Commission Bill (HRCB) entering the final stages of passage. Notwithstanding the tradition of "Ombudsman" offices, first established in Scandinavia in the early nineteenth century to field citizen complaints against state law and bureaucracy, the idea of Commissions or National Human Rights Institutions (NHRI) at a national level to govern implementation of international human rights principles was a relatively new one. Canada and New Zealand became the first nations to adopt a Human Rights Commission in 1977, and legislation was first prepared to create a similar body in Australia during that same year.[125] Introduced in June 1977 by Fraser's attorney general, Bob Ellicott, the Bill would check the compliance of Commonwealth legislation with the ICCPR, but it was widely criticised as a "toothless tiger" that merely duplicated

---

[121] Dennis Altman, *Homosexual: Oppression & Liberation* (Sydney: Angus & Robertson, 1972 [1971]).

[122] Craig Johnston, "Radical Homosexual Politics Today: A Legacy of the Seventies", *Australian Left Review* 74 (1980), 24.

[123] Ibid., 24.   [124] Ibid., 29.

[125] On the rise of National Human Rights Institutions, see Jeong-Woo Koo and Francisco O. Ramirez, "National Incorporation of Global Human Rights: Worldwide Expansion of National Human Rights Institutions, 1966–2004", *Social Forces* 87, no. 3 (2009), 1321–53; Ryan M. Welch, "National Human Rights Institutions: Domestic Implementation of International Human Rights Law", *Journal of Human Rights* 16, no. 1 (2017), 96–116.

178   Implementing Rights

the fact-gathering powers of Kirby's Australian Law Reform Commission, established in 1973.[126] The Bill lapsed with the elections of December 1977 and was reintroduced in September 1979 by Ellicott's successor, Peter Durack. This second iteration again restricted the Bill's prerogative to Commonwealth affairs but was framed more in terms of ensuring the government's ratification of the ICCPR later that year, alongside providing a clearer process for complaints handing and education. "We have no cause to hide anything in the area of human rights, and should be willing to ratify the central human rights covenant of the United Nations" Durack impressed on his fellow parliamentarians. "Unless we ratify the Covenant ourselves, and agree to be bound by it, we are hardly in a position to exercise influence" on Australia's neighbours to follow suit, he added.[127] Fraser had won the 1977 election on a platform that included establishing a human rights commission, which had been referred to in the governor general's opening speech of the 1978 parliamentary year – making it a promise his government had to deliver on.

Responses to the 1979 bill were even more virulent. ACOSS castigated the Bill as "window dressing to make Australia's position look better internationally".[128] Why did the Bill only focus on traditional "negative" rights instead of economic ones "like the right to work [and] to a minimum income", without which "how can there be any commitment to civil and political rights?"[129] Michael Gorton of the United Nations Youth Association labelled it a "token gesture", the powers of which are limited to "conciliation, publicity and reports to parliament (presumably to gather dust)". It was a "pale, weak, timid pussycat" in the words of Gareth Evans, while the Women's Electoral Lobby invoked Mao Zedong when describing the Bill as a "paper tiger, invented by paper pushers to keep themselves and an army of lawyers employed".[130] Conservative as well as progressive forces raised criticism as well, with the rights of the unborn child yet again becoming a cause of disagreement. The Right to Life movement employed its favoured strategies of mass correspondence, petitions and lobbying to force an amendment to the Bill. William Daniel of Parkville, Victoria, seized on the universalist language of the human rights revolution, questioning in a letter to *The Age* whether the refusal of "legal rights" to the unborn in the 1977 final report of the Royal

---

[126] *Canberra Times*, 29 December 1976, 2; *Canberra Times*, 11 July 1977, 7.
[127] *CPD* (House), 25 September 1979, 918–9.
[128] *Human Rights? That Is the Question* (Sydney: Australian Council of Social Services, 1979), 1–4.
[129] Ibid.
[130] Michael Gorton to Members of Parliament, 9 October 1979, AMP, MS 7528, Box 238, NLA. *Sydney Morning Herald*, 19 February 1980, 5; "Women's Electoral Lobby – Press Release", 8 March 1981, AMP, MS 7528, Box 240, NLA.

The Human Rights Commission and Its Discontents 179

Commission on Human Relationships meant that their human rights were to go unprotected– "do I have no more rights than the law allows me?"[131] James Nash of Victoria appended a copy of the 1959 Declaration on the Rights of the Child and its protection of human rights "before as well as after birth" – language excluded from the 1979 draft covenant – to a letter to pro-choice Liberal senator Alan Missen.[132] "The most blatant denial of human rights occurring in Australia today is the deliberate killing of an estimated 80,000 pre-born children each year," Margaret Tighe wrote to Missen, and to "deny that they are human ... is an act of gross discrimination and injustice against the smallest and weakest members of our community".[133]

Conservative lobbying proved successful in March 1980, with the "Simon Amendments" added to the HRCB by a conscience vote in the House of Representatives, specifically protected the "human rights of the unborn".[134] The Senate quickly rejected this amended legislation, putting the two houses at odds for the first time since Whitlam's dismissal in 1975, a decision that Missen was particularly instrumental in. One of the few Liberals with a strong civil liberties pedigree, as a 26-year-old vice president of the Victorian Young Liberals Missen had created a national stir in 1951 by labelling the party's proposed communist ban "totalitarian", for which his party membership was suspended.[135] After his election to the Senate in 1974, Missen embarked on international human rights endeavours, including a trip to Moscow in 1976 to meet leaders of the Helsinki Network and AI.[136] The senator's strong opinions and terse manner were evident in the written reasons the chamber provided for blocking of the proposed amendments, which were "irrelevant to the major tasks of the commission and, in their obscurity and uncertainty, will not advance the major purposes of the Bill". By requiring the commission to "define the human rights of the unborn", they would step away from the wording of the ICCPR, imperilling proposed ratification.[137] Missen took equal umbrage with pro-life letter writers, whose missives in "the same stereotyp[ical] terms" displayed "no concept or understanding of what is involved in the ... Bill itself", and with those parliamentarians who make faint praise of human rights but "do not bother to belong to the parliamentary branch of the Amnesty International or any human

[131] *The Age*, 17 April 1980, 12.
[132] James Nash to Alan Missen, 18 April 1980, AMP, MS 7528, Box 240, NLA.
[133] Margaret Tighe to Alan Missen, 11 April 1980, AMP, MS 7528, Box 240, NLA.
[134] *Canberra Times*, 5 March 1980, 1.
[135] Anton Hermann, *Alan Missen: Liberal Pilgrim* (Canberra: Poplar Press, 1993), 7–21, 1.
[136] Ibid., 117–18.   [137] *Senate Journal*, no. 176, 13 May 1980, 1309–10.

180   Implementing Rights

rights organisation".[138] The Bill finally passed unamended in 1981, and social movements were beginning to pay attention.[139]

In March 1981, Johnston joined two other veteran campaigners – Sri Lankan-Australian Paul Van Reyk and Sydney University professor Lex Watson – in announcing the formation of the GRL, whose "objectives were to be understood in a broad sense".[140] The organisation's "focus on specific issues which can readily be understood and supported by 'the public' as democratic objectives, and achievable in relation to the state" hinted at the group's socialist inclinations, an attempt to bridge the gap between the radical 1970s and the more conservative 1980s.[141] While the group's methods – lobbying politicians, compiling reports and appealing to the media – aped those of the emerging human rights movement, Johnston saw the GRL as an "independent, extra-parliamentary, radical and democratic movement [that] supports nothing which implies the inferiority of homosexuals or homosexuality". "The desire to achieve one 'very minor reform' is part of a strategy for liberation", as Johnston put it.[142] Not wasting any time, the GRL took advantage of Australia's ratification of the ICCPR in August 1980 and lodged the first ever domestic human rights complaint in an Australian jurisdiction via what was then the Human Rights Bureau (HRB), a small body within the attorney general's department created to perform the tasks of a NHRI while parliament wrangled over a long-term solution. The GRL wanted to test the consistency of Article 26 of the ICCPR, which mandated that "[a]ll persons … are entitled without any discrimination to the equal protection of the law", with the Australian Capital Territory (ACT) Law Reform (Sexual Behaviours) Ordinance 1976, that imposed a higher age of consent and greater fines for homosexual acts.[143] The ordinance was seen as a progressive move by many after its original passage, but it fell afoul of the GRL's philosophy of "nothing less than full equality".[144] This was a carefully prepared and reasoned complaint: in targeting a specific article of the ICCPR, it displayed an increased rights consciousness amongst activists, and by limiting its parameters to the

---

[138] *CPD* (Senate), 20 March 1980, 881.   [139] *Canberra Times*, 6 August 1980, 3.

[140] Craig Johnston, Paul Van Reyk and Lex Watson, "Proposal for a Campaign for Homosexual Law Reform", 3 March 1981, Gay Rights Lobby Records (henceforth GRL), MLMSS 4875, Box 1, State Library of New South Wales (henceforth SLNSW).

[141] Ibid.

[142] Craig Johnston to Ernie Chaples, 15 December 1981, GRL, MLMSS 4875, Box 10, SLNSW.

[143] Human Rights Bureau, "Complaint by the Gay Rights Lobby: Laws Relating to Homosexual Acts in the Australian Capital Territory", 5 August 1981, GRL, MLMSS 4875, Box 8, SLNSW.

[144] "Full Equality, Nothing Less", 14 July 1981, GRL, MLMSS 4875, Box 1, SLNSW.

The Human Rights Commission and Its Discontents   181

ACT – one of two territories under direct Commonwealth jurisdiction – the issue of federal competence in state matters was avoided.

In their report on the complaint, the HRB described it as "an extremely difficult inquiry", not only as this was their first case but also because of "the difficulty of interpreting and applying Article 26".[145] The Bureau focused on two key concerns: did homosexual persons constitute a "status" under Article 26; and did the complaint itself fall within the purview of that Article? While excluded from the eleven statuses provided in the ICCPR, and lacking any domestic or international precedent on the point, the Bureau turned to the European Court of Human Rights' (ECHR) decision to take a broad definition of status: "a personal characteristic (status) by which persons ... are distinguishable from each other".[146] Homosexuality could conceivably hold such status under a similarly formulated instrument, and a case then under appeal in the ECHR had ruled as such. Employing this precedent, the Bureau found that as medical evidence increasingly attested to the biological and psycho-social origins of sexual orientation, that homosexual individuals "pursue and protect an 'alternative lifestyle'" and had experienced historical group oppression, "they appear to the Bureau to present a compelling case to warrant the conclusion that homosexual persons should be accorded a status".[147] Despite finding that the status of homosexuality was acceptable within the ICCPR and that the law in question was indeed discriminatory as such, the Bureau was unable to find in the GRL's favour. This arose from the careful and specific manner in which Australia ratified the Covenant: owing to the nation's common law heritage, only the application and not the letter of the law could be adjudicated upon.[148] Painstakingly analysing the cases that had so far been heard in the ACT since the 1976 Ordinance came into effect, the Bureau could only conclude that, as no person had yet been tried in a way that revealed an inconsistency with the ICCPR, the ordinance must stand.[149] While able to celebrate a partial victory – the recognition of homosexuality as an (albeit limited and stereotyped) status under international law – the GRL decried the Bureau's "legalistic sham".[150] A *Canberra Times* correspondent claimed the case "raised disturbing questions": if "it is alright if laws have discriminatory provisions, as long as the discrimination is not carried out into practice", then "one is left wondering how many ways the fine words of the covenant ... can be

---

[145] Human Rights Bureau, "Complaint by the Gay Rights Lobby: Laws Relating to Homosexual Acts in the Australian Capital Territory", 5 August 1981, 2.
[146] Ibid., 4.   [147] Ibid., 6–7.   [148] Ibid., 11.   [149] Ibid., 12–14.
[150] Jamie Gardiner, "Gay Rights are Human Rights", GRL, MLMSS 4875, Box 8, SLNSW.

182   Implementing Rights

interpreted".[151] This also raised questions as the effectiveness of the Bureau's successor, "which is also dominated by the legally trained".[152]

The Human Rights Commission opened its doors on 10 December 1981 in Canberra's AMP Building, appropriately distant from the Parliamentary Triangle, under part-time chair Roma Mitchell, a well-known Adelaide lawyer and feminist. Peter Bailey, public servant and head of the former Bureau, became deputy chair, while five part-time commissioners were appointed to represent Indigenous and ethnic people, women, and the disabled in line with the Commission's obligation to check compliance with not only the ICCPR but also Declarations or Covenants on race, children, and the physically and mentally disabled.[153] The position of Al Grassby, former immigration minister under the Whitlam government and inaugural commissioner of Community Relations under the Racial Discrimination Act, was amalgamated with the HRC amidst protests that this would limit his effectiveness.[154] Twenty-five full-time staff were allocated, with ten assigned to Grasbby's Community Relations portfolio. The HRC's first annual report, covering the period from 10 December 1981 to 30 June 1982, gives a sense of its activities: receiving and handling complaints from individuals and groups within its purview, producing reports on the compliance of specific legislation with human rights law and educating the public on their rights.[155] In its first seven months, the commission received ninety-seven complaints on human rights matters and some 377 on racial discrimination, of which roughly 60 per cent fell outside its jurisdiction.[156] Of those that were investigated, the largest number concerned the application of Commonwealth law rather than inter-personal or workplace matters. The Commission's educational role consisted of publishing a monthly newsletter – *Human Rights* – while a glossy pamphlet entitled *The Human Rights Commission and You* was widely distributed.[157] Another of the Commission's tasks was the cultivation of a human rights NGO sector, first attempted in a Sydney meeting of twenty-five diverse community organisations in April 1982 attended by ethnic, refugee, religious, women's, homosexual and several self-professed human rights organisations.[158] While the commission happily reported that that "the

---

[151] *Canberra Times*, 13 December 1981, 4.   [152] Ibid., 4.

[153] As well as the RDA, the four Covenants and Declarations the HRC administered were the *ICCPR* (1966), *Declaration on the Rights of the Child* (1959), *Declaration on the Rights of Mentally Retarded Perso*ns (1971) and the *Declaration on the Rights of Disabled Persons* (1975).

[154] *The Age*, 24 September 1981, 13.

[155] *Human Rights Commission Annual Report: 1981–82, Volume 1. Report for the period 10 December 1981–30 June 1982* (Canberra: Australian Government Printing Service, 1982), xii–xiii.

[156] Ibid., 19–20.   [157] Ibid., 32   [158] Ibid., 60–2.

The Human Rights Commission and Its Discontents   183

organisations present ... agreed the meeting had been of value in bringing a wide range of organisations together in the human rights context", Jamie Gardiner of the GRL found that "not only NGOs but also members of the commission were very worried by the government's hamstringing of the HRC".[159] Alongside the ever-present concern of federalism, attention was drawn to the Bureau's earlier decision on the GRL's complaint, which another participant in the meeting called "a mockery of the whole Human Rights Act". "By the same logic", the participant declared, "apart-heid would not be a breach".[160]

High Court rulings in what have colloquially become known as the Koowarta and Tasmanian Dams cases of 1982 and 1983, respectively, provided solutions to the ongoing federalist impasse. Indigenous man John Koowarta had asked the federal Aboriginal Land Fund Commission to purchase the Archer River Cattle Station in far north Queensland at the behest of his community in 1976, and against the wishes of the Queensland Government. Koowarta took his case to the-then Office of Community Relations and eventually the High Court as a breach of the Racial Discrimination Act, to which the Bjelke-Petersen government responded by joining the states of Western Australia and Victoria in challenging the RDA itself as outside the Commonwealth's competence. In a narrow decision, the High Court upheld the rights of the Commonwealth to enter into treaties concerning topics of "international concern" without the consent and in fact potentially overriding certain authorities of indivi-dual states.[161] As discussed in Chapter 1, the idea of "domestic jurisdic-tion" had functioned as the basis of Australia's approach to international institutions since the 1940s but now seemed not just politically but legally defunct. The Tasmanian Dams case, concerning the Constitutional valid-ity of the Hawke government's World Heritage Protection Conservation Act (1983) that had interceded to halt Tasmanian state government plans to build hydroelectricity facilities in the World Heritage–listed Franklin River region, confirmed the Commonwealth's power to implement inter-national treaty obligations.[162] The decision also spelt a new period in Australia's negotiation of international treaties. No longer would Australia need to place federal reservations on its ratification of interna-tional treaties, as had been done in the case of the ICCPR to ensure that while the Commonwealth would "use their best efforts, [they would] not

---

[159] Ibid., 38; Gardiner, "Gay Rights Are Human Rights".
[160] Gardiner, "Gay Rights Are Human Rights". Underlining in original.
[161] My reconstruction of this case relies on Hilary Charlesworth, "Internal and External Affairs: The Koowarta Case in Context", *Griffith Law Review* 23, no. 1 (2014), 35–43.
[162] Ann Genovese, "Critical Decision 1983: Remembering *Commonwealth v Tasmania*", *Griffith Law Review* 24, no. 1 (2015), 1–15.

184   Implementing Rights

be required to comply with obligations that fell outside their jurisdiction".[163] The Hawke government amended Australia's ratification of the ICCPR in 1984, replacing the earlier federal reservation with a federal declaration that was "descriptive only and would not affect Australia's obligations under the relevant treaty".[164] Problems of federal–state jurisdiction in the enforcement of universal liberty seemed at an end.

The HRC's first foray into state politics, however, quickly demonstrated the limitations of its newfound powers. On 19 February 1985 Queensland again made national headlines, this time for terminating the employment of some 1,200 unionists working at the South East Queensland Electricity Board (SEQEB) amidst ongoing industrial action. Thanks to a system of "gerrymandering" electoral districts and a vociferous anti-communism, Bjelke-Petersen was enjoying his seventeenth year in office at the head of a Country Party that had ruled the state for nearly three decades, and his hostility to critics only worsened with age.[165] Commonwealth Attorney General Lionel Bowen instructed the HRC to investigate whether the Electricity (Continuation of Supply) Act 1985 – hurriedly passed legislation which had allowed the Electricity Commissioner to terminate the employment of any person who refused to "maintain or restore a supply of electricity", effectively barring trade unionists from employment – contravened the ICCPR's prohibition of "forced or compulsory labour". Again drawing on precedent of the ECHR, the Commission found that any legislation which contained "an element of compulsion, coupled with a penalty for, non-compliance", both of which featured in the 1985 Act, would constitute forced labour.[166] The HRC recommended that this inconsistency "be brought to the attention of the Queensland government", and if no action was taken to remedy the situation the Commonwealth should "make the provisions of Article 8 applicable as part of the law of Australia", transforming what was a "declaratory obligation" into a "specific 'Bill of Rights' provision".[167] While clearly researched and firm in its recommendations, the report made little difference: Bjelke-Petersen won the dispute, and the Electrical Trades Union was left licking its wounds. The federal ALP government – mindful of the damage Bjelke-Petersen had done in 1975 by filling a Labor Senate vacancy with dissatisfied party member Albert Field, creating the conditions for Whitlam's dismissal – was reticent to act against

---

[163] Madelaine Chaim, "*Tasmanian Dams* and Australia's Relationship with International Law", *Griffith Law Review* 24, no. 1 (2015), 93.

[164] Ibid., 94.

[165] See Raymond Evans, *A History of Queensland* (Melbourne: Cambridge University Press, 2007), chapter 21.

[166] Human Rights Commission, *Report No. 12: The Queensland Electricity (Continuity of Supply) Act 1985* (Canberra: Australian Government Publishing Service, 1985), 3–7.

[167] Ibid., 17.

The Human Rights Commission and Its Discontents

Queensland's increasingly violent and corrupt government. Without Evans' Bill of Rights, the Commission remained largely powerless. Even in the case of his defeat in *Koowarta*, the premier simply declared the area under dispute a national park, the only one created under his government.[168] States' rights again trumped international law.

The HRC also faced challenges. Launched with fanfare in 1981, by 1986 it was labelled a "monster" by the National Conference of the Young Liberal Movement, reflecting the party's new (or rather re-established) orthodoxy "that human rights could not be protected by a bureaucracy".[169] Having added the Convention on the Elimination of Discrimination against Women to its enforceable instruments in 1984, after the Hawke government made its swift ratification a priority, the Commission was now receiving some 2,000 complaints a year. Pamela O'Neill, Australia's first Sex Discrimination commissioner, drew on findings of the recently concluded third UN conference on women in Nairobi to label the "denial of Human Rights to women on an equal basis with men ... the most universal of all human rights struggles".[170] Its educational program for primary and high schools was expanding, despite being banned in Queensland public system, initiatives that were described, by a gathering of international human rights educators in 1985, as "more comprehensive and more closely tailored to classroom use than are materials available elsewhere".[171] The problem was less the organisation's success than the quickly shifting political climate. Much as John Howard's dismissal of a Makarrata was a heavy blow to campaigners for a bipartisan treaty, issues on which a political consensus existed from the mid-1970s were becoming freshly contested. Historian Geoffrey Blainey's incendiary 1984 speech questioning levels of Asian immigration became a matter of huge national attention, as the ideological offensive of the "New Right" got underway.[172] In the Commission's final two years, it was variously accused of enforcing rights "drawn up by overseas socialist countries", encouraging homosexual immigration, working as a star chamber and "destroying our society" through challenging traditional values.[173] The organisation's dissolution – owing to a "sunset clause"

---

[168] Charlesworth, "Internal and External Affairs", 5.
[169] *Canberra Times*, 8 January 1986, 1.
[170] Pamela O'Neill, "Women and Rights", *Human Rights* no. 15 (November 1985), 1.
[171] Human Rights Commission, *The Human Rights Commission: Its Educational Program and 'Teaching for Human Rights'* (Canberra: Australian Government Printing Service, 1986), 5–6.
[172] Frank Bongiorno, *The Eighties: The Decade that Transformed Australia* (Melbourne: Black Inc., 2015), 63–5.
[173] Peter Bailey, "In Answer to Some Specific Allegations", *Human Rights* no. 15 (November 1985), 11–12.

186   Implementing Rights

built into initial legislation – saw it amalgamated with the Equal Opportunity Commission as the Human Rights and Equal Opportunity Commission (HREOC) in 1986. Viewed as a saving grace by some and an emasculation by others, the HREOC had to perform more duties with fewer personnel and less funding, an announcement to which staff responded by going on strike "to protect the human rights of staff, complainants and minority groups".[174] Human rights, it seemed, remained as controversial as ever.

Conclusion

By 1984, the GRL was at an impasse. The organisation had been formed to decriminalise homosexuality, particularly in the Crimes Act (NSW) 1900, and the passage of a 1984 amendment seemed to have achieved this. The GRL had supported the amendment, despite its provision for unequal age of consent laws, recasting equality as a "principle [which] we must get as close to as possible" or as "stage one in a long campaign", for in the end people wanted action. Standing up for full equality, potentially imperilling partial legalisation, would see the GRL "cop a lot of flack from the gay sub-culture" that they represented.[175] On the other hand, some lambasted such moves as an abandonment of the group's commitment to "basic human rights" for "some liberal crumbs from the parliamentary do-nothings". "Either freedom of sexual expression is a right or it isn't", one member protested.[176] Reflecting on this debate and the partial victory, one scribe in the group's newsletter asked, "[I]s there life after law reform?" "Surely no-one ever believed that law reform was the beginning and end of the gay rights struggle"; after all, a range of issues still needed addressing. Differing age of consent rules, as well as de facto and immigration law issues – and ongoing demands for a Bill of Rights – constituted "a large workload for the future".[177] Garry Bennett used this moment of introspection to ask a different, more conceptual question: "what happened to gay liberation?"[178] Bennett worried what had been lost in the seeming abandonment of early ideas of abolishing sexual differentiation, the replacing of a desire to "liberat[e] everyone's sexuality" with "a more realistic, a more

---

[174] *Canberra Times*, 19 November 1986, 24; *Canberra Times*, 18 November 1986, 3.

[175] "Gay Rights Lobby Meeting – 30th November 1981", GRL, MLMSS 4875, Box 8, SLNSW.

[176] Jerry Davies, "No Partial Law Reform", *GRL: A Periodical Newsletter of the Gay Rights Lobby* no. 2 (September 1983), 6–7.

[177] "Is There Life after Law Reform?", *GRL: A Periodical Newsletter of the Gay Rights Lobby* no. 5 (June 1984), 7–8.

[178] Garry Bennett, "What Happened to Gay Liberation?", *GRL: A Periodical Newsletter of the Gay Rights Lobby*, no. 6 (September 1984), 3–5.

Conclusion

pragmatic, gay politics". The GRL had been established to seek liberation through legality, but Bennett's hindsight presented rights discourse as a necessarily mainstreaming operation – creating an often narrowly defined rights bearing sexual constituency by "focus[ing] on the symptoms of the problem" while "the cause is left unchallenged".[179]

Bennett's scepticism of human rights in the 1980s is reflective of the idea's trajectory during its moment of final, gradual implementation. Keith Suter's suspicions towards the overly quick embrace by governments of human rights in the late 1970s seem prescient, as the term's entering of the political mainstream saw it become a plaything of party leaders and political operatives, while its adherents found outcomes lacking. The year 1978 was one of possibility: both major parties endorsed the need for greater protections of human rights, while calls for a treaty or Makarrata with Indigenous Australians and a constitutional Bill of Rights seemed not just possible but inevitable. These halcyon days soon gave way to harsh reality, however. The Bill of Rights again fell foul of conservative arguments, in which the idea appeared as either inherent pointlessness in a system of common law rights, on one hand, or a threat to the very existence of Western society on the other. Equally, the growing and assertive land rights movement saw a Liberal Party increasingly under the sway of neoliberal ideas propose not a binding treaty but what would soon become known as "practical reconciliation". The Human Rights Commission proved another victim of mid-1980s cultural sparring matches, moving from a proud emblem of Australia's commitment to international law into a conniving player in a global conspiracy. Bennett's observations speak both to the inability of human rights to address the concerns of minority groups – whether because their particular demands failed to chime with dominant readings of the term's meaning or because their status had an unclear bearing on the category of human – and the more general but equally pressing question of constructing an ideal society. "[T]he promotion of the rights of a limited few who happen to identify as gay or be labelled as such" not only "does not mean that people have to like us or understand us", but also did not guarantee that "homosexuality, or indeed any form of sexual expression [would] become an accepted part of the daily lives of most people".[180] How did one move from having rights to be able to enjoy them in a society free from prejudice, let alone free from the need for minorities in the first place? Could, to borrow a term from contemporary human rights literature, the attainment of individual rights "cascade" into a rightful – indeed righteous – society?

[179] Ibid., 4–5.   [180] Bennett, "What Happened to Gay Liberation?", 4.

Epilogue: Cascade or Trickle?

On 10 December 1992 – forty-four years since the Universal Declaration of Human Rights was presented to the world – Australian Labor Party (ALP) Prime Minister Paul Keating launched the International Year of the World's Indigenous People. That such an event occurred in the first place showed how far the idea of human rights had developed, mutated and transformed in the intervening years, with Keating telling his audience – at "the Block" in the inner Sydney suburb of Redfern, an Indigenous-administered housing project – that it would "be a year of great significance for Australia".[1] Why that was required little explanation, whether to the First Nations people Keating was addressing or to those other Australians who heard it on the nightly news. Six months earlier, a case regarding the ownership of a small plot of land on a tiny island off the coast of Queensland had concluded after a decade of legal argument. *Mabo* vs *Queensland No. 2,* known simply as the Mabo judgement and named for its chief plaintiff, Eddie Mabo of Mer Island in the Torres Strait, saw the High Court finally extinguish what Keating called on that day the "bizarre conceit" of *terra nullius,* that Australia prior to European settlement had been a land without people.[2] In rapid-fire staccato statements, Keating told those assembled of something that Indigenous people knew all too well yet had not previously passed the lips of an Australian politician:

> We took the traditional lands and smashed the traditional way of life.
> We brought the diseases. The alcohol.
> We committed the murders.
> We took the children from their mothers.[3]

---

[1] Paul Keating, "Redfern Speech (Year of the World's Indigenous People)", 10 December 1992, available at https://antar.org.au/sites/default/files/paul_keating_speech_transcript.pdf.

[2] Ibid. For more on the Mabo judgement in international context, see: Peter H. Russell, *Recognising Aboriginal Title: The Mabo Case and Indigenous Resistance to English-Settler Colonialism* (Toronto: University of Toronto Press, 2006).

[3] Paul Keating, "Redfern Speech".

Epilogue: Cascade or Trickle? 189

This was an act of recognition – not an apology, which would take another fifteen years – that British colonialism and the Australian nation-state had been far from a universal good. As treasurer, Keating had presided over economic reforms – deregulation, privatisation and the ending of trade tariffs in exchange for a scaled-down Scandinavian-style social wage. Having unseated Bob Hawke in a long-running leadership contest a year earlier, he was turning his mind to "big picture" issues. Keating invoked Herbert Vere Evatt's words of some forty years before, cautioning that, if Australia was "truly the land of the fair go", the nation must "extend opportunity and care, dignity and hope to the indigenous people of Australia".[4]

The idea of a "justice cascade" has entered the human rights nomenclature of late, particularly owing to Kathryn Sikkink's 2011 book of that title, which used the term in specific reference to a trend from the 1990s onwards towards "holding individual state officials, including heads of state, criminally accountable for human rights violations". The idea of such accountability and the spread of normative rights frameworks more generally "started as a small stream, but later caught on suddenly, sweeping along many actors in its wake".[5] Keating's statement, and the subsequent acts of his government, could be read as the beginnings of just such a cascade. With Mabo having created the possibility that every inch of Australia sat on un-ceded Indigenous land, the Native Title Act 1993 was passed to provide mechanisms to "determine where native title exists, how future activity impacting upon native title may be undertaken, and to provide compensation where native title is impaired or extinguished".[6] While not the land rights that Indigenous Australians had long demanded, and subject to various restrictions that were only to become more contentious, this marked the first recognition of Indigenous sovereignty in an act of parliament. The flow seemed to be strengthening. In 1993, Keating's government subscribed to the first optional protocol of the International Covenant on Civil and Political Rights (ICCPR) allowing individual petition, and two men – Rodney Croome and Nicholas Toonen – promptly petitioned the UN's Committee on Human Rights that the continued criminalisation of homosexuality in the state of Tasmania breached the Convention's first article. Deciding in the pair's favour, the Committee "rejected the suggestion that moral issues were exclusively a matter of domestic concern".[7] Keating

---

[4] Ibid. See Chapter 1 for Evatt's expression of the UDHR as congruous with the Australian notion of the "fair go".

[5] Kathryn Sikkink, *The Justice Cascade: How Human Rights Prosecutions Are Changing World Politics* (New York: W.W. Norton & Co., 2011), 5.

[6] *Native Title Act*, no. 110 (1993).

[7] See Katharine Gelber, "Treaties and Intergovernmental Relations in Australia: Political Implications of the Toonen Case", *Australian Journal of Politics and History* 45, no. 3 (1999), 330–46.

190   Epilogue: Cascade or Trickle?

rushed the Human Rights (Sexual Conduct) Act 1994 through parliament, ensuring that private sexual acts would not be subject "to any arbitrary interference with privacy within the meaning of Article 1 of the [ICCPR]". Tasmania soon rescinded its non-complying legislation, amidst conservative criticism that a "faceless group of people" in the United Nations Human Rights Commission were overriding Australian sovereignty.[8] Michael Kirby, by this stage a controversial appointment to the High Court, welcomed the decision as "[n]ot pie in the sky [but p]ractical human rights protection.[9] In 1997, the Human Rights and Equal Opportunity Commission (HREOC) released the *Bringing Them Home* report, commissioned by Keating to unearth the extent of child removal policies targeting Indigenous Australians between 1910 and 1970.[10] The 700 oral testimonies of separation, neglect and generational trauma therein reduced then-ALP opposition leader Kim Beazley Jnr to tears on the floor of parliament.[11]

Outside of mainstream politics, human rights appeared to be becoming an everyday vernacular. Yothu Yindi, an Indigenous/settler rock band, released their breakthrough single "Treaty" in 1991, reaching number eleven on the Australia Recording Industry Association charts, and the group's album *Tribal Voices* of the same year debuted at number four.[12] Reacting to the Fraser and Hawke government's failure to keep their promises, particularly those contained in the Barunga Statement of 1988 requesting land rights and compensation, the song pointed out that

> Words are easy, words are cheap
> Much cheaper than our priceless land
> But promises can disappear
> Just like writing in the sand.[13]

Yet, the last verse struck a hopeful note. "Now two rivers run their course / Separated for so long", yet it was possible to dream "of a brighter day / When the waters will be one", and the song quickly won numerous

---

[8] *Canberra Times*, 14 April 1994, 13.

[9] Michael Kirby, "Global Moves to Legal Protection of Human Rights", paper presented at the International Bar Association Conference, Boston, USA, 2 June 1999, available at www.hcourt.gov.au/assets/publications/speeches/former-justices/kirbyj/kirbyj_belfast.htm #FOOTNOTE_1.

[10] Ronald Wilson, *Bringing Them Home: Report of the National Inquiry into the Separation of Aboriginal and Torres Strait Islander Children from Their Families* (Sydney: Australian Human Rights and Equal Opportunity Commission, 1997).

[11] Phillipa McGuinness, *2001: The Year Everything Changed* (North Sydney, NSW: Penguin, 2018), 84.

[12] Aaron Corn, "Treaty Now: Popular Music and the Indigenous Struggle for Justice in Contemporary Australia", in Ian Peddie (ed.), *Popular Music and Human Rights Volume II: World Music* (Farnham: Ashgate, 2011), 17–26.

[13] "Barunga Statement", 1988, available at www.barungafestival.com.au/1988-statement/.

Epilogue: Cascade or Trickle? 191

awards, including a 1991 Human Rights Award from the HREOC.[14] Equally hopeful was Philip Alston – a professor of law, appointed the UN's special rapporteur on extreme poverty in 2017 – when he remarked in 1994 that "in light of recent developments, it seems reasonable to predict that, within a decade at most, Australia will have a Bill of Rights". That 72 per cent of Australians felt a Bill of Rights was a necessity coupled with "the inevitable evolution of the judicial role in protecting individual rights in response to changing attitudes within society" and the "emergence of an authentically universal and increasingly effective International human rights regime" gave Alston cause for optimism.[15] More was being said on the topic as well, with the number of books published under the keyword "Human Rights – Australia" expanding from seventy-three in the 1980s to 181 a decade later.[16] The subject of rights was also growing – with a Disability Discrimination Act passed in 1998 and a new focus on the rights of the elderly evident in the HREOC's publications.[17]

Larissa Behrendt, the first Indigenous Australian to study at Harvard Law School, heard Keating's Redfern speech as a sign of real possibility: "she needed to finish her studies quickly because so much was changing at home, so fast, and she wanted to be a part of it".[18] This euphoria was, as Berhendt later put it, "naïve". For while scholars are beginning to locate the 1990s as the true apogee of human rights' ascendance, this occurred in the context of a world order that facilitated only the most limited of utopias. As Stefan Ludwig-Hoffman argues, "It was only after the end of the Cold War that 'human rights' emerged as an explanatory framework for understanding what had just happened". Human rights were not the "cause but a consequence" of the end of Cold War rivalries and the sudden disappearance of a world outside of capitalism.[19] The tiny, exhausted Communist Party of Australia followed many of its global

---

[14] Jill Stubington and Peter Dunbar-Hall, "Yothu Yindi's 'Treaty': Gantna in Music", *Popular Music* 13, no. 3 (1994), 243–59.

[15] Philip Alston, "An Australian Bill of Rights: By Design or Default", in Philip Alston (ed.), *Towards an Australian Bill of Rights* (Canberra: Centre for International and Public Law, 1994), 1–4.

[16] Trove Advanced Search – Subject: "Human Rights – Australia", available at https://trove .nla.gov.au/book/result?q=subject%3A%22Human+rights+–+Australia.%22.

[17] On disability rights in Australia, see Rachel Carling-Jenkins, *Disability and Social Movements: Learning From Australian Experiences* (Abingdon: Routledge, 2014). For examples of HREOC reports concerning age discrimination, see *Age Matters: A Report on Age Discrimination* (Sydney: Human Rights and Equal Opportunity Commission, 2000).

[18] McGuinness, *2001*, 69.

[19] Stefan Ludwig-Hoffman, "Human Right and History", *Past & Present* 232, no. 1 (August 2016), 282.

192   Epilogue: Cascade or Trickle?

namesakes by dissolving in 1992, while the ranks of those seeking women's, gay or black liberation continued to dwindle in the face of an ever-growing professional NGO sector that spoke the language of compromise and expediency.[20] These movements were a thing of the past: gay liberation "or whatever it is called these days", as one writer for University of New South Wales student newspaper *Tharunka* put it, served as a "catalyst for the movements [of] today" and little more.[21] Yet, the rise of human rights as the lingua franca of a newly borderless world, facilitating unrestricted trade flows and "humanitarian" interventions in Africa and the Middle East – not to mention East Timor, where Australia played a leading role in ending the Indonesian occupation it had previously acquiesced to – co-existed with what Stephen Hopgood calls their "endtimes". Drawing a distinction between the everyday *human rights* activism of grassroots movements and the *Human Rights* of international institutions and NGOs, Hopgood argued that the latter's "global structure of laws, courts, norms, and organizations" became hostage to a post–Cold War liberal internationalist order, "opening a legitimacy gap" between promises and practical outcomes.[22] Rather than a cascade, the openings of the mid-1990s – for international law, truth and reconciliation – appeared more as threat than promise to Australian leaders who, as this book has demonstrated, have long viewed transnational forums and ideas with suspicion.

* * *

Given the wide scope within which human rights are today understood, readers of this book may be surprised as to its narrow contours. Following Lora Wildenthal, I have sought to unearth the "language of human rights" in a period when the term was often only barely audible.[23] I have located the Australian experience as not divorced from the goings-on of the world but instead responding to and in some ways precipitating the term's reinvention and contestation in local and global settings. While few agitators found it meaningful in the nineteenth century, Australia's particularly powerful and electorally successful labour movement brought human rights into public discussion in new ways by the beginnings of the twentieth century. Their conflation with the goal of full

---

[20] A history of the final few decades of the CPA remains to be written; for basic facts, see Tom O'Lincoln, *Into the Mainstream: The Decline of Australian Communism* (North Carlton, VIC: Red Rag Publications, 2012).

[21] *Tharunka*, 8 April 1991, 5.

[22] Stephen Hopgood, *The Endtimes of Human Rights* (Ithaca, NY: Cornell University Press, 2013), ix.

[23] Lora Wildenthal, *The Language of Human Rights in West Germany* (Philadelphia: University of Pennsylvania Press, 2013), 2.

employment and growing standards of living in the darkest days of the world war, and the inability to force constitutional change to enlarge Australia's limited welfare state, saw Australian Attorney General Herbert Vere Evatt advocate for their meaningful inclusion in the United Nations charter and the Universal Declaration of Human Rights. While the postwar focus on social and economic rights proved rather unpopular amongst civil libertarians in the 1950s, who largely steered clear of its universalist aspirations, the refocusing on self-determination and cultural rights by the Third World UN spoke to radicalising Aboriginal activists of the 1960s and 1970s. Women's liberationists, on the other hand, questioned whether the "human" in human rights had a chromosomal limitation that made their concerns only secondary to the overriding ambitions of equality, development and peace at global forums supposedly held in their name.

In locating human rights and its often-small groups of adherents in their historical contexts, this book has necessarily adopted a selective case-study approach: many causes – from opposition to the death penalty in the 1960s to events culminating in the independence of Papua New Guinea in 1975, for example – have not been given the attention they deserve. By locating groups and thinkers from across the political spectrum who have often only fleetingly found the idea of universal humanity a meaningful one, it has necessarily unsettled some presentist assumptions about human rights, which are neither as ancient nor as inherently progressive as many of the term's contemporary advocates would have it. While many of the groups and individuals here surveyed spoke of the millennia-old wellsprings of their activism, highlighting the oft-made critique of human rights as a "secular religion", this was as much a rhetorical as a self-justificatory exercise.[24] Rather than (or perhaps as well as) standing for ancient ideals, groups like Amnesty International or the Right to Life movement sought to make novel interventions on behalf of new categories of humanity: prisoners of conscience or unborn children – "to force others to confront a specific claim of injustice" as Wildenthal has it.[25] For Catholics, human rights were a way of attempting to secure church doctrine within a secular system that had been long viewed with suspicion. Human rights were a way of problematising old assumptions and relationships for others. The Communist Party of Australia's dismissal of human rights as bourgeois ideology gave way to an understanding of the ideas as "more than an abstract principle" in the

---

[24] This argument is made in Stephen Hopgood, *Keepers of the Flame: Understanding Amnesty International* (Ithaca, NY: Cornell University Press, 2006).

[25] Ibid., 3.

194   Epilogue: Cascade or Trickle?

turbulent 1960s for a party looking to refashion itself in light of a crisis of faith in Soviet-style communism.[26] The power of the conservative Returned Services League of Australia was confronted with similar claims to universality by the Ex-Services Human Rights Association of Australia, with the former's long-held status as defenders of the nation's freedom questioned as their continued support for undemocratic and racist politics became outmoded at home and abroad.

For Australian governments, human rights always appeared as a double-edged sword. Evatt, champion of rights and of a still-unrealised international court in their name, invoked the power of domestic jurisdiction to ensure that the nation-state on which the UN system was built remained inviolable against the protests of those, like Chinese seamen in the late 1940s, who lacked what Arendt thought to be that most precious right: nationally bounded citizenship.[27] As the years went by and the UN's composition and complexion changed, domestic jurisdiction became insecure in a world of increasingly interconnected and confident self-determination struggles. While quick to crow of its record on civil and political rights, the increasing dominance of more "emotionally charged" issues like race and global inequalities at global forums spelt self-imposed isolation during the 1950s and 1960s.[28] Both Whitlam and Fraser sought to break this deadlock, but each was unable to truly transcend Australia's economic and geopolitical position. Labor's push to make Australia a bridge between the first and third worlds was viewed with suspicion by neighbouring states, for whom the humiliations of white Australia were all too recent, and broke against the rocks of a New International Economic Order which threatened the nation's privileged global economic position. The human rights revolution of the late 1970s compelled a Liberal party that had long questioned the key tenets of multilateral order to think afresh, rejoining the UN's Commission on Human Rights in Geneva and creating a national version in Canberra. The long-delayed implementation of rights in Australia, however, proved to be a false dawn: The rise of conservative John Howard – first to opposition leader in 1985 and then prime minister in 1996 – marked the New Right's ascendency and the reimposition of international ambivalence, while the seeming promise of international law as a saviour proved only its continued enchainment to a world of nation-states. "Ordinary" Australians – if such a category truly exists – continued a long tradition of resisting greater

[26] *Charter of Democratic Rights* (Sydney, NSW: Communist Party of Australia, 1967), 1.
[27] Hannah Arendt, *The Origins of Totalitarianism* (San Diego, CA: Harcourt, Inc., 1968), 295–6.
[28] "Draft Instructions to the Australian Delegation to the International Conference on Human Rights, Tehran, 22nd April – 13th May, 1968", NAA: A1838, 929/1/5 PART 4.

Epilogue: Cascade or Trickle? 195

restrictions on their loosely defined rights. This is an inclination apparent from the narrowly defeated anti-Communist referendum of 1951 to the Hawke government's proposed Australia Card in 1986, while a willingness to extend rights – British, civil, equal or more rarely "human" – appears in such instances as the 1967 referendum. Anxiety, however, remained the more commonly response from government.

* * *

With the benefit of hindsight, it is clear that Australia's human rights cascade was only to be a trickle. While quick to pass the necessary legislation overriding Tasmania's archaic homosexuality laws, Keating reacted angrily to a High Court decision in 1995 that international instruments, even when not domesticated through legislation, could have an impact on immigration decisions.[29] That the appellant – Mr Teoh, a Malaysian citizen appealing his deportation on the basis of his being provider for a young family – had not even invoked the treaty under which the High Court ruled his deportation order to have been improper, the International Convention on the Rights of the Child (UNCRC, 1989), was considered particularly egregious.[30] While reiterating that "the Government remains fully committed to observing its treaty obligations", the decision declared that simply "entering into an international treaty is not reason for raising any expectation that government decision-makers will act in accordance with the treaty", and the government rushed to pass legislation plugging this newly found gap in Australian law.[31] That the Teoh case concerned (unauthorised) migration was no accident: just as the spectre of Chinese refugees who "contrive to enter Australia" had animated such opposition and resistance in the 1940s, unauthorised 'boat people' were again making headlines.[32] The 2,100 boat people, most Vietnamese, who had arrived in Australia from 1976 until 1981 were welcomed as Cold War refugees fleeing persecution at the hands of the "enemy".[33] The arrival of an additional 735 Chinese, Cambodian and Vietnamese asylum seekers on Australian shores from

---

[29] On the case, see Wendy Lacey, "In the Wake of Teoh: Finding an Appropriate Government Response", *Federal Law Review* 29, no. 2 (2001), 219–40; Margaret Allars, "One Small Step for Legal Doctrine, One Giant Leap towards Integrity in Government: Teoh's Case", *Sydney Law Review* 17, no. 2 (1995), 204–41.

[30] "Joint Statement by the Minister for Foreign Affairs and the Attorney-General, 'International Treaties and the High Court Decision in Teoh'", 10 May 1995, available at https://foreignminister.gov.au/releases/1995/m44.html.

[31] Ibid. The Administrative Decisions (Effect of International Instruments) Bill 1995 failed to pass. The Howard government tried and failed to pass a similarly worded Bill in 1997.

[32] *Koon Wing Lau v Calwell* [1949] HCA 65.

[33] Zoe Anderson, "Borders, Babies and 'Good Refugees': Australian Representations of 'Illegal' Immigration, 1979", *Journal of Australian Studies* 36, no. 2 (2012), 499–514.

196   Epilogue: Cascade or Trickle?

1989 to 1994 coincided with an economic downturn, and Keating took two pivotal actions. An Immigration Detention Centre (IDC) in Port Hedland, Western Australia, was opened specifically to house maritime arrivals in 1991, and a policy of mandatory, indefinite detention for so-called unlawful arrivals began one year later.[34] The flow of unauthorised arrivals soon ebbed, before picking up in 2000 under Liberal Party Prime Minister John Howard, elected in 1996 on a platform of making Australians "comfortable and relaxed" after Keating's attempts to unsettle the nation's past and forge connections with Asia.[35]

In 2001, regional instability in Iraq and Afghanistan saw the numbers of "illegal" arrivals by boat again increase, and the "Pacific solution" came into being. Australia's assessment of asylum seeker applications were outsourced to impoverished island nations such as Nauru, furthering longstanding semi-colonial relationships.[36] Refugees continued to be held in "on shore" detention, at Port Hedland and the infamous Woomera IDC – opened in 1999 to house 400 detainees but by mid-2001 holding some 1,500 – while those that arrived after the MV *Tampa* incident of August 2001 were held "off shore".[37] Opposition, previously limited to "small numbers of concerned individuals and core refugee, human rights, professional and church groups", soon mushroomed.[38] Phillip Ruddock, Howard's minister for Immigration who had chaired Amnesty International's first parliamentary group meeting in 1973, was publicly stripped of his membership in October 1999 over the mandatory detention policy. "It's in breach of the UN convention and it's in breach … of international law," national President Kathy Kingston

[34] Dawn Donghua Bolger, "Race Politics: Australian Government Responses to Asylum Seekers and Refugees from White Australia to Tampa" (PhD Thesis, Western Sydney University, 2016), 208–10; Adele Garnier and Lloyd Cox, "Twenty Years of Mandatory Detention: The Anatomy of a Failed Policy", paper presented to the Australian Political Studies Association Conference, Hobart, 24–26 September 2012, available at www.auspsa.org.au/sites/default/files/twenty_years_of_mandatory_detention_adele_garnier_and_lloyd_cox.pdf.

[35] See Judith Brett, "Relaxed and Comfortable: The Liberal Party's Australia", *Quarterly Essay* 19 (2005), 1–79.

[36] On the "outsourcing" of detention as part of a program of "Authoritarian Neoliberalism", see Cameron Smith, "'Authoritarian Neoliberalism' and the Australian Border-Industrial Complex", *Competition & Change* 23, no. 2 (2019), 192–217. On Australia and Nauru, see Cait Moor, *Nauru: Imperial Form, International Status and the Histories of International Law* (Cambridge, Cambridge University Press, 2019).

[37] David Marr and Marian Wilkinson, *Dark Victory: How a Government Lied Its Way to Political Triumph* (St Leonards, NSW: Allen & Unwin, 2004) remains the authoritative account of *Tampa* and the subsequent "children overboard" affair.

[38] Diane Gosden, "'What If No One Had Spoken Out against This Policy?' The Rise of Asylum Seeker and Refugee Advocacy in Australia", *Portal: Journal of Multidisciplinary International Studies* 3, no. 1 (2006), 1.

Epilogue: Cascade or Trickle? 197

protested.[39] Groups such as ChilOut – short for Children out of Detention – highlighted the policy's incompatibility with "Australia's human rights obligations, especially those contained in the UN Convention on the Rights of the Child".[40] Yet by focusing on children – a long-standing humanitarian tactic – or adherence to international norms, protesters arguably played into the hands of a government that insisted its "hard border" policy discouraged "people smugglers" from risking the lives of children. Much as 1950s assimilation policies were presented as meeting international obligations of fostering equality between peoples, an explanatory memorandum accompanying 2014 amendments to the Migration Act insisted that "the government has treated the best interests of the child as a primary consideration".[41] Protesters at Woomera in March 2002 also encountered the practical limitations of inmates' calls that "we are human beings" for those who exist in what Giorgio Agamben dubbed the "state of exception".[42] Calls for "more humane incarceration" – the removal of children or the adherence to international law – proved inadequate, and protesters instead demanded "the free movement of people ... [and] a real globalization, based not on the freedom of capital to exploit the world's people with ease, but on global solidarity and justice".[43] ChilOut ceased operations in June 2018, having "seen thousands of children finally freed from detention" since 2001; however, 112 children remain incarcerated on Nauru at the time of writing.[44]

Indigenous Affairs proved to be another desultory experience for rights campaigners. The hope solicited by the Mabo decision was crushed by government responses to the High Court's decision in *Wik Peoples* v *The State of Queensland* (1996), which established that native title was not extinguished by the granting of crown leases over pastoral lands.[45]

---

[39] "Ruddock stripped of Amnesty International badge", *AM*, 18 March 2000, available at www.abc.net.au/am/stories/s111533.htm.

[40] "ChilOut: Our Goals", available at https://chilout.org/our-goals/. For more on ChilOut, see Roumen Dimitrov, "ChilOut [Children Out of Detention]: Strategic Communication by Small Advocacy Groups", *Australian Journal of Communication* 34, no. 3 (2007), 129–43.

[41] Jordana Silverstein, "Why Do We Talk about Child Refugees?", *Australian Critical Race and Whiteness Studies Association*, 3 August 2018, available at https://acrawsa.org.au/2018/08/03/1910/.

[42] Giorgio Agamben. *States of Exception* (Chicago, IL: University of Chicago Press, 2005).

[43] Jessica Whyte, "'We Are Human Beings': The Woomera Breakout", in *We Are Everywhere: The Irresistible Rise of Global Anticapitalism* (London: Verso, 2003), 435–6.

[44] Susanne Legena, "Nauru's Children Are Self-Harming, but Ordinary Australians Can Stop the Horror", *ABC News*, 29 August 2018, available at www.abc.net.au/news/2018-08-28/nauru-imprisoning-traumatised-kids-is-child-abuse/10174688.

[45] On the case, see David Godden, "Attenuating Indigenous Property Rights: Land Policy after the Wik Decision", *The Australian Journal of Agricultural and Resource Economics* 43, no. 1 (1999), 1–33.

198   Epilogue: Cascade or Trickle?

Howard's government developed a "10 point plan" to amend the Native Title Act 1993, dubbed by one commentator as "not amending legislation [but] a total rewrite" that removed from potential claim vast swathes of land and made it harder for Indigenous groups to make them.[46] Self-determination gave way to "practical reconciliation", focusing on "socio-economic disadvantage", which was to be ameliorated by neoliberal projects targeting Indigenous workforce participation and school attendance.[47] While the Hawke and Keating government had engaged in a project of "consensual neoliberalism" – undertaking market reforms in exchange for an expanded social wage – Howard's sung from the New Right playbook.[48] "Responsibility" became a buzzword, both for Howard and for his supporters in the Indigenous community, namely prominent Cape York leader Noel Pearson, who in 2000 wrote that "our right to self-determination is ultimately the right to take responsibility", particularly for replacing "passive welfare" with engagement in the "real economy".[49] Announcing that "the economic is the social", Pearson argued that Indigenous society had always functioned on a strong economic imperative that had dissipated with the arrival of "handouts" in the 1970s. "[W]hy has a social breakdown accompanied ... advancement in the formal rights of our people?" Pearson also asked. Rates of Indigenous incarceration – today the highest in the world – and limited life expectancy due to alcohol and drugs had resulted from post-1970 self-determination policies, a cascade that left Indigenous people with only "the human right to misery, mass incarceration and early death".[50] Attempts by scholar Sarah Holcombe to facilitate the translation of the UDHR into the Anangu language of central Australia were problematized not only by the euro-centric assumptions that underlay the document but because very few locals had ever even heard the term "universal human rights", let alone sought to make meaning of it in their own conditions.[51]

Such critiques aside, it was the Howard government in 2007 that responded to a Northern Territory government report into child sexual

---

[46] *Courier-Mail*, 9 September 1997, 11.

[47] On the "neoliberalisation" of Indigenous policy, see in particular Elizabeth Strakosch, *Neoliberal Indigenous Policy: Settler Colonialism and the "Post-Welfare" State* (Basingstoke: Palgrave Macmillan, 2015).

[48] Elizabeth Humphrys, *How Labour Built Neoliberalism: Australia's Accord, the Labour Movement and the Neoliberal Project* (London: Brill, 2018).

[49] Noel Pearson, *Our Right to Take Responsibility* (Cairns, QLD: Noel Pearson & Associates, 2000), 1–10.

[50] Noel Pearson, "On the Human Right to Misery, Mass Incarceration and Early Death", Dr Charles Perkins Memorial Oration, The University of Sydney, 25 October 2001, available at www.kooriweb.org/foley/pearson/charles_perkins_oration.pdf.

[51] Sarah Holcombe, *Remote Freedoms: Politics, Personhood and Human Rights in Aboriginal Central Australia* (Stanford, CA: Stanford University Press, 2018), 65.

Epilogue: Cascade or Trickle?   199

abuse by suspending the Racial Discrimination Act (RDA) and launching
the Northern Territory Emergency Response (NTER) or "Intervention"
into remote Indigenous communities.[52] The *Little Children are Sacred*
report, co-authored by leading Indigenous lawyer and human rights
advocate Pat Anderson, deployed the language of the UNCRC to con-
demn what was called an outbreak of child sexual abuse in Indigenous
communities: what was said to be a 78 per cent increase between 2001–2
and 2005–6.[53] "[T]he compulsory acquisition of townships; the suspension of the permit system to access Aboriginal communities; the removal
of customary law or cultural practices in any legal considerations in
sentencing ... and the quarantining of a proportion of welfare benefits
for all recipients in designated communities" followed.[54] The NTER
was attacked both domestically – including by the report's authors, who
distanced themselves from Howard's actions – and internationally as
a violation of numerous treaties, as well as the newly minted United
Nations Declaration on the Rights of Indigenous Peoples (UNDRIP).[55]
While the ALP government of Kevin Rudd finally made a formal
apology to the "stolen generation" in 2008, adopted UNDRIP in 2009
and restored the RDA in 2010, the NTER remains ongoing, and the
much-vaunted goals of "closing the gap" between Indigenous and settler Australians remain as distant as ever.[56]

In the more traditional terrain of domestic civil and political rights,
stalled progress on a bill of rights has coupled with dramatic escalation
of anti-terror legislation "in great haste, in stunning scope and number"
to see the emergence of what scholars now dub a "national security
state".[57] The horrific attacks of 11 September 2001 and Australia's

---

[52] On how much of the evidence to justify the "Intervention" was a deliberate political
concoction, see Chris Graham, "Bad Aunty: 10 Years On, How ABC Lateline Sparked
The Racist NT Intervention", *New Matilda*, 23 June 2017, available at https://newma
tilda.com/2017/06/23/bad-aunty-seven-years-how-abc-lateline-sparked-racist-nt-inter
vention/.

[53] Rex Wild and Pat Anderson, *Little Children are Sacred: Report of the Northern Territory
Board of Inquiry into the Protection of Aboriginal Children from Sexual Abuse* (Darwin, NT:
Government Printer, 2007), 239.

[54] Peter Gale, "Rights, Responsibilities, and Resistance: Legal Discourse and Intervention
Legislation in the Northern Territory in Australia", *Semiotica* 209 (2016), 167.

[55] For example, James Anaya, United Nations Special Rapporteur on the situation of
human rights and fundamental freedoms of indigenous people, *Observations on the
Northern Territory Emergency Response in Australia*, February 2010, available at www
.ncca.org.au/files/Natsiec/NTER_Observations_FINAL_by_SR_Anaya_.pdf.

[56] For a critique of the "close the gap" policy, see Kerryn Pholi et al., "Is 'Close the Gap'
a Useful Approach in Improving the Health and Wellbeing of Indigenous Australians?"
Australian Review of Public Affairs 9, no. 2 (April 2009), 1–13.

[57] George Williams, "A Decade of Australian Anti-Terror Laws", *Melbourne University Law
Review* 35, no. 3 (2011), 1136–7.

200   Epilogue: Cascade or Trickle?

own experience of terror on the popular Indonesia resort island of Bali on 12 October 2002 sparked a globally "unprecedented" wave of legislation. By 2011 over fifty new statutes restricting freedom of speech, creating new sedition offences, tightening citizenship rules and allowing the weeklong detention of suspects without charge or trial had passed parliament with overwhelmingly bipartisan support.[58] The case of Indian national Mohamed Haneef – unjustly detained without charge for twelve days on suspision of providing support to a terrorist organisation – is amongst the only time such laws have faced a public challenge.[59] While discussion of a bill of rights has only grown during this period, helped by popular interventions from well-known Australians such as expatriate human rights lawyer Geoffrey Robertson, an equally vociferous counter-campaign from conservatives as to the unde-mocratic potential of an empowered "activist judiciary" now leaves Australia the only Western nation to lack such safeguards.[60]

Indeed, the idea's discussion seems to have had somewhat of a cooling effect on popular opinion: when surveyed recently, 61 per cent of Australians were found to believe the nation already enjoyed such a document and its codified freedoms, symptomatic of what Australian Human Rights Commission President Rosalyn Croucher bemoaned in 2018 as the lack of "human rights literacy" amongst Australians.[61] The term is usually discussed in "negative space", Croucher remarks, with human rights presented as restricting personal freedoms or the nation's right to follow its domestic policy directives. Liberal Prime Minister Tony Abbott, who in 2015 declared Australians to be "sick of being lectured to by the United Nations" as part of a broader ideological offensive targeting the Australian Human Rights Commission President Gillian Triggs' "political stitch-up" of the government's refugee policy, exemplifies this approach.[62] The ongoing fracas at the time of writing concerning a potential Religious Discrimination Act, a conservative response to the

---

[58] Ibid.

[59] See Mark Rix, "The Show Must Go On: The Drama of Dr Mohamed Haneef and the Theatre of Counter-terrorism", in Andrew Lynch et al., *Counter Terrorism and beyond: The Culture of Law and Justice after 9/11* (Oxford: Routledge, 2010), 199–215.

[60] For the opposing arguments, see Geoffrey Robinson, *The Statute of Liberty: How Australians Can Take Back Their Rights* (North Sydney, NSW: Random House Australia, 2009); Jullian Lesser and Ryan Haddrick (eds.), *Don't Leave Us with the Bill: The Case against an Australian Bill of Rights* (Barton, ACT: Menzies Research Centre, 2009).

[61] Rosalind Croucher AM, "Rights Mindedness: The Alice Tay Lecture in Law and Human Rights 2018", 25 September 2018, available at www.humanrights.gov.au/news/speeches/ alice-tay-lecture-law-and-human-rights-2018-rights-mindedness.

[62] *Sydney Morning Herald*, 10 March 2015, 1. The HREOC was renamed the AHRC in 2008.

Epilogue: Cascade or Trickle?

overwhelming endorsement of gay marriage by Australians in September 2017, shows that, while critical of rights at times, conservatives remain aware of their potential to cloak reactionary sentiments.[63]

* * *

Upon informing colleagues, friends and family that I was writing an Australian history of human rights, the most common response has been something along the lines of "that shouldn't take long". Australia's contemporary reputation as a pariah, indeed acting as a role model for a wave of far-right nationalism in Europe, also informs a less commonly remarked-upon theme: that Australia has abandoned the leadership position it held in the 1940s.[64] One of this book's objectives has been to fill the gap between Evatt's supposed internationalism and today, showing that, while not a major topic of discussion, there has always existed a rights tradition in Australian politics, intricately tied to local peculiarities and global movements. Moreover, there is no more pressing time to be discussing this often-subterranean legacy. On the one hand, there is substantial cause for hope. The release of the Uluru Statement from the Heart in May 2017 – fifty years after the 1967 referendum – demanding a constitutionally enshrined "voice" in Australian parliament, a national treaty system and process of "truth-telling" marks perhaps the best-organised and most representative attempt for meaningful change since 1788.[65] Already, Victoria and South Australia are negotiating state-based treaties that aim to create meaningful systems of representation and compensation.[66] Victoria, Queensland and the Australian Capital Territory have also each adopted bills of rights, though these are heavily restricted in their usability

---

[63] For details on the Marriage Equality vote, see Simon Copland, "The Australian Marriage Law Postal Survey and the Limitations of Vulnerability-based Politics", *Australian Feminist Studies* 36, no. 96 (2018), 261–74. For details on the as-yet unreleased Religious Freedom Review, see "Religious Freedom Review", available at www.pmc.gov.au/domestic-policy/religious-freedom-review.

[64] Sasha Polakow-Suransky, "How Europe's Far Right Fell in Love with Australia's Immigration Policy", *The Guardian*, 12 October 2017, available at www.theguardian.com/world/2017/oct/12/how-europes-far-right-fell-in-love-with-australias-immigration-policy.

[65] Megan Davis, "The Long Road to Uluru: Walking Together – Truth before Justice", *Griffith Review* 60 (2018), 13–32, 41–5; Eddie Synot, The Universal Declaration of Human Rights at 70: Indigenous Rights and the Uluru Statement from the Heart", *Australian Journal of International Affairs*, published online 16 June 2019.

[66] For a critique of these processes, see in particular Dominic O'Sullivan, "Victoria's Treaty with Indigenous People Must Address Vexed Questions of Sovereignty", *The Conversation*, 25 June 2018, available at https://theconversation.com/victorias-treaty-with-indigenous-peoples-must-address-vexed-questions-of-sovereignty-98758.

202 Epilogue: Cascade or Trickle?

within the legal system and, much like state-based treaty initiatives, must necessarily play a secondary role to eventual Commonwealth legislation.[67]

On the other, contemporary Australian rights talk remains both conceptually and intellectually impoverished. The post-1970s focus on civil and political rights, for example, has meant that economic, social and cultural rights are "notably absent" from Australian debates, as Philip Alston put it in 1993.[68] While NGOs overtly concerned with human rights have blossomed in Australia in the new millennium, the idea finds little resonance in Australia's largest social movement: the trade unions.[69] The idea of human rights as purely limiting powers on government means that rights to work, education, social security, rest and leisure – so central in 1948 and more vital than ever after the financial crisis of 2008 – remain largely undiscussed, to both advocates' and society's detriment.[70] Iranian journalist Behrouz Boochani, held on Manus Island without trial for the past five years, remarked in October 2018 that "superficial" critiques of offshore detention needed to give way to "deep research into how a human ... is forced to live between the law and a situation without laws".[71] Indeed, his own book – tapped on a mobile phone and smuggled from the island – endeavours to do just this type of vital intellectual work, towards which I hope that the present volume provides only a small contribution.[72]

---

[67] For an overview of the *Victorian Charter of Human Rights and Responsibilities* (2006), see George Williams, "Victoria's New Charter: Human Rights and the Community", *Just Policy: A Journal of Australian Social Policy* 43 (April 2007), 6–10. The Australian Capital Territory's Human Rights Act 2004 is analysed as part of a new "parliamentary rights" model in Janet L. Hiebert, "Parliamentary Bills of Rights: An Alternative Model", *Modern Law Review* 69, no. 1 (2006), 7–28.

[68] Alston, "An Australian Bill of Rights", 14–16.

[69] One notable exception is the Australian Institute of Employment Rights, see "Australian Charter of Employment Rights", available at www.aierights.com.au/resources/charter/.

[70] Samuel Moyn, *Not Enough: Human Rights in an Unequal World* (Cambridge, MA: Belknap Press of Harvard University Press, 2018).

[71] "Statement from Behrouz Boochani in support of the Academics for Refugees National Day of Action, 17 October 2018", available at https://academicsforrefugees.wordpress.com/nda-public-read-ins/.

[72] Behrouz Boochani, translated by Omid Tofighian, *No Friend but the Mountains: Writing from Manus Prison* (Sydney: Pan Macmillan Australia, 2018).

Index

Aarons, Eric, 90, 95, 98
Aarons, Laurie, 91–92, 93, 98
Abbott, Tony, 200
Aboriginal Legal Service, 119, 132, 166
Aboriginal Treaty Committee, 166, 171
Abortion, 120, 145–150, 151, 168, *See also*
   Right to Life Movement
Alston, Phillip, 191, 202
Alston, Richard, 162, 165
Altman, Dennis, 176
Amnesty International, 116, 149
   Campaign against Torture, 156–159
   Conscientious objection and, 112–116
   Criticisms of, 112, 165
   Formation of, 109
   Indigenous Australians and,
      109–112, 171
   Parliamentary group of, 157
Anderson, David, 169–171
Anderson, Patricia, 199
Andrews, Shirley, 1–2, 3–5, 83–84, 121
Anti-Slavery Society, 2, 84
Anzac tradition, The, 100
   Critique of, 101, 103
   Human rights and, 106–107, 108
Apartheid, 1, 5, 80, 111
   Parallels to Australia, 80, 183
Arendt, Hannah, 20, 194
Ashbolt, Alan, 101, 106–108
Atlantic Charter, 21, 37, 42
   Indigenous Australians and, 75, 76–78
Attwood, Bain, 9, 123, 126
Australia Card, 175, 195
Australian Broadcasting Commission,
   37–39, 59, 99–101
Australian Capital Territory, 149–150,
   180, 201
Australian Constitutional League, 40
Australian Council for Civil Liberties
   Attitude towards human rights of, 61
   Communist Party Referendum (1951)
      and, 71

Founding of, 57–59
Indigenous Australians and, 79
Links to American Civil Liberties Union
   (USA), 58, 59
Links to National Council for Civil
   Liberties (UK), 58–59, 79
Sharkey trial and, 64
World War II and, 60
Australian Council of Churches, 106
Australian Council of Salaried and
   Professional Associations, 126
Australian Council of Social Services, The,
   173, 178
Australian Council of Trade Unions, 68
Australian Human Rights Commission,
   200–201
Australian Labor Party
   Bill of Rights and, 168, 174
   Communist Party of Australia and,
      64–65
   Early rights talk of, 32–35
   Federal Parliamentary Labor Party,
      35, 96
   Founding of, 31
   Indigenous Australians and, 131,
      188, 199
   Makarrata (Treaty) and, 176
   Postwar Reconstruction and, 36–37
   Women's Liberation and, 136
Australian Law Reform Commission,
   173, 178
Australian Security Intelligence
   Organisation, 93, 102

Bailey, Peter, 182
Barwick, Sir Garfield, 2
Batman Treaty, 170
Beazley, Kim (Junior), 190
Beazley, Kim (Senior), 47, 112
Behrendt, Larissa, 191
Belloc, Hillaire, 26
Beneson, Peter, 109, 116

204 Index

Bennett, Gary, 186–187
Bennett, Mary, 11, 78
Bill of Rights, 30, 61, 68, 154, 187, 191, 199–200
  1973 Legislation, 168–169
  1986 Legislation, 173–176, 185
  Agitation for, 167–168, 169
  Critique of, 168
Bjelke-Petersen, Johannes, 155, 165, 184
Blackburn, Doris, 78
Blainey, Geoffrey, 185
Bongiorno, Frank, 65
Boochani, Behrouz, 202
Bowen, Lionel, 184
Bradley, Mark Phillip, 3, 44
Bringing Them Home Report (1998), 190
Britain, 6, 13, 17, 56, 58, 75, 146
British Commonwealth League, 76
British Empire, 12, 13, 20, 46, 76
Burke, Roland, 7, 87, 159
Burton, Henry, 58, 59

Cairns Aborigines and Torres Strait
  Islander Advancement League, 122
Calwell, Arthur, 45, 46–50, 96
Campaign Against Moral Persecution, 176
Canada, 6, 11, 166, 170, 177
  Bill of Rights (1960), 117
  Charter of Rights and Freedoms (1982), 174
Carter, Jimmy, 154, 156, 162
Castles, Alex, 117
Castley, Shirley, 137, 140
Catholicism, 37
  Australian history of, 24–25
  Conscientious objection and, 107–108
  Critique of modern society, 26–27
  Fascism and, 25–26
  Humanae Vitae and, 120, 143
  Labor Party Split (1955) and, 71–73
  Postwar rights talk and, 23–30
  Right to Life Movement and, 143–144, 147
  Second Vatican Council and, 107
Catholics for Peace, 106, 107, 108
Chalidze, Valery, 91
Chesterman, John, 9, 123
Chifley, Ben, 43–44, 47, 64, 81
Children out of Detention (ChilOut), 197
Chile, 157, 160
China, 17, 46, 80, 91, 133
Chinese Seaman's Union, 46, 48–50
Civil Liberties. *See also* Australian Council
  for Civil Liberties
  Australian origins of, 55

Conscription and, 56–57
Indigenous Australians. *See* Indigenous
  Australians, Civil Liberties and
Clinton, Hillary, 133
Coe, Paul, 119, 132
Cold War, the, 108, 165
  Australia and, 64, 71, 85
  Communist Party of Australia and, 93–94
  Effect on rights talk, 54–55
  End of, 191
Colombo Plan, The, 127
Commission on the Status of Women, 133, 135
Communist Party of Australia, 45, 53
  Anti-Semitism and, 92–94
  Attitude towards rights, 62, 66–68
  Charter of Democratic Rights and, 95–97
  Civil Liberties and, 58, 60
  Communist Party Referendum (1951), 70–71
  Dissolution of, 191
  Gay rights and, 176–177
  Indigenous Australians and, 80–83, 121–123
  Prague Spring and, 98–99
  Trial of Lance Sharkey. *See* Sharkey,
    Lawrence Louis Lance
Communist Party of Italy, 91
Communist Party of the Soviet Union, 90, 92, 94
  Stalin Constitution (1936), 35, 54, 81
Communist Party of the United States of
  America, 62
Constitution of Australia, 30, 31, 35, 65, 69, 126, 187
  Bill of Rights and, 168
  External Affairs power of, 154, 183
  Indigenous Australians and, 74, 169, 171
  *Constitutional Alteration (Aboriginals) Act
    1967*, 120, 126, 195, 201
  Implications of, 166
  Limitations of, 127
Convention on the Elimination of all forms
  of Discrimination against Women, 134
Coombs, H. C. (Nugget), 171–172
Council for Aboriginal Rights, 111, 121, *See
    also* Andrews, Shirley
  Founding of, 80
  Influence of the UDHR on, 82
Croucher, Rosalyn, 200
Curtin, John, 30, 36–37, 40, 60
Czechoslovakia, 89, 98

de Costa, Ravi, 10, 14, 123
Decolonisation, 6, 88, 118, 139, 143

Index

Democratic Rights Council, 80–82
Department of External/Foreign Affairs, 125, 129, 139, 159
Department of Information, 30
Devereux, Annemarie, 10
Domestic Jurisdiction, 43, 50, 70, 183, 194
Du Bois, W. E. B., 75
Dubcek, Alexander, 89, 98
Duguid, Charles, 78, 80, 111, 122
Dunn, Bill, 164
Dunstan, Donald, 125, 131
Durack, Peter, 178
Duranti, Marco, 28

East Timor, 164–165, 192
Ecumenical Movement, 144, 152
Elimination of all forms of Discrimination against Women, 143
Elkin, A. P., 77
Ellicott, Bob, 177
Ennals, Martin, 158
Eureka Stockade, 16–17, 53, 63
European Court of Human Rights, 181, 184
Evans, Gareth, 174–175, 178, 185
Evatt, Herbert Vere, 6
    Atlantic Charter and, 37, 77
    Communist Party Referendum (1951), 70
    Human rights and, 37
    Labor Party Split (1955) and, 72
    United Nations and, 42–43
    White Australia Policy and, 49–51
Evatt, Mary Alice, 68
Ex-Services Human Rights Association of Australia, 101
    Catholicism and, 108
    Conflict with Returned Services League, 105–106
    Human rights and, 103–104

Federal Council for the Advancement of Aborigines and Torres Strait Islanders, 84, 110, 121
Fitzpatrick, Brian, 58–59, 60, 63, 71, 79
Fraser, Malcolm, 101, 151, 194
    Campaign against Torture and, 158
    Human rights and, 153, 154, 156, 161, 178
    Indigenous Australians and, 170, 172, 190
Freedom of contract, 38, 55, 197
Freedom of movement, 45, 70, 111
Freedom of religion, 28, 171
Freedom of speech, 31, 56, 59, 64, 171, 200

Freedom Ride (1965), 124, 132
Freney, Denis, 164

Gandhi, Mohandas, 75
Gay Liberation Movement, 150, 176, 186, 192
Gay Rights Lobby, 177
    Appeal to Human Rights Bureau, 180–182
    Founding of, 154, 177
    Reform of the NSW *Crimes Act*, 186–187
Genocide. *See* Indigenous Australians, Genocide of
George, Henry, 32
Germany, 36
Germany, East, 110, 113
Germany, West, 3
Globalisation, 12, 80, 142, 197
Grassby, Al, 162, 182

Harris, Stewart, 166–167, 171, 173, 176
Hasluck, Paul, 1, 83–84, 87, 126, 161
Hawke, Robert, 154, 174, 176, 183, 185, 189, 195, 198
Helsinki Watch/Network, 155, 179
Hewett, Dorothy, 94, 97
High Court of Australia, The, 42, 47–48, 50, 53, 63, 69, 154, 183, 188, 195, 197
Hill, Edward (Ted), 92
Hirst, John, 65
Hoffman, Stefan-Ludwig, 4, 191
Holcombe, Sarah, 198
Holland, Alison, 11
Holt, Harold, 105, 126
Hope, Robert, 167
Hopgood, Stephen, 192
Horn, Robert V, 114–115
Horne, Donald, 100
Howard, John Winston, 131, 176, 185, 194, 196–199
Hughes, William Morris (Billy), 60
Human Rights and Equal Opportunity Commission, 186, 190–191
Human Rights Bureau, 180–181
Human Rights Commission (Australia), 143, 153, 154–155, 177–178, 182–183, 187
Human Rights Council of Australia, 163–164, 172
Human Rights Day, 67, 113, 161, 165, 171
Human Rights Movement, 88, 118, 121, 162, 180
Human Rights Revolution, 116, 159, 178, 194

206 Index

Human Rights Watch, 155
Humanitarianism, 12–14, 61, 79, 150, 192, 197
'Humane Empire', 13, 20
Hunt, Lynn, 13

Indigenous Australians
1967 Referendum. *See Constitutional Alteration (Aboriginals) Act 1967*
Citizenship rights and, 14, 20
Civil liberties and, 73–75, 79
Feminism and, 151–152
Genocide of, 128–129
Government attitudes towards, 83–84, 129–130
Human rights and, 79–83, 109–112, 121–123, 127, 197–198
International status of, 170–171
Makarrata (Treaty) and, 166–167, 171–173, 176
Racial discrimination and, 131–133
Indonesia, 46, 80, 157, 164, 192, 200
Institute of Public Affairs, 175
International Commission of Jurists, 132, 163, 169
International Convention on the Elimination of all forms of Racial Discrimination, 119, 120, 124, 128
Australian adoption of, 125
Australian ratification of, 131
International Covenant on Civil and Political Rights (ICCPR), 154, 156, 159–160, 167
As 'Litmus Test', 173
Australian ratification of, 179–182
Indigenous Australians and, 174
Optional Protocol to, 189–190
International Covenant on Economic, Social and Cultural Rights (ICESCR), 159, 174
International Development. *See* New International Economic Order
International Labour Organization, 123
International League of the Rights of Man, 61
International Women's Year. *See also* Reid, Elizabeth
Australia and, 136
Debate of, 137–138
Legacy of, 141–143
Mexico City conference, 138–141
National Advisory Committee, 136, 137, 142

Japan, 1, 30, 36, 45
Jefferson, Thomas, 40, 105
Jensen, Stephen, 88, 118
Johnston, Craig, 176–177, 180

Keating, Paul, 188–190, 195–196, 198
Kenny, Dennis, 107
Keys, Barbara, 88, 157
Khrushchev, Nikita, 67, 90–92
Kirby, Michael, 173–174, 178, 190
Koowarta v Bjelke-Petersen (1982), 154, 183, 185
Korean War, 53–54, 84

Lake, Marilyn, 9, 17
Lang, Jack, 44
Latham, John, 50, 69–70
Law Reform (Sexual Behaviours) Ordinance 1976, 180
Lawyers, 1, 62, 91, 96, 108, 138, 167, 168, 173, 178, 182, 199, 200
League of Nations, 44, 59, 76, 78, 145
Leibler, Isi, 93
Liberal Party of Australia, The, 41, 44, 65, 131, 151, 176, 179, 196, 200
Little Children Are Sacred Report (2007), 199
Lydon, Jane, 11

Mabo v Queensland No. 2 (1992), 188, 197
Mabo, Eddie, 188
MacBride, Sean, 157
Macintyre, Stuart, 21, 31, 37, 58, 61, 71, 79
Magna Carta, 22, 32, 68–69
Makarrata (Treaty). *See* Indigenous Australians,
Makarrata (Treaty) and
Manus Island, 202
Marriage
Human rights implications of, 46–50, 123, 201
Marx, Karl, 81, 85
Rights and, 67
McGinness, Joe, 122, 123, 127, 128, 139
McKenna, David, 114–115
McKerras, Michael, 112
Menart, Vladimir, 162
Menzies, Robert Gordon, 36, 60
Atlantic Charter and, 21
Bill of Rights and, 168
Communist Party Referendum (1951) and, 70–71
Forgotten People speech and, 40–41
Legacy of, 106
Millar, Thomas, 163

Index

Missen, Alan, 179–180
Mitchell, Dame Roma, 9, 182
Mortimer, Rex, 91, 93
Moyn, Samuel, 3, 15, 26, 40, 121
Multiculturalism, 154, 162, 163
Murphy, Lionel, 168–169
Murray, Les, 175

National Aboriginal Conference, 166, 172–173
National Aboriginal Consultative Council, 166
National Human Rights Institutions, 177, 180
Native Title Act 1993, 189, 198
Nazism, Spectre of, 21, 47, 48, 53, 94
Neoliberalism, 156, 187, 198, *See also* New Right, The
New International Economic Order, 134
Australia and, 140
Feminist critique of, 141
New Right, The, 155, 175, 185, 194, 198
New South Wales, 11, 14, 44, 57, 68, 102, 145
New Zealand, 1, 15, 166, 177
Nicholls, Yvonne, 79–80
Nichols, Doug, 79, 122
Non-Government Organisations, 4, 140, 155, 182, 192
Noonuccal, Oodgeroo, 121–122, 127
Northern Territory, 79, 82, 84, 128, 130–131, 149, 199
Northern Territory Emergency Response (Intervention), 198–199
Northern Territory Welfare Ordinance (1953), 84

O'Donnell, Denis, 106
O'Keefe, Annie, 47–48
Oppenheimer, Lincoln, 113
O'Shane, Pat, 131–132
Overduin, Daniel, 148

Papua New Guinea, 124, 193
Paris Peace Conference, 34
Parliament of Australia, 21, 29, 36, 46, 48, 50, 112, 115, 119, 131, 150, 172, 176, 177–178, 189, 200
Parsons, Geoffrey, 73–75
Peacock, Andrew, 160–161
Pearson, Noel, 198
Pedersen, Susan, 76
Perkins, Charles, 125, 132, 169
Poverty, 23, 32, 37, 39, 51, 107, 191
Powers Referendum (1944), 31, 35

Queensland
Conflict with the Commonwealth, 183–185
Indigenous Australians and, 127, 188, 197
Resistance to human rights of, 125, 162, 165

Racial Discrimination Act (1975), 131, 161, 183
Critiques of, 131
Suspension of, 199
Refugees, 163
Mandatory Detention of, 195–197
Wartime, 45–46, 48
Reid, Elizabeth, 133, 135
Critique of Development, 140–141
Role in International Women's Year, 136–137
Returned Services League, 65, 77, 99–103, 104, 107, 108
Rich, Harold, 63
Right to Life Movement
Emergence of, 148–149
Human rights and, 144–147
Tactics of, 149–150, 178
Rights
As secular religion, 109, 193
Citizenship, 19–20, 41, 57, 77, 83, 116, 123, 129, 150, 194
Cultural, 120, 127, 128
Economic, 8, 28, 42, 45, 81, 93, 134, 139–141, 172, 173
Human needs and, 140, 169
Land, 130–132, 172, 187, 189, 190
of the British Subject, 8, 12–16, 17–19, 20, 35, 46, 65, 152
of the Child, 18, 144, 146, 150, 178, 195, 196–197, 198–199
Property, 6, 14, 16, 28, 32–34, 37, 66, 70, 72, 171
Social, 40, 67, 81, 84, 172
To life, 27, 113, 144–145, *See also* Right to Life Movement
Robertson, Geoffrey, 200
Robertson, Mavis, 96
Roosevelt, Franklin, 21, 27, 41, 75
Rosenboim, Or, 30
Royal Commission into Human Relationships, 149–151, 179
Rudd, Kevin, 199
Ruddock, Phillip, 157, 196

Santamaria, B. A., 27, 29, 72
Sarian, Emma, 146

208 Index

Scalmer, Sean, 15, 66
Schreiber, Marc, 160
Scutt, Jocelyn, 173
Seaman's Union of Australia, 45
Sedition, Charge of, 57, 200, *See also*
    Sharkey, Lawrence Louis 'Lance'
Self-determination, 21, 116
    Communist Party of Australia and, 98
    Indigenous Australians and, 123, 128,
    172–174, 198
Senate Standing Committee on
    Constitutional and Legal Affairs,
    173, 175
Sex Discrimination Act (1983), 143, 185
Sexism, 133, 137–141
Seymour, Alan, 101
Sharkey, Lawrence Louis 'Lance', 92–93
    Sedition trial of, 53, 61–64
Solzhenitsyn, Alexander, 149
South Africa. *See* Apartheid
South Australia, 78, 125, 131, 146
Soviet Jews, 93
Steinbeck, John, 23
Street, Jessie, 2, 81–82, 122, 135
Summers, Anne, 17
Suter, Keith, 153, 162, 187

Taft, Bernie, 91–93, 96, 97
Tasmania, 138, 154, 183
    Decriminalisation of homosexuality,
    189–190, 195
Tasmanian Dams Case (1983), 154,
    174, 183
Television, importance of, 92, 100
Tennant, Kyle, 23
Terra Nullius, 172, 188
Third World, The
    Australia and, 136, 142
    Indigenous Australians and, 172, 193
    Project, 120
    United Nations and, 134
Thomas, Pete, 97
Torture
    Awareness of, 164
    Campaign against, 156–159
Totalitarianism, 6, 23, 31, 37, 71, 85,
    112, 179
Transnationalism
    Indigenous Australians and, 10, 166, 172
    Theory of, 3
Triggs, Gillian, 200

Uluru Statement from the Heart, 201
Unemployment, 23, 35–36, 39, 42, 173
United Australia Party, 36, 40–41

United Nations
    Australia and, 1, 6, 34, 62, 104, 120
    Commission on Human Rights, 128, 159
    Creation of, 42–44
    First World Conference on Human
    Rights (Tehran, 1968), 87, 116, 128
    General Assembly, 87, 115, 125, 128,
    133–134, 156–158, 160
    Indigenous Australians and, 78–80, 112,
    127–130
    International Year of Human Rights
    (1968), 87, 106, 117
    International Year of the World's
    Indigenous People (1992), 188
    Wartime Refugees and, 47–50
United Nations Association of Australia,
    117, 138, 153, 162, 165
United Nations Declaration on the Rights
    of Indigenous People (UNDRIP), 199
United States of America, 39, 50, 62, 137,
    148, 156, 158, 165
    As model, 29, 34, 40, 103
    Civil Rights and, 88, 122
Universal Declaration of Human Rights,
    54, 73, 115, 144, 174
    Australian Influence on, 42–43, *See also*
    Evatt, Herbert Vere
    Commemoration of, 4, 87, 161
    Communist Party Referendum (1951)
    and, 69–71
    Distribution of, 68, 104, 161
    Indigenous Australians and, 3, 79–83,
    126, 171
    Vernacularising of, 6, 43, 48, 68–71, 198
    Women and, 146, 150

Victoria, 18, 56, 59, 64, 71–72, 73, 80,
    110–113, 114–116, 179, 183, 201
    Abortion and, 147
    Anti-Chinese laws in, 11, 16–17
Vietnam War, The, 144, *See also*
    Ex-Services Human Rights Association
    of Australia, Amnesty International
    Australian involvement in, 102
    Opposition to, 106, 114
Von Luckner, Felix, 59

Waddington, Leslie, 101–102, 104,
    107, 113
War on Terror, The, 199–200
Waterside Workers Federation, 62, 68, 70,
    98, 123
Welfare State, The
    Feminist critiques of, 152
    Indigenous Australians and, 84, 130, 198

Index

Labour movement and, 30, 34–35
UDHR and, 21, 22, 51
Western Australia, 46, 63, 80, 82, 125, 183, 196
White Australia Policy, 23, 43, 44–49, 87, 163
White, William 'Bill', 105, 112–114
Whitlam, Gough Edward, 96, 179, 182, 184, 194
  Abortion and, 147–148
  Campaign against Torture and, 158
  Dismissal of, 155
  Election of, 119–121
  Indigenous Australians and, 166, 170
  International Women's Year and, 135–136, 138
Whitlam, Margaret, 140
Whyte, Jessica, 54, 197
Wik Peoples v The State of Queensland (1996), 197
Wildenthal, Lora, 3, 7, 164, 192–193
Wilenski, Peter, 100

Wilson, Woodrow, 21, 31, 34
Wives of Chinese Seamen Association, 48–49
Women's Charter Movement, 134, 135, 145
Women's Electoral Lobby, 178
Women's Liberation Movement, 139, 146,
  See also Reid, Elizabeth
  Foundation of, 135
  Sexism and, 137, 140
Women's suffrage, 17–19
World Council of Indigenous Peoples, 166
  Third General Assembly, Canberra (1981), 172–173
Wositzky, Clare, 111
Wright, Tom, 83

Yothu Yindi, 190–191

Zarb, John, 114
Zedong, Mao, 80, 91–92, 178

CPSIA information can be obtained
at www.ICGtesting.com
Printed in the USA
LVHW011151040821
694433LV00017B/1965